INTIMATE MEM

INTIMATE MEMORIES
The Autobiography of Mabel Dodge Luhan

EDITED BY
Lois Palken Rudnick

UNIVERSITY OF NEW MEXICO PRESS
ALBUQUERQUE

Library of Congress
Cataloging-in-Publication Data

Luhan, Mabel Dodge, 1879–1962.
Intimate memories: the autobiography of Mabel Dodge Luhan/
edited by Lois Palken Rudnick—1st ed.
p. cm
ISBN 0-8263-1857-6—ISBN 0-8263-2106-2 (pbk)
1. Luhan, Mabel Dodge, 1879–1962.
2. Intellectuals—United States Biography.
3. Taos (N.M.) Biography.
I. Rudnick, Lois Palken, 1944–
II. Title;
CT275.L838A3   1999
973.9'092–dc21
[B]
99–24085
CIP

Designed by Sue Niewiarowski

CONTENTS

Introduction

> I started out to try & show the inward picture of a person of my own period; what heredity and environment had made of her. I did not believe, & do not believe, that she was inwardly so different from a lot of others. She was a 20th century *type*.[1]

> When she started to write her memoirs, she wrote incessantly, without stopping, day after day, lying on her sofa with a copybook and pencil. She poured herself untiringly into those books. The energy concentration was boundless, until all of a sudden the book was finished and Mabel resumed normal life—which was energetic enough, Heaven knows.[2]

Mabel Dodge Luhan (1879–1962) began to write her autobiography in 1924, a process that took over a decade and resulted in a 1,600-page, four-volume opus that was published serially under the title *Intimate Memories*. Luhan's memoirs are a fascinating eyewitness account of the United States's entrance into modernity that take us from Victorian Buffalo, through *fin de siècle* Florence, into the radical heartland of pre–World War I Greenwich Village, and end with her "discovery" of the Indian Southwest as a place of personal and cultural renewal. Luhan wrote her memoirs from the point of view of a rebel who had spent much of her adult life constructing a series of utopian domains that were intended to overturn "the whole ghastly social structure" under which she felt the United States had been buried since the Victorian era.[3]

Intimate Memories is an extraordinary achievement for a woman of Mabel Dodge Luhan's time, especially for a woman with no claim to any particular professional accomplishment. Luhan made her mark primarily as a patron of social and cultural radicals and reformers who have achieved far greater renown than she in the annals of twentieth-century history. At the time she published her memoirs, however, Luhan was a well-established figure, variously described in the regional and national popular press as the "first lady of Taos"; one who "foresaw in Taos an American Florence of American art"; a "hostess and angel to numerous writers, and the modern incarnation of the French dames who ran their salons for the struggling and successful writers of all nationalities"; one of the few women in the country who could be called "national institutions." Her character and life story had been borrowed by numerous writers—including Gertrude Stein, D. H. Lawrence, and Carl Van Vechten—who saw her, as she saw herself, as a 20th century type.[4]

The fact that Luhan's publisher, Harcourt Brace & Company, allowed her the luxury of four volumes in which to tell the story of the first forty years of her life is testimony to her national prominence, particularly given their publication during the heart of the Great Depression. Yet both the sales figures and the reviews of her memoirs were (on the whole) disappointing. It is one of the ironies of Luhan's life that the publication of *Intimate Memories* reinforced the worst impressions of some of the leading leftist critics of the 1930s, who read her autobiography as a parable of the social decline and economic fall of the United States. Malcolm Cowley summed up her life as "the case history of an art patroness under capitalism—a fable told round the fireside to edify and frighten little Russian children," while Granville Hicks recommended the book as an incomparable account "of the destruction that can be wrought by money when it is in the hands of intelligence and determination."[5]

The irony of these critics' responses lies in the fact that Luhan self-consciously constructed herself to serve as just such an example. One of her overriding purposes in writing her memoirs was to present her life as a paradigm for the decline and fall of Anglo-American civilization and, in her final volume, to provide her fellow Americans with an alternative model of self- and cultural transformation. Luhan focused her self-construction on those elements of her past that supported the thematics of her narrative: her emotionally deprived childhood in Buffalo, the self-indulgent aestheticism of her expatriate years in Florence, the anomie that resulted from the host of revolutionary causes and free love ethic she adopted during her salon days in Greenwich Village, and, finally, her salvation through the love offered her by Tony Luhan.[6]

If Luhan's memoirs were criticized in her own day, they have rarely been addressed since then. Their historical demise can be partly attributed to the ways the kinds of "woman's work" that was her métier have been viewed. In the estimation of historians and biographers like Christopher Lasch and Emily Hahn, and literary scholars like Patricia Spacks, Luhan did not contribute anything of "significance" to American history. She was a culture carrier rather than an originator. She did not do her own work but depended for her identity on the work of creative artists, mostly men. She did not, in other words, either achieve in the masculine realms of public activity or formulate a clear identity that could serve as a model for other women.[7]

I have come to regard Luhan as an artist of life whose realm of work has been undervalued, like that of many other women who have invested time and energy in the creative use of space and place, who have nurtured the genius of others, and who have provided arenas for the rich and contrapuntal discourse of the avant-garde. Although not nearly as well known as the autobiographies of Edith Wharton, Charlotte Perkins Gilman, and Mary Austin, Luhan's memoirs can fruitfully be read with theirs to illuminate the conflicts faced by turn-of-the-century American women of the middle and upper classes. I would also place Luhan within one of the most important traditions of American women's utopian and reformist writing and activism. This tradition began in the nineteenth century with the idea of the home as "a haven from the heartless world" and evolved into a vision of the home as a model for national redemption, of the world *as* home.[8]

If there is one metaphor that ties together Luhan's four volumes of memoirs it is that of a woman in search of a universe in which she can be "at home." Throughout her autobiography, the dwellings in which she lives serve as objective correlatives for the state of her interior being, as well as for the various cosmoses that she spends her adult life designing in the hope of establishing a place where individual creativity is rooted in community. Thus she tells us early in her first volume, *Background:*

> I have never had a room merely "arranged" in any house I have ever
> lived in, from the time I first wrestled with death in our house—wrestled
> and won a room to "fix up," above on the third floor. . . . So the houses
> I have lived in have shown the natural growth of a personality struggling
> to become individual, growing through all the degrees of crudity to a
> greater sophistication and on to simplicity. Of all these houses I shall
> try to tell, for they are like the shells of the soul in its progressive
> metamorphoses—faithfully revealing the form of the life they
> sheltered until they were outgrown and discarded.

Initially Luhan was motivated to write her memoirs for personal reasons, as part of the therapy prescribed by her Freudian analyst, A. A. Brill, who was Freud's American translator and the father of the American Psychoanalytic movement. Brill had been one of the first to disseminate Freudian psychology to the avant-garde, and one of his earliest venues was at Mabel's salon in Greenwich Village. Although Brill encouraged Mabel to write, the Freudian theories to which he introduced her insisted on the fulfillment of woman's "nature" through love and motherhood, while the radical sexologists Havelock Ellis and Edward Carpenter, whom Mabel was also reading during this time, insisted that women's primary vehicle of fulfillment lay in "mothering" male genius.

Some of the most painful passages in *Intimate Memories* for a modern reader are the ones where Luhan tells us that women are not capable of being "self-starters"(*Background*), that the only time she felt assured about her womanhood was when she was pregnant (*European Experiences*), and that she would not have so many pages to write had she not been so "unlucky in love" (*Movers and Shakers*). Luhan was, however, inspired to write her memoirs by Freud's theory of catharsis. Reliving the past through language, the painful emotions associated with the "experience" would presumably be exorcised and cease to cause disturbances. Through verbal expiation Luhan hoped she might free herself from her still-existent neuroses and find the psychic equilibrium denied her by her past. Perhaps for the first time in her life, she understood the act of writing as an active and creative use of her intelligence to give shape to her own life, rather than depending upon others to do that for her.[9]

At some point in the late 1920s, Luhan recognized that her life's story could serve a public as well as a private purpose. By showing the "crude and unflat-tering aspects of the past," as she puts it in the foreword to her second volume, she could practice therapy on a national scale. She may have been supported in this mission by the responses she was getting from the friends and acquaintances to whom she circulated her manuscript: Havelock Ellis, Willa Cather, and especially D. H. Lawrence. Lawrence did not believe that Mabel had the discipline to write fiction, but he encouraged her to write her memoirs because he saw her life as paradigmatic of American culture. After reading the manuscript of her first volume, he wrote her: "I should say it's the most serious 'confession' that ever came out of America, and perhaps the most heart-destroying revelation of the American life-process that ever has or will be produced. . . . Life gave America gold and a ghoulish destiny."[10] Luhan hoped that her memoirs would lead to an improved future by helping others to exorcise the sins of the nation's past. She wrote movingly to Leo Stein about the broader intentions of her work:

> How any of us have ever survived at all the system we inherited & were conditioned by, is more than I can understand. Of course we are crippled & malformed & always will be, but I do *not* see why those who come after us go on in this same pattern, if some of us try & expose the way . . . we thought & felt & how we were motivated: the lack of suitable outlets, ambition, activity, stimulation; the sensory and psychic insufficiency. . . . The whole ghastly social structure under which we were *buried* & that must be torn down, exposed, so those who follow us will have peace & freedom to make a different one.[11]

It infuriated Luhan that critics typically did not understand her intentions when she exposed herself as foolish, destructive, and unlikable in order to accomplish her larger purpose. What Mabel did not realize was that then (as now) readers demand of female biographical subjects a "niceness" that has never been expected of men.

The first volume of Luhan's memoirs, *Background,* is an insightful account of the social formation of America's "ruling class": its substitution of "power, prestige, and possession" for love, which begins in the nursery and culminates in the production of individuals invested in conquest and domination: the men seeking to master the earth, the women seeking to master the men.[12] Luhan's grandparents achieved social and economic prominence as businessmen and bankers. The Mabel Ganson who grew up in the high noon of the Gilded Age lived in a city of 244,000 on a street that housed the economic elite of Buffalo and in a neighborhood where many of its sixty millionaires resided. They lived in the city with the baronial splendor of a landed gentry, only two or three miles from the industries, wharves, row houses, and slums of the inner city— the "other America" that housed the working class and indigent, who suffered greatly in the two serious depressions that occurred during Mabel's childhood.

Mabel's parents had the misfortune of living on inherited wealth, products of the "conspicuous consumption" that Thorstein Veblen would write about in his 1899 treatise, *The Theory of the Leisure Class.* Sara and Charles Ganson's lives were clearly damaged from having "nothing to do," while Mabel suffered from what I have come to call upper-class child abuse. She was not physically punished, but she was psychologically damaged by parents whose emotional frigidity was compounded by the child-rearing practices common to their class. In *Background,* Luhan sets the stage for the willful, manipulative, and selfish woman who appears throughout her memoirs as a symbol of the confusion of values generated by her family dynamics and class position. But here, too, Luhan presents a Mabel whose passionate desire for love, experience, and knowledge led her to defy the cultural scripts for Victorian womanhood, most interestingly in her explorations of lesbian identity.

European Experiences, volume two of *Intimate Memories,* begins with Mabel's marriage to her first husband, Karl Evans, but is devoted primarily to the years she spent abroad in Florence with her second husband, Edwin Dodge. Although she shows herself as choosing a heterosexual identity, it is still a profoundly conflicted one, as she describes her first marriage in terms of an abduction, marries Edwin on the condition that he provide her with a milieu in which she can devote herself to art and beauty, and engages in sexual flirtations with both men and women. As in volume one, Luhan constructs a symbolic self, in this case an expatriate American who could have stepped out of the pages of a Henry James novel. Rejecting the spiritual, emotional, and cultural shallowness of her American background, she embraces the Renaissance past. The extreme aestheticism of Mabel's life in Florence, her life for art's sake credo, epitomizes the fin de siècle philosophy of European decadence, which also influenced her experimentation with the role of the femme fatale.

The magnificent Medicean villa that Mabel and Edwin Dodge reconstruct and furnish, the clothes Mabel wears, the "Gran' Salone" in which she entertains émigré royalty, writers, and artists, the very consciousness she applies to daily living—all are materials for her first cosmos, a world in which she tries to create permanent values and a secure identity by erasing her American past. Luhan's descriptions of her behavior at the Villa Curonia often reach self-parodic proportions that are very amusing—"I so deep, so fatal, so glamorous—and he [Edwin] so ordinary and matter-of-fact!" This is but one of several examples of what Luhan meant when she told Leo Stein that in writing her memoirs she tried not to be "any other than the one I was at the time I write about," and that during her reign in Florence, "I was very stupid, and unhappy, indeed quite desperate, with no heart at all nor any brains." While this is an overly self-disparaging assessment, it is also an indication of the ways Luhan was willing to sacrifice herself on the public altar, critics be damned.[13]

At the end of *European Experiences* Luhan tells her readers that by 1912 she had finally come to a "dead end" with the forms of the past. It is clear from her construction of her life up to this point that both the Victorian and fin de siècle worlds she rejected left as their legacy a generation of men and women who craved a deeper emotional sustenance, a broader social base, and a freer range of expression. In her third volume of memoirs, *Movers and Shakers,* Luhan suggests that she returned to the United States at just the right moment to become part of the revolution of radical innocents who infiltrated Greenwich Village with their exuberant optimism and will to believe that they could create a brave new world of social justice, artistic and personal freedom, and sexual egalitarianism.

During the eight years Mabel had lived in Europe, the industrial system that her grandfathers had helped to build reached its apotheosis. In 1912, two percent of all Americans controlled sixty percent of the personal wealth of the nation, while one-third to one-half lived in poverty or so close to it that they were pushed over the line anytime they suffered extended illness or industrial accidents—in which the United States led the world. During these same years, the ruthless exploitation of human and natural resources and the economic oppression of child and adult laborers created among different segments of the population calls for reform and revolution.

The radicals who formed the inner core of the Mabel Dodge circle were sweeping in their condemnation of the basic ill health of bourgeois America and industrial capitalism, even though they participated in many reformist efforts. Like other "clean government" reformers, Lincoln Steffens worked to expose urban corruption by pointing up the collusion between American businesses and political party machines. But he also lectured and wrote about the debilitating social and psychological effects of the Horatio Alger success myth. Walter Lippmann shared with elitist Progressive intellectuals the belief that social scientists should regulate the nation's industrial economy because their commitment to rational principles would lead them to adjust the disparity among goods, services, and human needs. But in his more visionary moments, he scorned the shibboleths of middle-class property and propriety. John Collier worked to improve the conditions of working-class people by supporting such causes as tenement and factory reform, unionization, and expanded educational opportunities for immigrants. But he also focused much of his energy on promoting ethnic hegemony for the millions of immigrants who were swarming to American cities, because he was convinced that the preservation of their communal traditions was a necessary counterbalance to the anomie of urban life. Socialists and anarchists like Max Eastman, Emma Goldman, and Bill Haywood demanded even more fundamental changes in America's political and economic system: from the redistribution of the national wealth, through a graduated income tax and federal regulation of wages, to workers' wresting the national wealth and the means of production from the hands of their owners.

Liberated by the aesthetic theories of Leo and Gertrude Stein, whom she met in her last years in Florence, Mabel immersed herself in the avant-garde spirit of radical antiformalism that seemed to suit the protean qualities of her personality. In *Movers and Shakers,* she portrays herself as the eye of a fascinating storm and her home as a center for "free speech" through which the various new ideas and practices that are aired will liberate herself and her fellow men and women from the shackles of the past. Just as she had tried to out-Florentine the Florentines in her attempt to re-create the Renaissance, here she portrays herself as the archetypal Modernist.

Joseph Singal has pointed out that the Victorians made "sharp distinctions" in all realms of life—between civilized and savage, superior and inferior classes, white and colored, male and female spheres—whereas the various "manifestations of Modernism had in common . . . a passion not only for opening the self to new levels of experience, but also for fusing together disparate elements of that experience into new and original 'wholes.'" Modernists privileged "authenticity" rather than "sincerity" as their most valued character trait, believing that "one must constantly create and recreate an identity based upon one's ongoing experience in the world."[14] Luhan shows herself taking up this Modernist credo with a vengeance, embracing everything from suffrage, birth control, and psychoanalysis to postimpressionist art, anarchism, and socialism.

The Mabel Dodge of these years appears prescient not only in her understanding that new forms of communication are abroad in the land but also in her awareness of how to use the media to build a national image and to promote her "causes" and her public persona as a "creature of importance in her own time." She becomes vice president of the Armory Show, the first major exhibition of postimpressionist art in the United States, at which she circulates her self-published "Portrait of Mabel Dodge at the Villa Curonia," written by Gertrude Stein; she contributes to *The Masses,* one of the finest radical journals of the time; she instigates the Paterson Strike Pageant, the first major left-wing labor pageant; she disseminates popular psychology through editorial pieces in the Hearst papers; and she takes as her lover John Reed, at the time a youthful bohemian and labor journalist, who would later found the Communist Labor Party.

Movers and Shakers also provides us with important insights into the transition of women from the Victorian to the Modern era, women who were reared, in Virginia Woolf's words, to be "looking glasses" for men, but whose adulthood coincided with the twentieth century's first wave of feminism. These "new women" were among the first feminists to openly address issues of gender roles and sexuality, along with the more traditional political and legal issues of women's rights. Luhan shows us how she became a leading symbol of these women: seemingly sexually emancipated, self-determining, and in control of her own destiny. She wished, in the words of Simone de Beauvoir, "to justify the universe by changing it, by thinking about, by revealing it," but she was convinced that what Beauvoir called the "desire to found the world anew" could only be actualized by men. Luhan's profound confusion and ambivalence about her gender and sexual identity, which lie at the heart of her memoirs, is highlighted here in the struggles she depicts of a generation of women who were attempting to create a new sexual politics that balanced "meaningful work and love in egalitarian relationships."[15]

Halfway through *Movers and Shakers,* Luhan acknowledges the widening gap between the public figure she cut as the symbol of the "New Woman" and the isolated and lonely Mabel Dodge who had yet to find a coherent identity and purpose in life. She was, indeed, emblematic of many feminist women who experienced a deep-seated conflict between their desire to have free and equal relationships with men and their need for emotional stability, a conflict compounded by the contradictory ideals and practices of the men in their lives.

Although the male radicals of Greenwich Village worked to subvert the bourgeois morality and capitalist economics that kept Woman in her place, they also wanted women who could give them the best of all possible worlds. They would be the mothers who provided the security they abandoned with their middle-class roots, the lovers who were always available to fulfill their sexual needs, and the muses who would inspire them to great works of creative endeavor.

As soon as John Reed becomes her lover, Luhan shows how she is rendered helpless and dependent in her desperate attempts to compete with his increasing fame—and to keep him faithful. When she gives him up for the postimpressionist painter Maurice Sterne, she fares no better and descends into a loveless struggle after she marries him in order to turn him into a sculptor. By the end of volume three, Luhan has not "solved" any of the personal, social, or cultural problems that she has shown as rooted in the self-assertive and egoistic individualism of Western culture, in both its elite and radical manifestations.

It is only when we come to Luhan's fourth and final published volume, *Edge of Taos Desert: An Escape to Reality,* that we realize the larger shape and intention of Luhan's autobiography. As she shows us how and why her "life broke in two" after her journey to New Mexico, we begin to see the ways she has embedded her memoirs within the genre of the conversion narrative. This is one of the paradigmatic genres of American literature, in which the hero imagines history as a journey from imperfection to perfection, often typified by a search for a paradise to be regained, where new beginnings are associated with new frontiers. One aspect of the originality of Luhan's autobiography is her subversion of this primarily male-defined tradition, through which she radically alters the mainstream American journey myth at the same time that she reverses the 500-year-old plot of the Indian captivity narrative.[16] *Intimate Memories* culminates with an Indian captivity narrative. Only here the white woman is not brought back to Christian civilization from the "savage" world of the Indian. It is the Anglo world that is the anti-Christ or, in Luhan's more secular language, that embodies the savagery of a civilization that exploits the earth and destroys human community. The light of true faith is shown to lie in the Pueblo Indian world, and it will be the duty of a new interracial Adam and Eve, Tony and Mabel, to bring that light to the Western world.

Mabel was not impressed with the town of Taos, a frontier community of about 2,000 people: its center, a dilapidated green enclosed by crumbling adobe walls; its shops and stores bearing the marks of its status as a crossroads for traders. But the Pueblo Indians offer her the antithesis of all she has known and found wanting: both the materialistic world she grew up in and the chaotic world of new freedoms in which she had matured. Throughout her memoirs, she shows us how she has been impelled by a desire to devour the world in her frantic search to connect her solitary ego to something larger than itself. As described in *Edge of Taos Desert,* the Pueblos offer her—and potentially her fellow Americans—what no so-called advanced twentieth-century society was able to: a model of a fully integrated society that is achieved through an intimate connection between individual and community, work and living space, play and art.[17]

Contemporary scholars who have written about white patronage of indigenous cultures in the Southwest have brought to the fore the less attractive elements of the Anglo fascination with Pueblo cultures: their tendency to view Native Americans in static, romantic, and essentialist terms; their undermining of tribal integrity by determining what forms of expression were culturally "authentic"; and their appropriation and marketing of Indian and Hispanic cultures to enhance their own well-being. Luhan's life and memoirs are implicated in these difficult and serious issues. We need to read *Edge of Taos Desert* in light of this critique, just as we need to acknowledge Luhan's elitism, and the racial and ethnic biases that are present in her other volumes, especially her antipathy toward African-American urban culture.[18]

Yet we also need to read Luhan's memoirs within their historical context, as well from the perspectives that recent theories of women's and postmodern autobiography have brought to bear on once marginalized texts like *Intimate Memories.* Viewed from the vantage point of a profoundly racist United States that had all but lost consciousness of Native America, the small but important achievements of Luhan and her friends in working with the Pueblo Indians to promote Native American health care, land rights, religion, and artistic expression were admirable. While Luhan can be criticized for constructing the Pueblos within a "noble savage" tradition and for her stereotyping of Hispanics as fatalistic, her respect for the native populations' careful use of the land's resources, her appreciation for the communal aspects of tribal and village cultures, and her belief that the folk cultures of the Indian and Hispanic Southwest were contributory to the creation of a vital national culture should be acknowledged [19]

Luhan's portrait of Tony suggests a way of being in the world that calls into question the Western myth of the self-made, "autonomous" man—or woman. If Mabel is finally restored to full humanity by Tony's love (at least during the "time" of the memoir), it is because he teaches her that the self can only "be made real" if it exists in relation to others and is responsible to a specific physical and cultural landscape. Unlike the Anglo male modes of knowing that Mabel had always imitated—prying, penetrating, analyzing—Tony teaches by suggestion and example and relies on an intuitive sense of his surroundings.

Unlike her previous lovers, he does not tap her creative energies for his own use, nor does he enshrine her as an idealized (or demonized) other. He is shown as devoted to helping her integrate her feeling, thinking, and acting selves. His nurturing of her is as much female as male during the nine months of "gentle organic growth" during which he sees her "into being."

Swept clean of the waste and sickness of civilization by New Mexico's "undomesticated" landscape, where life is reduced to its "bare essentials," Luhan shows in *Edge of Taos Desert* how her newly adopted home and lover influence the rebirth of her imagination. In fact, it was in New Mexico that Luhan found her voice as a writer, just as other strong women, such as Mary Austin, Willa Cather, and Georgia O'Keeffe, were drawn to its allure as a seemingly masterless frontier in which they could inscribe an original, creative vision. These three women were also friends and admirers of Tony Luhan, at least in part, I am convinced, because he offered Anglo women who sought success in male-dominated domains an alternative vision of maleness.

At the end of *Edge of Taos Desert,* Luhan admits she has turned the tables on the field of anthropology by telling "all" about her own tribe of white folk but refusing to play this role with the Pueblo Indians, the secrets of whose ceremonial culture she will not reveal. Like all other autobiographers, of course, there is much that she leaves unsaid (as she acknowledges in her foreword to *European Experiences*). It is telling, for example, that she ends her memoirs at the moment when she and Tony are about to consummate their relationship— before any of the serious problems occurred that marked their loving but difficult forty-two-year partnership. Luhan also chose not to publish the more tragic aspects of her adult life, which included a traumatic affair with Karl Evans's family doctor, Dr. John Parmenter, who delivered her son, John Evans. Nor did she reveal her multiple exposure to venereal disease, beginning with Dr. Parmenter, who infected her with gonorrhea, and marking her marriages to Edwin Dodge, Maurice Sterne, and Tony Luhan, from whom she contracted syphilis. (Given the extraordinary social stigma carried by venereal disease, it is hardly surprising that Luhan suppressed this information.) Reading her memoirs in light of this knowledge allows us to better understand both her psychological suffering and the deep-seated hostility that underlay her dependency on men.[20]

Luhan was as self-conscious about the stylistics of her autobiography as she was about what subject matter she included—and excluded. After the publication of *Intimate Memories* was completed, she explained in an interview that in each of her four volumes she attempted to imitate through language and syntax the particular phase of her life she was reconstructing. Thus her European and New York volumes were written with complex sentences; highly charged, allusive phrases; and uneven, sometimes frenetic, prose rhythms. This style was intended, she said, to indicate the complex world of ideas and the intensity of emotional entanglements in which she was engaged. In *Edge of Taos Desert*, she wished to call her readers' attention to the stripping away of her civilized veneer, and thus she simplified her diction and syntax so that they could view her new world through eyes no longer encumbered by the weight of "dead" philosophies and books.

In spite of her conscious efforts at crafting her autobiography, Luhan is often rhetorically excessive and sometimes tediously repetitive. Yet her prolixity, narrative discontinuities, and self-contradictions are not unlike those found in many of the memoirs and diaries written by women that have been recovered from the past. As Estelle Jelinek has pointed out, women's autobiographies are often "disconnected, fragmentary, or organized into self-sustained units rather than connecting chapters." Luhan's memoirs also fit Anna Walters's description of women's life studies as portraying a "paradoxical self-image of denial and assertion. Essentially the self is fragmented in the conflict between social conditioning and natural impulse." Those who read autobiography from a postmodern perspective argue for the necessity of understanding the subject as being "positioned in multiple and contradictory discourses" that challenge our belief in the rational, coherent, and unified (male) self that "is powerfully linked to American traditions of individualism." Luhan's *Intimate Memories* challenges those traditions, even as she reveals herself as deeply implicated in the system that her "representative" self sets out to destroy.[21]

Throughout the writing of *Intimate Memoirs,* Luhan is engaged in what Sidonie Smith calls women's "transgressive desire for cultural and literary authority." Smith notes that in the twentieth century, "the ambiguities and confusions of modernism" offered the autobiographer the possibility of grappling "self-consciously with her identity as a woman in patriarchal culture and with her problematic relationship to engendered figures of selfhood." The one contemporary scholar who has written extensively on *Intimate Memories* has made a good case for its inclusion in the Modernist canon, on the grounds of Luhan's self-reflexive play with language, her multivocal discourse, and her extensive use of mixed genres that include letters, newspaper articles, poems, fiction, and dramatic fragments.[22]

What finally is most compelling about *Intimate Memories* is Luhan's vibrant and life-affirming, if sometimes infuriating, voice. It offers us a richly elaborated argument for the centrality of women's experiences to an understanding of modern America's emergence by showing us how the seemingly private domain of women's "intimate" lives continually shapes and is shaped by the public sphere. Ever since I first read *Intimate Memories,* some twenty-five years ago, I have thought that Luhan needed a good editor. It is my hope that she has found one and that this highly condensed version of her autobiography reveals enough of the original's flavor and value that readers will find their historical imaginations captivated and their knowledge of American social and cultural history enhanced.

A Note on This Edition

I have focused my text selections on aspects of Luhan's life story that I believe are central to understanding the complex facets of the persona she created and that are most revealing of the historical moments she engaged. Because of the anecdotal and self-contained nature of Luhan's narrative, it has been possible to make radical reductions in the text and still maintain continuity. In order to increase that continuity and maintain readability, I have not indicated where I have deleted text or restructured paragraphs. All ellipses in the text are Luhan's. Where deletions of the original text have resulted in a shift of topic, I have used double-spaced paragraph breaks. The entire text, with the exception of what is placed in brackets, is taken from *Intimate Memories* as it was originally published. I have, however, modernized and standardized spelling and punctuation in order to create a uniformity that does not exist across the original volumes. At the end of the book, I have added an alphabetized Glossary of Names, with brief biographical descriptions of the chief historical figures who appear in the text.

Notes

1. Mabel Dodge Luhan to Hutchins Hapgood, 5 November ?, Hapgood Collection, Beinecke Library, Yale University.
2. Dorothy Brett, "Autobiography: My Long and Beautiful Journey," *South Dakota Review* 5, no. 2 (summer 1967): 41.
3. Some literary theorists differentiate memoir from autobiography on the grounds that "memoir emphasizes the personal rather than the public." I use the terms interchangeably to discuss Luhan's *Intimate Memories* because the personal and public dimensions of her volumes are so closely intertwined. One of the arguments her memoirs makes is that the personal and the political cannot be separated, particularly sexual and cultural politics. See Kathleen Woodward, "Simone de Beauvoir: Aging and Its Discontents," *The Private Self: Theory and Practice of Women's Autobiograph-*

ical Writings, ed. Shari Benstock (Chapel Hill: University of North Carolina Press, 1988), pp. 90–113.

4. *Washington, D.C., News,* August 18, 1934; *Town and Country,* n.d.; Henry McBride, "Exhibition of New Mexico Paintings Holds Interest," *North Carolina Observer,* May 5, 1935; James Gray, *St. Paul Minnesota Dispatch,* August 16, 1934. Newspaper clippings in Scrapbook vol. 11, Mabel Dodge Luhan Collection, Beinecke Library, referred to hereon as MDLC.

5. *Background* was published in 1933 and sold 2,699 copies; *European Experiences* in 1935 and sold 2,968 copies; *Movers and Shakers* in 1936 and sold 3,022 copies; and *Edge of Taos Desert* in 1937 and sold 3,660 copies. See Malcolm Cowley, "Fable for Russian Children," *New Republic* (November 15, 1936): 122; Granville Hicks, Portrait of a Patroness," *New Masses* (November 24, 1936); clippings in Scrapbook, vol. 8, MDLC. Both reviews were in reference to *Movers and Shakers.* Luhan's first volume received generally positive reviews, as did her last volume, at least in the Western press.

6. Mabel changed the spelling of her name to "Luhan," purportedly because Anglos did not pronounce the Spanish *jota* correctly. Tony Lujan's name was spelled variously throughout his life with both the *j* and the *h.* In the few of his (dictated) letters available, his name is spelled "Lujan," which is also how it appears in Mabel's will. On his tombstone in Taos Pueblo, however, his name is spelled "Luhan." For consistency's sake, I have chosen the "Luhan" spelling.

7. See Christopher Lasch, "Mabel Dodge Luhan: Sex as Politics," *The New Radicalism in America: (1889–1963): The Intellectual as a Social Type* (New York: Vintage Books, 1967), pp. 104–40; Emily Hahn, *Mabel: A Biography of Mabel Dodge Luhan* (Boston: Houghton Mifflin, 1977); Patricia Spacks, *The Female Imagination* (New York: Knopf, 1975). See also my essay "The Male-Identified Woman and Other Anxieties," in *The Challenge of Feminist Biography: Writing the Lives of Modern American Women,* ed. Sara Alpern, et al. (Urbana: University of Illinois Press, 1992), pp. 116–38, where I argue that "in terms of certain feminist and leftist notions of 'correct' scholarship," Mabel Dodge Luhan is the "wrong kind of woman" to write about.

8. I am grateful to Melody Graulich for the suggestion that Luhan's memoirs should be read in conjunction with these writers. For a discussion of the idea of the world as home, see Lois Rudnick, "A Feminist American Success Myth: Jane Addams' Twenty Years at Hull-House," in *Traditions and the Talents of Women,* ed. Florence Howe (Urbana: University of Illinois Press, 1990), pp. 145–67; and Dolores Hayden, *The Grand Domestic Revolution: A History of Feminist Designs for Homes, Neighborhoods, and Cities* (Cambridge: MIT Press, 1983).

9. See A. A. Brill, *Basic Principles of Psychoanalysis* (New York: Pocket Books, 1960 [1921]), p. 8; also Luhan to Leo Stein, October 23, 1925?, Stein Collection, Beinecke Library, where she explains that her memoirs will record "no more or less content than the moment held. It is what the analysts call 'abreaction' in writing."

10. D. H. Lawrence to Mabel Dodge Luhan, December 5, 1927, D. H. Lawrence Collection, Humanities Research Center, University of Texas, Austin.

11. Mabel Dodge Luhan to Leo Stein, November 30, 1935?, Stein Collection. According to Luhan's close friend Frank Waters, one of the primary models for her autobiography was Marcel Proust's multivolume *Remembrance of Things Past,* in which sin, selfishness, pride, and envy abound as the hero probes his evolving consciousness (with sometimes excruciating detail) in a search for truth and redemption.

12. See G. William Domhoff, *The Higher Circles: The Governing Class in America* (New York: Random House, 1970).

13. Mabel Dodge Luhan to Leo Stein, November 30, 1935?, Stein Collection.

14. Joseph Singal, "Towards a Definition of American Modernism," *American Quarterly* 39, no. 1 (spring 1987): 12.

15. Simon de Beauvoir, *The Second Sex* (New York: Bantam Books, 1961)(1949), p. 671; Ellen Kay Trimberger, "The New Woman and the New Sexuality: Conflict and Contradiction in the Writings and Lives of Mabel Dodge and Neith Boyce," in *1915, The Cultural Moment: The New Politics, the New Woman, the New Psychology, the New Art, and the New Theatre in America,* eds. Adele Hellerand and Lois Rudnick (New Brunswick: Rutgers University Press, 1991), p. 113.

16. See William Spengemann and L. R. Lundquist, "Autobiography and the American Myth," *American Quarterly* 17, no. 3 (fall 1965): 501–19; Jane Nelson, "Journey to the Edge of History: Narrative Form in Mabel Dodge Luhan's *Intimate Memories,*" *Biography* 3, no. 3 (summer 1980): 240–52; Jane Nelson, *Mabel Dodge Luhan,* Western Writer's Series, no. 55 (Boise: Boise State University Press, 1982), pp. 24–46. Nelson argues that the autobiography combines the confessional and epic genres.

17. See Annette Kolodny, *The Land Before Her: Fantasy and Experience of the American Frontiers, 1630–1860* (Chapel Hill: University of North Carolina Press, 1984).

18. See Jackson Rushing, "Feminism, Mysticism, and the Fourth World: Mabel Dodge Luhan on Pueblo Art," paper presented at the New Mexico Art History Conference, Taos, New Mexico, October 1988; Sylvia Rodriguez, "Art, Tourism, and Race Relations in Taos: Toward a Sociology of the Art Colony," *Journal of Anthropological Research* 45, no. 1 (spring 1989): 79–97;

Helen Carr, *Inventing the Primitive: Politics, Gender and the Representation of Native American Literary Traditions, 1789–1936* (New York: New York University Press, 1996), ch. 5. Some recent interpretations of the relationships between Anglo patrons and Pueblo painters have emphasized the mutual collaboration between these groups as well as the influence of Pueblo aesthetic traditions on Anglo artists. See, for example, J. J. Brody, *Pueblo Indian Painting: Tradition and Modernism in New Mexico 1900–1930* (Santa Fe: School of America Research Press, 1997).

19. See Lois Rudnick, "Re-Naming the Land," ch. 1, *The Desert Is No Lady: Southwestern Landscapes in Women's Writing and Art,* ed. Vera Norwood and Jan Monk (New Haven: Yale University Press, 1987; Tucson: University of Arizona Press, 1997). On the socioeconomic situation of the Pueblos and the beginnings of the "Pueblo crusade," see Lawrence Kelly, *The Assault on Assimilation: John Collier and the Origins of Indian Policy Reform* (Albuquerque: University of New Mexico Press, 1983).

20. Luhan's son, John Evans, put restrictions on several manuscripts that are among the 1,500 pounds of papers she donated to the Beinecke Library at Yale, in 1954. These restrictions will be lifted in the year 2000. Information on Luhan's experiences with venereal disease is taken from a manuscript labeled "Doctors: Fifty Years of Experience" (no. 56, dated 1954) in MDLC. Luhan tells a very different story about her meeting with Dr. Parmenter here than she does in *Background.* I discuss the implications of this document, which was not available while I was writing my biography of Mabel Luhan, in "The Male-Identified Woman," pp. 134–36.

21. Estelle Jelinek, *Women's Autobiographies: Essays in Criticism* (Bloomington: Indiana University Press, 1980), pp. 7–8, 17; Anna Walters, "Self-Image and Style: A Discussion Based on Estelle Jelinek's *The Tradition of Women's Autobiography from Antiquity to the Present,*" *Women's Studies International Forum* 10, no. 1 (1987): 89–90; Albert E. Stone, *Autobiographical Occasions and Original Acts: Versions of American Identity from Henry Adams to Nate Shaw* (Philadelphia: University of Pennsylvania Press, 1982); and Betty Bergland, "Postmodernism and the Autobiographical Subject: Reconstructing the 'Other,'" in *Autobiography & Postmodernism,* ed. Kathleen Ashley (Amherst: University of Massachusetts Press, 1994), pp. 135, 161.

22. Sidonie Smith, *A Poetics of Women's Autobiography: Marginality and the Fiction of Self-Representation* (Bloomington: University of Indiana Press, 1987), pp. 50, 56; Suzanne Cleary-Langley, "Mabel Dodge Luhan's *Intimate Memories*: A Life Suffused with Language," Ph.D. diss., Indiana University of Pennsylvania, 1996.

VOLUME ONE

❧

Background

(1879–1897)

Dedicated to Buffalo, New York

Life in Buffalo has changed a great deal in fifty years. Children have a good time there now, and the grown-ups themselves have many more interests to occupy them. People understand themselves and their families better, and there is more talk about life and what it means. There are fewer taboos, fewer fears, and less unhappiness. But there is a corresponding lack of savor and of charm. It almost seems as though to lose the glamour and the intensity that form a large part of the dark ages is too great a price to pay for understanding better how to live.

Even with all its melancholy, my childhood had a wild, sweet, enthralling zestfulness that seems to be missing from the lives of my grandchildren, and I would not live it over again in their happy circumstances if I had the chance to choose between my past and their present; for their present seems to me dim and leveled down to a contentment that has no high moments such as I knew.

So these few words are just put here to show that I feel I must stand up for all I had—both of darkness and of light; and that it was all all right, and I would not have had it different. We are all, inevitably perhaps, loyal to our own. I like my Buffalo as I knew it, just as I like and understand and admire now those grown-ups who surrounded me and who endured so gallantly, and with such a robust courage, the terrible emptiness of their lives.

CHAPTER ONE 🖎 BUFFALO

In 1880 Buffalo was a cozy town. At least it was for those who formed the nucleus in the center of it, that central part made up of Delaware Avenue and the avenues parallel to it and the cross streets that intersected the privileged area. This fashionable part of Buffalo, where one knew practically everyone one met on the street, was only a small portion of it, but it seemed to us to be the only real Buffalo. On the other side of Main Street, where all the stores were, it was just an outer wilderness.

Our instinctive feeling towards the East Side was one of contempt that had something inimical in it. Charlotte Becker made one of her jokes about the beautiful Reinhardt girls whose German father came to live in our part of town when they began to grow up. Because they had lived on the East Side, everybody snickered at Charlotte's remark that the Reinhardt girls didn't "come out" like other girls—they just "came over."

Within the narrow limitations of life in Buffalo, where the occupations were so unvaried and the imaginations so little fed, there came to be many queer characters and people with curious ways. Although everybody knew everybody else and all there was to know about everybody else, yet by a kind of mutual agreement they all pretended to ignore each other's inward lives. People never talked to each other except of outward things, but about each other they exchanged many conjectures. There was hardly any real intimacy between friends, and people had no confidence in each other. People in this town neither showed their feelings nor talked about them to each other. To their neighbors or to their families, they only talked of other people's feelings. Inside the house or outside, no one ever talked about how *she felt* . . . her own pain and fear—she just felt and buried it.

Life flowed on in an apparently commonplace way until, once in a while, something happened. Donald White would be found hanging to the gas fixture in his bedroom, naked except for a pair of white gloves; Caroline Thompson would suddenly be seen no more among her friends and her mother would not mention her absence. But people would whisper: "They say they had to take her out to the insane asylum"—and she would never be seen again. It would not be long before she was forgotten by everyone except perhaps her parents, who seemed to go on as they always had, though their faces changed almost unnoticeably from the hidden grief.

Scattered among the houses that made up Buffalo for us lived our doctors and our ministers, and that was about all of Buffalo, except the shops. There was Boyce's on the corner of Main Street and Allen, where all the women in our neighborhood met every morning to pick out their groceries and meat, and Allen's drugstore, on the corner opposite. Next to Boyce's was Miss O'Brien's, a tiny shop containing tiny dolls and dolls' furniture, knitted mittens and mufflers, hairpins and kid curlers, and many little oddities. Farther down on Main Street there stood Flint & Kent's, a large refined drygoods store. It had attractive things in it; all our ribbons and ginghams for summer dresses came from there, and when people bought some new furniture covering or things for their houses they bought them upstairs in that store.

Still farther down Main Street were other, larger department stores—Jay & Adams, and Adams & Meldrum's—but these were not pleasant stores to go to. One met fewer people one knew there. These stores were full of people we didn't know and never would know, and the air was close and had a disagreeable, common smell we always associated with common people.

When I was ten years old my grandfather Cook gave me a Shetland pony named Cupid, with a tiny two-wheeled cart, and some of the other girls and I used to range all over Buffalo, galloping as fast as we could go. We knew all sorts of places in that way that other children never could have known in that town. We used to drive out to Forest Lawn, the new cemetery that took the place of "the old burying ground" on the corner across from our house that held the first graves of people—many of them Indians.

We used to be allowed to take things out to eat and picnic there in Forest Lawn sometimes, and once we forgot to notice the shadows growing longer as we played behind a tomb, and when we realized it was late we made a dash for the gate and found it locked! Three small girls not yet in their teens and locked up in the cemetery for the night! We were instantly filled with a thrilling, delightful terror. We knew we were scared but yet how we enjoyed it!

From the very earliest days in Buffalo any accidental heightening of feeling was welcome. No word reached us of any way to live beyond the routine of sleeping, dressing, and "going outdoors to get fresh air." Until we began to read books, our need for change and variety was gratified only by our companionships and expeditions around town. And these companionships were comparatively few. However, I think we savored to the utmost the qualities and differences we found in each other, and while we were still children we used to talk about each other and call each other's attention to the slightest change or alteration in those whose backs were turned for a moment!

So we savored each other and fed upon each other a little. Later we played a game together called Truth, in which we had to answer every question truthfully or not at all. In this game we grilled each other, probing into the most hidden corners, laying bare preferences, analyzing each other and ourselves until we were in a tingling excitement. But it helped us by letting off steam and it helped us, too, to call by name the vaguer thoughts and feelings that we carried about inside us, as well as by airing those secrets that were all too defined for comfort. The unloading of secrets—what a pleasure that always was! Since that time I have been indiscreet. Everybody says I tell everything, my own and everyone's secrets, and it's true! I cannot, to this day, resist that peculiar urge to tell what is not really mine to tell. Just a little interesting news and an interested mind nearby, and "My dear, do you know . . . ?" and the secret's out! I used to be sorry I did it and ashamed that people knew it and said it and called me a sieve. But I don't know that I feel particularly sorry anymore. The less secrets the better—of my own or anybody else's. Need anyone *ever feel ashamed?* I doubt it.

Besides the cemetery, of course we made excursions in all the other directions about town. Once in a while, on a gray, dull day when hearts sank and seemed to beat more slowly, we would whisper to each other: "Let's go to that street." "My dear, that's a bad place. No one ever goes there!" "What of it? Let's go and look at it." And so rarely—maybe it only happened two or three times—we turned down from the street where the General Hospital stood and we searched out Grove Street, the bad place where the "men" went. It did not look any different from any of the other streets, either east or west of our part of town. Wooden houses painted gray or brown, little yards, verandas with rocking chairs on them, that was all. But to us it seemed to be masking another world altogether. Life of some kind, other than that of our own houses, went on behind those windows. We *had* to taste it all—all the flavors the town had in it.

I do not need to say that every street and house in our quarter of Buffalo had for us its particular look and character. The houses of the people we knew were all big, solid houses, each standing on its own and having flowers about it in the summer. Buffalo always grew northwards and people beginning life down on Lower Delaware Avenue or Franklin Street, where my grandparents first lived in Buffalo and where I was born in 1879, people already living in comfortable brick or stone houses, following some urge, from time to time would build new and larger houses farther uptown. So that when I was little my parents moved up to Delaware and North Street to live in the square red-brick house that Grandpa Cook bought for my mother.

It seems an obvious thing to say, yet how many people know that beauty and reality in a house come from a sharp personal feeling for all the things in the house—and for a *need* to have them there either for use or merely to live in through the eye? I have never had a room merely "arranged" in any house I have ever lived in, from the time I first wrestled with death in our house— wrestled and won a room to "fix up," above on the third floor. I have never, thank God, regarded things as merely inanimate. They have always lived for me or else I did not have them about. And every house I have ever lived in has been a reflection of myself as I lived in it, sometimes changing noticeably year by year. There has never been any setting for a personality unfelt or any longed-for grandeur. When I had grand surroundings I *felt* grand and that was why I had them. *They* did not make me so. So the houses I have lived in have shown the natural growth of a personality struggling to become individual, growing through all the degrees of crudity to a greater sophistication and on to sim-plicity. Of all these houses I shall try to tell, for they are like the shells of the soul in its progressive metamorphoses—faithfully revealing the form of the life they sheltered until they were outgrown and discarded.

CHAPTER TWO 🐚 IN OUR HOUSE

It stood on the corner of North and Delaware—that's the way everyone spoke of streets in Buffalo. There it was of red brick and half covered with an am-pelopsis vine in the summertime. It was square and had a cupola on top. In the center of the neat lawn there was a circular bed of flowers that held, through the warm months, different kinds of blooming things.

My mother was rather proud of this flower bed on account of its hard, un-failing precision. First the hyacinths would come up in rows: pink, blue, white, and deeper pink. With no expression at all, they just came up in large healthy spikes. In tulip time the tulips would radiate in symmetrical circles of white, red, yellow, and pink—every bloom a perfect, unblemished success, every leaf strong, aggressive, and tailored, and the whole thing so mathematical and so ordered that all the spontaneity and flowerness of growth couldn't be felt at all. It was like a slaughter of innocents to plant those hardy bulbs there and make them come up in unbroken and undifferentiated rows. Because every flower is a thing, a special individual thing in itself. A hundred specimens of it is only a hundredfold camouflage of singleness and identity. So that I, who loved flowers so much and who used to try to assimilate each into myself by a passionate sniffling, followed often by a more passionate tasting, could never bear that flower bed. Besides, the colors in those rigid rows were so hard and ugly, planted willfully like that.

The tulip bed was a symbol for the rest of our house. It was all ordered and organized, nothing was left to fortuitous chance, and no life ever rose in it taking its own form. My mother was too good a housekeeper for that.

The rooms were filled with furniture that had no significance for me either. Not even before my mother "did over" the house, when I was maybe ten, nor after, can I recall any object in it that was, so to speak, mine. Excepting the possible case of the wallpaper in the nursery where I slept in the early years, and this became mine from many nights' association with it, rather more than from the days, for in the early evening summer twilight I used to lean my head against the wall and press my mouth to the small figures in the paper until I had aroused in myself some feeling of comfort. The scenes were from Mother Goose and the simple outlines of the forms were filled in with a light wash of pinks and blues. I can only recall the kind of thing they were and not any detail. They were simple, cozy, and familiar, and I was so used to them that I could trace their outlines on the wall when dark had settled down altogether over the room and blotted out everything except myself and my everlasting need to rest—for nothing in my actual life about me did anything to lessen the ache and the hunger. I believe if there had been one picture in the house that I could have looked at from which I could have drawn some of the spirit of life, I would have been satisfied by it. One thing, if it had been true, would have been enough to slake me. Or one face that had real feeling in it for me would have answered. But there was nothing and no one.

I would gladly have exchanged what I felt to be finer in myself for the kind of perception that would have let me enjoy the things I had to live with. Besides, I suffered very much from my failure to hide my lack of interest and feeling for my world, or for the world into which I was pitched at birth, for the people in our house felt my criticism, no matter how I tried to dissemble it. Anyway, I could not always pretend an enthusiasm that was singularly absent, for them and all their ways, and at the earliest age they revenged themselves upon me by sarcastic utterances in my hearing, such as: "Oh, she was born old!" . . . "She was born bored." . . . "She's always blasé." That I showed no feeling was of course supposed to be due to a lack of it, and no one ever suspected—or if they did they never showed it—that feeling was there, accumulating in me all too fast in the absence of anything to which to attach it. Only on the nights when the west wind blew down North Street and loosened the perfume of the hyacinths, only at moments like that could my own perfume leave me and spend itself on the warm night.

Probably most people have some memories of their earliest years that contain a little warmth and liveliness, but in my own I cannot find one happy hour. I have no recollections of my mother's ever giving me a kiss or smile of spontaneous affection, or of any sign from my father except dark looks and angry sound. I know now they must both of them have been cheated of happier times than they found under their own roof, and that they had no happiness to radiate to a solitary child. We all needed to love each other and to express it, but we did not know how.

My mother was married to a man whose years passed in an increasing inner torment and whose temper grew worse with these years. She was a strong, energetic woman with ruddy hair and truly no words in her mouth. She was of the purest Anglo-Saxon blood. She was not tall—about five feet six, I think—and her small bones were padded with the whitest, firmest flesh. Always plump, in the later years she grew quite stout. She had no imagination and no fear and she seemed to live without love, though both my father and she loved their animals. They each had a dog, usually little longhaired Yorkshire terriers or Boston bulls, and they always had a tenderness for these.

My mother spent herself in ordering her household and in controlling the servants. Everything was carried out according to *"what was what."* No unhappy maid was ever allowed a visitor in the evening, though there was a servants' dining room that could easily have harbored an occasional addition to the dull domestic discipline. No, my mother knew "what was what," as she had been heard to announce. Any servant who ever had a beau was dismissed—and yet she herself had beaux. Quite early I sensed this and was terrified by it. I didn't know why. Not for my father's sake, certainly, for when he flew into a storming rage of jealousy and stamped and shouted and called her names, and I saw her cold, merciless, expressionless contempt behind her book or newspaper, I tried to imitate her look, for that was what he made me too feel.

My father would shout and fling his arms about and his face would seem to break up into fragments from the running passion in him, but my mother behaved as though she were not alive, and when he could shout no more he would stamp out of the room and mount the stairs and presently we would hear his door slam far away in the house. Sometimes, then, she would raise her eyes from the pretense of reading and, not moving her head, she would glance at me sideways and drawing down the corners of her mouth, she would grimace a little message of very thin reassurance to me, upset as I must have looked. For these storms shook me through and through, menacing the foundation of a life that, unsatisfactory though it was, still held all the security I knew.

So that was why I feared that my mother had secrets, because it made my father so wild, and me so afraid that someday our whole life would fall apart, and I could not conceive any other than the one we had so miserably together.

I would have had to stay with him, as I had heard him threaten her, when he swore he would leave her and never come back and that if he left I would leave too. That I was to be used merely as a weapon to overcome her I quite clearly understood, for I knew with all the prescience of a child that my father had no love for me at all. To him I was something that made a noise sometimes in the house and had to be told to get out of the way. So that a change which would have resulted in a house containing just him and me and his nerves was a frightful thing to look forward to. Or should a change mean that my mother and I would be alone together, it was scarcely less to be feared, for would that not mean, perhaps, that then she and I would go and live all the time with Grandma Cook, that old woman who didn't like me either?

My father was taller than my mother by several inches and he was well built. He had a nicely shaped head and his hands and feet had a great deal of individuality until they grew deformed from rheumatism and gout. His irritable nature had spoiled his whole being. And yet . . . and yet . . . he was kind. He always followed up an attack of swearing at Andy, the coachman, with a present of long black cigars. Everyone seemed to know instinctively that he was not really mean and that something tortured him so that he gave vent to it upon anyone who happened to be near. His life was so terribly empty of interest or activity—since he wouldn't work in the bank with his father or at the law for which he was trained—nothing remained for him in Buffalo but to grow cross. His empty life! The energy in him turned to poison, stagnating in his veins, and his only outlets were anxiety, jealousy, and querulousness. No child could have taken to him. Of course I didn't like him.

But I didn't want a change, I wanted things to stay as they were because I had my own nursery with the colored English Christmas prints in it, and though it wasn't ever happy, it was safe. Besides, I didn't know what happiness was; I only knew what safety was.

People didn't divorce in those days. We knew only one woman who had ever done so, and when she reached the pinnacle of resolution that enabled her to jump off into the uncharted realm, she was without a guide in the conduct that was required, so she had to invent her procedure. What she did was to put on deep mourning and, ordering a closed carriage, she drove from house to house announcing her divorce to her friends and showing her papers.

So, since this realization of the safety of the unchanging, even if unhappy, environment grew in me, it made room there for that power to grow which would effect a change for myself as soon as the right time came. For very soon after I was born, I must have known anxiety, a fear that, without the stability of my surroundings, my ego could not grow and develop unless some assurance of a kind of continuity was found. And when the cunning watchfulness of childhood made out that the two antagonists were helpless and bound, from that time on I was at liberty, in myself, to find my escape from them both. And all the years that I have to tell of are but a record of that search.

If the long quiet hours in the nursery were dull with Mary Ann [her nurse-maid] for my sole companion, anyway they were better than the times when I was left there alone. For often she would say: "Now you be good till I come back. I have to go and iron," or some other excuse like that, and off she would go for a gossip with the other "girls." I found this out very soon by summoning the courage to follow her on tiptoe down the back stairs, and there she would be in the cozy kitchen with a cup of hot tea in one hand and on her pale, thin face a shadow of faint animation hardly ever to be seen in our room.

There was always some play going on among the girls down there. And once they had a visitor, a fat gay female who roistered and teased them and chuckled and nagged until they retaliated with some daring rejoinder, when, to my inexpressible amazement, I saw her rip open the front of her dress and drag her great breast out from the shelving corset that supported it. With a quick pressure she directed a stream of pale milk right across the room onto the three squawking servant girls, who hid their faces from this shower. Such a novelty as this became a matter of conjecture to me that lasted for . . . who knows how long? I couldn't get the picture out of my mind. Continually I saw again the fine stream of grayish milk striking across the room, and I longed to see it again in actuality. That it came like that out of a woman allured my imagination and was fascinating to think about because it stirred something hidden inside me and gave me new feelings.

Sometime later I tried to make it happen again. My mother was away visiting Grandma Cook in New York. I do not remember Mary Ann's being about anymore at this time, but we had for a "second girl" a big fair Swedish girl named Elsa. I was attracted by her; she seemed to me to have so much life in her. I begged her to sleep with me. I told her I was afraid at night with my mother gone from the room next to mine, so she sat with me until she thought I slept and later she came and got into my big bed: the bed where Mary Ann had slept beside me for years. But I had not gone to sleep. I had been waiting for her; I had no plan, no thought, of what I wanted—I just wanted.

I waited, quiet, until I knew she was asleep and then I drew nearer to her. She lay on her back and in the darkness I felt her soft breath coming from her open mouth. I felt, rather than saw, how stupid she looked, but I liked her so:

I liked her stupid, fair, gentle presence that was yet so throbbing and full of life. With a great firmness, I leaned over her and seized her big warm breast in both hands. It was a large, ballooning, billowing breast, firm and resilient and with a stout springing nipple. I leaned to it and fondled it. I felt my blood enliven me all over and I longed to approach the whole of my body to her bosom, to cover her completely by my entire surface and have the bounding breast touch me at every point. I rolled it ecstatically from side to side and slathered it with my dripping lips. As my sudden new, delicious pleasure increased, I grew rougher. I longed now to hurt it and wring something from it. I wanted to pound it and burst it.

Suddenly I remembered that other breast seen long ago in the kitchen and I wanted to force from this one the same steely stream of milk that I felt within it, resisting me. However Elsa slept through all this is more than I know, but she never became conscious. I and that breast were alone in the night and that was what I wanted. I worked it back and forward; I approached my body to it in every way I could think of doing to see how it would feel. I held it, pushed it up hard and taut between my two small cold feet, and finally I had enough and, relinquishing it, I fell asleep. Of the awakening the next day I remember nothing; only that night, that first battle and thunder of the flesh, I remember as though it were yesterday.

My mother's room had always for me the same atmosphere both before she did over the house and after. After her breakfast she threw herself energetically out of bed and one could hear the movements of her morning toilet all over the house—such splashing and coughing and bustle she made! Only on Sunday mornings she stayed in bed longer and the Sunday (illustrated) Buffalo paper would be brought up to her and the bed would be covered with the tossed, open sheets, but any further delay in rising after the paper was read was disastrous. A half hour's idleness and time to think with nothing to do brought the mood to the surface that the weekdays were spent in crushing back, the discouragement and self-pity that she was too gallant all the week through and all the year round to allow to take possession of her thoughts. But on Sunday mornings the tears would pour down her face, and when I would go in to see her after my own breakfast on my own little table in the nursery, her eyes would be stained a bright red.

My mother, a speechless woman herself, had set an example of mute endurance and I had modeled myself upon her. So it was, in our house, as though we believed that by ignoring and never speaking of the misery we caused each other we would thereby blot it out from our hearts. And though knowing so well what weight of woe was pressing the rare and difficult tears from her blue eyes, I could find no better way to show her I was interested and sympathetic, struck more dumb than ever by the sight of her, than to squeeze out in a small voice: "What's the matter, Mamma?" "I feel so blu-u-e," she would quaver, burying her face in her handkerchief, but not before I had a glimpse of her disciplined countenance breaking up into a wholly new group of curves and contours forced upon it by the inner upheaval. It was like watching the ice break up in the river.

The outstanding feeling that comes to me from those days is of *désœuvrement* [idleness], of having nothing to do, and with the recollection comes, in long waves that reach away back into that very time, the dread of that feeling, so heavy, so desolate, and so deeply painful that nothing is quite so hard to bear. Better a real pain, better a danger to life itself, than this negation of living that comes from not having anything to do. So to escape from that burden became the great problem in the first five years and has remained so ever since, and to escape the *fear* of the pain for idleness has led me in curious deviations away from the true chances of escape into occupation, all for lack of an intelligent word now and then from my mother, whom I scarcely ever saw, or from Mary Ann, whom I saw all the time. A very little girl alone is not often, I am sure, ingenious in invention; boys probably can amuse themselves more readily and "think up" all kinds of things to do, but a girl needs someone to take the initiative and to suggest things to her. A word is enough to set the whole psychic process moving, but that word is necessary, for she is rarely, I believe, a self-starter.

There were so many hours like this in those first years that later on my principal prayer for a long time was *to be used*. No one had ever taught me how to use myself; I didn't know how to begin. My only hope was from fortunate outside initiative until I developed my own, which later I did.

The first toys in that early time, I remember, were the hollow blocks that begin large and, fitting into each other, grow smaller and smaller. They were gay colored with pictures pasted on them and big letters on some sides of them. A small child on the floor with a set of these graded blocks is limited in what she can do with them. But the years, following on one another's heels from then right down to today, bring me faithfully again the feeling of an extra-big flop of the heart in the middle of its ache that was induced by a great kick at the tall tower of squares, built up one on another as high as my own head.

Now, to discover the thrill and leap of the heart that one can produce from kicking over this construction so carefully built up was an awfully bad discovery for me, and if someone had helped me find this accelerated life by another route, I would have been saved many troubles. This was the time when I became destructive and liked it because I got more feeling of life excitement from it.

I look back and grasp at any lighter days among the many heavy months and years that went by. There were not many that I can bear even to think about. The trouble is, there just wasn't any fun in those days. In our family, all plodded along one day after another and two of us accepted it, while I tried to plot a way out of it. Esther Goodyear and I, eating supper on the tray up in my room, would talk of what we wanted to do when we were grown up. She wanted to be married and have children, but—oh, my goodness—I didn't!

"I'm going to be a hospital nurse," I announced, for these were the only women I had ever seen who were free and not married. I had seen many of them coming and going in our house. They worked in nice clean starched clothes and then they changed their clothes and put on their hats and coats and went out into the dazzling world, free to enjoy all the things, whatever they were, that we didn't have in our house and yet must be waiting somewhere outside our environment. In those days a hospital nurse represented the most desirably situated woman alive!

CHAPTER THREE ✎ GROWN-UP PEOPLE
AND A DINNER PARTY

There was always, for me, a great feeling of mystery about my mother. I suppose her reserve, combined with the appearance of free and unchecked movement through life, made her seem a creature of secrets. Maybe she was. Anyway, she didn't care how she appeared to anyone. That was evident. She has moved unhampered and even unaware that others watched her through the years from my babyhood until now—strange, hidden, determined, and free within the narrow boundaries of her life.

I wanted to be as free. Someday I would be. But I never did succeed in becoming so unconscious or so indifferent to those outside myself. She made her plans and told them to no one. She never, I am sure, had a confidante. She was extremely respectful to my grandmother and grandfather Cook, and when almost daily letters of counsel came from the former, she read them and carried out the numerous suggestions for housekeeping, for dosing a child, or for the care of animals that my grandmother passed her mornings in compiling for her daughters. But for her own secret psychic needs my mother never received any advice. In those days, only the outermost rim of life was given any conscious attention. People, especially children and parents, never spoke together about or even thought of their hearts and souls, and as for their bodies, I think a pill was about the limit of their consideration! If it were true, as my father hinted to me darkly once or twice, that my grandmother had tried to separate my mother and me from him when I was a baby, it must have been in only the most practical qualities that he seemed to my grandmother unable to satisfy my mother. No lack in the inner life would ever be sufficiently important to justify a move like that. Only some external, practical deficiency.

My mother naturally had no intimacy with Grandma Cook. One is not intimate about food and clothing and houses, but about the affairs of the heart. All this was left untouched between them, and left untouched by my mother and me in turn. Example is so strong! If only a mother here and there would be herself, act on her own feelings, and break the chain that holds her to the past and makes her emulate her own mother in every way!

And so I do not know my mother's secret life. I only felt she had one. Sometimes little signs would make me feel she knew, intimately, people whom we never saw. For instance, she took me to New York when I was very little. We drove in a carriage to a large hotel, a place filled with what seemed hundreds of gay people. Everyone seemed to know everyone else. It was like a party at our house at home, and I felt there like the stranger that sat at the top of the stairs and watched the gaiety below.

Apropos of this, I remember the way I tried once, at home, to get into things, to be a part of it, and not to have to stay up on the second floor away from it all, outside of life. They had put me to bed early to get me out of the way, so that Mary Ann could help in the pantry, where there was so much to do. I had gone into my mother's room in my night drawers and, sitting with my knees drawn up and my feet under me to keep warm, I watched her put on her jewels, which meant that she was ready. She pinned a life-sized emerald lizard on one shoulder and a dragonfly of colored jewels on the other. She had a diamond necklace from which a complicated ornament was suspended, and in her dark red hair a large diamond star whizzled at the end of a long, strong gold hairpin. For rings she had a set of three in rows of rubies, sapphires, and diamonds, her solitaire engagement ring, and a large single pearl.

I have watched her jewels alter through the years, for she was always exchanging them to follow the fashion. And now she has scarcely anything but pearls. She has accumulated pearls as I have accumulated experience, all these years since she pinned on herself an emerald lizard and I, determined not to be excluded from all that, sat and planned how to get into the swim of life that she so imperturbably enjoyed. And now, so longer after, I have no pearls or emeralds but I do not mind, for I have had the years.

Before she was quite finished she turned to me and said: "Now you go to bed and go to sleep. Don't call Mary Ann. She is going to be very busy. Have you had your drink of water? Well, go to sleep then and be a good girl." She held out a cold cheek and I kissed it and made off out of the room through the dressing room to the nursery. There the light was turned low and the bed was waiting for me, but I crept out on tiptoe and down the stairs. Quiet as a mouse, I crept on through the still rooms to the dining room.

The loaded table stood in the subdued light of the room, glistening and portentous, like a sumptuous altar before the god descends upon it. I heard the maids in the pantry conversing in the low, serious voices that the occasion produced in them. Such a party was always a severe ordeal for them all in the kitchen. Twelve guests and nearly twelve courses of food, dozen and dozens of delicate glasses to be cared for, dozens and dozens of costly china plates; and all these dishes to be served promptly without a break in the rhythm—one thing followed another smoothly, inevitably. The wine bottles standing in rows ready to be uncorked, for every glass must always be full; the accessories ready waiting at the side; the crackers and cheeses and jellies and sauces, the pickles and sauces and olives and relishes.

I stood an instant and gazed, then lifted the long tablecloth that hung almost to the floor and crept under at the right hand of my mother, closest to the pantry door through which the feast arrived. The table was wide enough for me, under there. I snuggled into the place between its legs and there I waited. It wasn't any fun at all. Never did I feel so out of things . . . it's too sad to tell about. Presently I think I fell asleep there. There was nothing else to do! When I woke up in the morning I was in my own bed. When I was found or how I never learned. No one said anything. In this way, too, grown-ups bar children out, by refusing to talk things over with them instead of behind their backs.

In the lively hotel in New York, in what I supposed was the middle of the night, I was hanging behind my mother and trying to look like everyone else, happy and gay. Soon after we came in, while my mother stood at the desk and talked to a man behind the counter, another man came up smiling and held out his hand to her. "Well, Sara," he said. He was rather old and fat. I had never seen him before but my mother called him Randolph. She said to him: "Wait till I take her up and put her to bed, Randolph, and then I'll come down again."

She went upstairs into a dark room and when the gas was lighted she told me to undress myself. While I did so she poured some water from a pitcher and washed her face and hands. When I was in bed, shivering and shaking with dread, she said to me: "Now you go right to sleep."

"Where are you going?" I asked in a choking voice. I was terrified. It seemed as though everything was going to pieces around me. What was she going to do? What was I to do alone in that room in that big bed that I had never seen before?

"Never mind about me. You go to sleep," she said, and turned out the gas. She went out the door, and my heart threatened to knock me to pieces. The dreadful, dreadful fear! Where was my mother and what was she doing? I felt it was secret and strange and shameful. How could a child have had any such knowledge of shame? Was it shame? And why?

I lay and quaked there in the bed. The linen sheets smelled queer and unfamiliar. I could not warm them and the bed remained cold and inhospitable to me. I could not sleep but lay awake for hours, it seemed to me, waiting for my mother, wondering who Randolph was and what they were doing together. The unknown street below me was full of the sharp clacking of horses' hoofs and people's voices rose from there. Again I was no part of it all. I was an unassimilated small atom of consciousness burning to live and unable to live wherever I found myself. Why? Why was I never a part of things like everybody else?

After ages passed, my mother came back and I sat up in bed with a bounce of relief. "Aren't you asleep yet? What's the matter with you? I never knew such a child!" she complained, then threw off her clothes vigorously and blew her nose with a loud noise and gave the window a great push until it was wide open and then climbed into bed and flung herself onto her side with her back to me and was asleep in a moment. I was all right again. Her cold, harsh, healthy presence in the bed reassured me and I breathed in long, slow, happy breaths. I didn't care anymore what she had been doing nor was I tortured and shamed by the thought of her guilt, whatever it was. I had her there and she made me comfortable, whatever she had done or whomever with.

Randolph appeared and disappeared throughout the years. I saw him again at Grandma Cook's. Just a friend, a family friend, the friend of all the Cooks. Why had I assumed some secret thing between him and my mother? Something hateful and terrifying? After I learned to read I found an English edition of Boccaccio in my mother's second bureau drawer under her handkerchief case. When I first found it and read it I could not understand it, but I felt it was shameful because it was hidden. This book threw a darker glamour over my mother. . . . It spoke of mysteries and far-off, strange things that I came to identify with her. Was she a deep and secret woman, ruthless and unashamed, imperturbable amidst the weaklings about her, or did I invent all that about her?

CHAPTER FOUR 🕮 BOOKS AND PLAYMATES

Nina Wilcox is one of those whose destiny and mine have been linked together from the earliest days. My connection with her began when, as they told me, my father fell in love with her mother. But he married my mother and she married Ansley Wilcox and Nina and I were the outcome. Nina was born in our house on the corner of North and Delaware, and my grandfather Cook bought that house from her family and gave it to my mother when I was a year or two old. So I was moved into the nursery Nina had occupied there, and her parents moved two doors down the street into the fine old brick house with the high Doric columns. It was always painted gray and the columns were white.

I liked playing with Nina because I could make her do just as I liked. Quite early I won the upper hand over her, though of course that isn't saying much— the poor child! Her *volonté de vivre* [will to live] and to branch out for herself had suffered a daily, almost hourly, setback from the discouraging contrast between her stepmother's feelings for [her stepsister] Frances and for her, whereas I in my loneliness at home had gathered my forces until I was strong. When I ran out of my empty nursery I felt I could conquer the world, although from the habit of silence no one would have guessed it from my face. So I was the leader and Nina followed after wherever I went.

[One] night I was going to stay over at Nina's for supper, so we had a nice long afternoon to play in. "What let's do?" I asked tentatively as I threw myself across the fence with gusto. "Let's do something different!"

"Well, what?" asked Nina, ready.

Frances came up with [her] rag doll and I got my new idea. I rushed Nina off alone and said: "I know. Let's s'prise Frances! Let's make her think her doll knows how to do number one!" Nina's eyes opened wide. "How do you mean?" she asked. "Oh, I'll show you! Let's get the doll away from her. Hey, Frances, come here! You give us that Dinah doll and we'll make you a wonderful s'prise." She thrust the lank and worn black doll out to us and we ran off into the house with it, after we got her to promise to wait out in the grape arbor till we came back.

The house was deathly still as we entered it and darkened as were all the other houses of the people we knew in Buffalo on warm summer afternoons. Mrs. Wilcox, we knew, was "resting" in her bedroom. The door was closed upon her. We crept into the bathroom opposite and shut the door quietly. Then I turned Dinah upside down and sent Nina out again into the danger zone to find a pair of scissors. She came back trembling, for by now we were both awfully excited with a queer delicious kind of pleasure, both mysterious and yet familiar. We experienced the secret, forbidden joy of arousing our own buried life.

I sat down on the floor and holding Dinah firmly between my knees I poked a hole into the seam between her dark legs in the place where the hole ought to be. Then I turned on the faucet in the washbowl and applied Dinah's newly made orifice to the stream of cold water. I suppose we thought that Dinah would just swell up and retain the water, but she didn't. She got danker and danker until she was a squishy bundle of rags and the colors ran together and into each other and into the washbowl. It was a dreadful mess and Dinah was done for!

"What will Frances say?" whispered Nina, for Frances adored Dinah and even had to sleep with her. "What will your mother say?" I asked in an awe-struck tone.

I quaked with such a strong quake that now it began to be agreeable. It seemed to us both that the Judgment Day might be like this, for we could not imagine a colder, harder judge of our action than Mrs. Wilcox would be, and we knew our offense was one of those unspeakable, those absolutely unmentionable and shameful deeds that would arouse in her that certain look which grown-ups have for children—that look of repulsion, disgust, that thrusts one into the outer darkness, the look of helpless disgust for the unexamined and unnamed deeds of childhood that lie in the ignored areas of the body. Oh, children well know this look on the faces of their parents! But why did I have to tell her? I didn't know then and I don't know now. It was a feeling that we must, it was unavoidable, we must go and tell Mrs. Wilcox.

Mrs. Wilcox simply couldn't say anything at first. She just looked and I looked back at her. The most frightening expression came into her face in the silence. She just looked baffled and unable to find words to punish us—me— as I deserved. I could see that to her we appeared to be the lowest form of animal life and she loathed having any connection whatsoever with us. Oh, how human beings can detest each other!

In a moment she spoke: "You naughty girls! You shall be punished for this. Take that doll right downstairs and show Frances what you have done and then give it to Norah to throw away. And tonight you shall not have any strawberries and cream for your supper. Now go!"

We went quietly downstairs and found Frances and we had no more feelings in us to experience any more. We just held out Dinah to her, where she sat waiting, that good, quiet blond child, in the cool grape arbor. "Here," we said again. "Here's Dinah."

"Guess I'll go home," I said. "This is no fun. Goo'-by!" And I went, crestfallen, over the fence.

That early energy of mine led me into many queer actions—into exhibitions of power, of prowess, and of courage that finally won me a dubious success, for while they impressed Nina and the other children with my surprising faculties, they affected the grown-ups with dismay. I recall that when I made Nina think that I could eat worms—by holding one in thumb and forefinger close to my mouth and then swiftly throwing it over my shoulder—Mrs. Wilcox really did think I was an out-and-out bad girl with who knows what strange perversions!

Somehow I learned to read, and then I passed right over into the book world. I became a member of the different families in those adorable little books, with their vivid, simple pictures. I was one of the little girls in the "Dorothy Dimple Series" and the "Flaxie Frizzle Series." I ate with them and slept with them, and when they were good girls and their dear kind mamma allowed them to have lemonade on warm afternoons under the shade tree on their lawn, I tasted it and enjoyed it with them. The "Lulu Books" too were full of nice little girls with kind mothers and manly papas. And as for the "Rollo Books," with Rollo's uncle George—well, I went all over the world with Rollo.

One of the disasters of my childhood, however, was when I became identified with Elsie Dinsmore in the "Elsie Books." Elsie certainly was a good girl and it took all kinds of courage to be as good as she—and so she was worth imitating. When Elsie sat all morning on the piano stool until she dropped fainting with fatigue before she would touch the keys on Sunday, when her bad, unprincipled father had asked her to play for him, I thought that was the most perfect behavior I had ever known. And I waited and watched until I too could be asked to do something on Sunday that my conscience wouldn't allow me to do, so that I too could be as noble and as strong as Elsie.

But oh, poor Mary Ann's life was all upset by that paragon of a child, for Elsie wouldn't button her own shoes! No, she was a southern child—a little lady—and she let it be known that no ladylike girl would button up her own shoes when she had a colored servant right there to do it for her. No, indeed! Well, after I read that, the very next day when Mary Ann was trying to hustle me and make me dress quickly, I sat down in a chair and stuck out my feet and said: *"I'm* not going to button my shoes anymore. I'm a little lady and you're my servant and you have to do it for me."

I remember Mary Ann's pale, impudent Canadian face to this day, when I said that. "Well, I never! A lady, is it? Well, you're mistaken, that's what you are if you think I'm hired to dress you at your age and button your shoes! I'd be ashamed—a great big girl like you, near nine years old. You set right down there and put on your shoes this minute or I'll call your ma in here and we'll see who's a lady!"

It didn't work at all, I must say. Early I learned the discrepancy between books and real life. What a lesson!

It was a sign that we were growing up when we began to keep our "little books"—the only bookkeeping I have ever done, let me add—tiny little note-books, and everyone had them, the boys as well as the girls. Every week we made lists, "us girls," of the boys we liked, in the order of their importance to us. No. 1 was the one we liked the best, and so on. The boys kept lists of the girls. All the girls wanted to be first on Bob's list, but he had Mary Forman there for a long time and I, for one, was very discouraged about it. He had been first on mine for a long time, just as he was on Mary's, on Esther's, and on many another.

And what changed him? Was it his mother's words one night? He came in breathless, as usual, and threw his fur cap down. His "little book" stuck out of his breast pocket and I looked at it longingly. I felt I *had* to get first in there. Mary was off down south with her parents and only that day I had had a let-ter from her and she told me that she had cut the letters B.C.R. in a tree down there. She liked him best and he liked her best! How hopeless it seemed! Mrs. Rumsey caught up my thoughts as I gazed at him standing moodily by the wood fire. "Bobkins, do you still like those pink cheeks and that auburn hair? Oh, Bobkins, you don't know how to choose! What you love doesn't lie in pink cheeks. Learn to read, little man, learn to *read*." And she turned to me and laughingly passed her hand over my hair—my straight brown hair. Noth-ing but that, but next day Conger Goodyear came to me late on the pond just as dusk was coming. Grouch, we called him, for he never smiled. He scowled and his bushy eyebrows nearly met over his blue eyes. Later he grew to look somewhat like Abraham Lincoln. He was Bob's faithful slave.

"Hey, Mabel, come over here a minute!" He beckoned to me with that mix-ture of patronage and contempt that the boys always adopted towards us. I suddenly saw Bob make off, running at top speed through the dusk on the path that ran around the whole garden and around the tall trees bordering the pond.

"Bob says to tell you he's put you first on his list. But he's not sure he's going to keep you there!" Oh, golly! Oh, glory! My heart rose in a thrust like a bird rising. I was first with him at last! Maybe I never again felt such triumph as in that moment. I had longed for it so hard. It had seemed unattainable.

Bob continued to race around the pond and he never came near me. It hadn't anything to do with nearness, anyway. It was abstract, pure, unalloyed experience having its rise, its life, and its decline in another realm than the one in which we moved and spoke. No—somewhere in the depths something that was Bob had something that was me first on the list in his little book. It was very delicate and powerful and we added to each other's stature by that obscure exchange of hidden life.

CHAPTER FIVE ☙ GRANDMA GANSON
AND HER HOUSE

Grandma Ganson lived on Delaware Avenue in a large square brick house with a cupola on top if it, with windows to the four corners. The house was painted what they called dun color, a fawn-gray tone. It had an iron fence and two large iron vases set in the lawn on both sides of the front steps. In the summer these vases always had "ornamental grasses," geraniums, and fuchsias growing in them. Some people had iron deer on their lawns.

On the left side of Grandma's house, the lawns running together, was the Buffalo Club, the club of the middle-aged and elderly gentlemen. Right opposite, close to the street, stood Trinity Church—"our church." At the corner of the block on Edward Street was the cozy-looking Saturn Club of red brick, the young men's club, which bore on its inner walls the device: "Where the women cease from troubling and the wicked are at rest!"

Grandma loved her neighborhood. In winter she used to sit in her bay window that was projected out into the world with its glass panes reaching to the floor. She sat in a fine light, shining cane rocking chair and knitted cotton washclothes. As she knitted she peered over her spectacles towards the Buffalo Club, or the Saturn Club, or towards the church. She knew all the men who frequented all these places, and she was openly and earnestly interested in them all. She knew them personally, most of them—their houses and their businesses and their families. And besides that she knew their club habits. And all the men knew her and always looked towards her bay window, and lifted their hats whether they saw her there or not, which depended on the year and the time of day.

Grandma Ganson had been a Batavia girl. Batavia is a small town about an hour away from Buffalo and it was settled before Buffalo, but it never grew up. I suppose Buffalo grew because it was on Lake Erie. When Grandma was a young girl the Iroquois Indians were all about in that country. I have heard it whispered, when I was quite small, that she had Indian blood, and this was fascinating to me. But in those days it was rather frequently whispered about people.

Grandma Ganson, then, as a girl used to walk past the bank in Batavia on her way to school and James Ganson, a stern young man of thirty-five, saw her pass and said to himself that she was the girl he would marry. And he did. James Ganson was a severe, humorless man—with a square white beard when he came into my life. He was in his bank all day until the middle of the afternoon, the Marine Bank of Buffalo.

Grandma Ganson certainly was plebeian. She hadn't a distinguished thing about her. She was the typical small-town woman with her church and her "Saturday class," where the ladies met to sew together, while someone read from *Littell's Living Age*. She had not ignoble but yet not elevated thoughts—about anything. She was like a bird, a chirping sparrow, undaunted because all unaware. But I loved her as much as a child ever loves anyone. That is, I liked to go to her house. It was warm and homelike and nourishing. I liked to go in there and feel secure and loose all over. At home I never could feel so at ease.

My father lived the most prosaic life imaginable, but he managed, out of his own queerness, to convey a feeling of the unknown to people. He used to drive downtown every morning in the buggy to an office somewhere and shut himself in there until twelve. Then he would be brought home again. What he did there no one in the world knew, for he had no business. He had studied the law, and he had refused to practice it. My grandfather had asked him to go into the bank with him, but he had refused that too. He had nothing to do and finally died of doing nothing.

My father was tortured by my mother's silent and inexpressive character. She rarely spoke or smiled. She had some inability for speech. There is a story of how she enraged my dignified grandpa Cook by her inarticulation as a child; that after a prolonged refusal to speak and reply to him, he seized a horsewhip and chased her round and round the garden in Bath until, catching her, he whipped her hard. This probably sealed her up more than ever. Anyway, when we all found ourselves living together in the cold, expressionless house on the corner of Delaware and North Street, there she was as silent as a sphinx. And she has always remained a sphinx to me. I know nothing of her or what goes on in her. She simply sat and wrote letters, or read the paper or a book.

We never had any talk in our house at meals or at any other time. My parents, like everyone else in their set, had dinner parties all the time. The women were occupied all day with housekeeping, and children, and sewing, and driving out, and the men were all downtown working. Then when the evening came there would be many dinner parties in Buffalo society. It was all divided up into sets and each set dined together a great deal. The dinners were usually of twelve people and the tables were loaded with glass and silver and lace centerpieces. People ate and drank very well in Buffalo. Often my father would look down the dinner table and see my mother looking at the man next to her with an expression in her cold eyes that he didn't like, and he would jump up from the table with a frightful black look at her, catch up a Sèvres plate and dash it on to the hardwood floor. Then, generally without a word, he would stamp upstairs and his door would bang through the house. The ladies on each side of his empty place would raise their eyebrows, smiling, and pass it off with some light joke to my mother. Everyone was used to my father. Most of them had always known him, except those who, like my mother, had come from out of town and married someone in Buffalo.

His peculiarly unsuitable marriage was taken as a matter of course. That he hated my mother was no news to anyone. He had one hobby—flags. He had the flags of all nations, and when anyone from another country came, he would hoist the foreign flag on our flagpole out on the front lawn. He had, too, his personal flag with his monogram C.F.G. on it. Whenever my mother went away to stay with Grandma Cook, he would run up his flag and keep it flying all the time she was away. The day she returned he kept it at half-mast. She herself paid not the slightest attention to this. Everyone in town knew the signal and smiled and shrugged and accepted it. "Charley Ganson is a crank." That's what they called it in those days forty years ago.

CHAPTER SIX ≈ GRANDMA COOK IN HER HOUSE

My grandfather Cook started life in Bath, New York. His father, Constant Cook, an English younger son, came over to this country from the family place in Surrey, called Wheatley, and bearing a grant of land from the king, he settled the town of Bath. He broke the earth, he built houses, he shod the horses. He had to do everything along with the other young men who joined him in the new country. So the Cooks became the whole thing in that place. Grandpa Cook was the president of the bank when he left it for New York because he couldn't keep his dollars occupied there.

Grandpa Cook stood six feet and some inches and was very slender, with broad shoulders. He had deep-set eyes, iron colored, with a distant, abstracted gaze on inner problems, a thin high-bridged nose that had a sudden curve to the hump, and a square white beard. He rarely spoke and hardly ever smiled. He was lost all the time in speculation. I admired him passionately, for there was, in his aloofness, a grandeur about him. Grandma Cook was an awesome person too. She grew crosser and crosser as she grew older. In her younger years she had lived in Bath in the large clapboarded house that stood far back from the village street, inside a white picket fence. Here in this village she had been an active, practical, managing woman, since to provide for her family all those luxuries and pleasures of the table recalled by their fathers in the life at home in the old country required great planning and ingenuity.

Grandmother was always superintending the kitchen, helping to prepare the splendid country meals, training the young country maids, overseeing the preserving, the many complicated puddings and cakes and pies, the roasting of the big joints and fowls, and attending to the thousand details of a hearty, comfortable living. Besides, she was always "bringing up" her four handsome girls while their father, down in the village, spun the whole countryside out of himself. Horseshoeing, banking, judging, railroad building, house building, town building!

There was plenty for everyone to do in America in those days. The Cooks were the town of Bath—the bank, the courthouse, the business—and money flowed to my grandfather Cook. He had a genius for money and it was mystical to him. He had a sense not only of its importance but of its holiness.

I remember his coming slowly down the grand, gloomy staircase in the house on Fifth Avenue one day when I was about eight years old. His slender, tall body held very straight—he always moved slowly, like a priest. When he reached the bottom of the stairs, where I stood looking up at him, he put his hand in his pocket and drew out a shining new silver coin and held it towards me on the palm of his bloodless, clawlike hand. He had a very deep look in his iron-colored eyes that had arched, dropping lids. He looked like a noble bird of some kind—the real American eagle. Some man like him, with a close affinity for that fowl, must have stamped this image on our currency, circulating himself into immortality.

"Here," he said to me loudly and impressively, "here is a silver dollar for you! Look at it! Now take it and never forget it. A silver dollar!"

I remember just how this felt—an important moment. And two conflicting emotions rose up in me: a sense of reverence, of deep veneration for my grandfather, a glad reverence that he was mine and his words were law, so that a silver dollar was indeed a thing to honor all one's life; and a willingness and a submission to this symbol, yes, a desire to be prostrate to it because of that noble old man, my lawgiver. And yet at the same time a feeling of revulsion and disdain and inward ridicule and irony that has rejected so many other symbols for me all though this life, the sense of clarity and irony that tears away veils and makes one see realistically—though indeed who knows whether more truly? So while I almost wanted to kneel down and accept that silver dollar from him like a sacrament, at the same time I wanted to cry out: "Oh, nonsense! What do I care for your old dollars!"

Grandma Cook lived, when I first remember her, in the somber stone mausoleum on the corner of Fifth Avenue and Seventh-eighth Street. [In the mornings she] would issue forth from her dressing room impeccably groomed, oiled, powdered, and swathed. To her Chippendale desk she would slowly move like a cheerful, soft-stepping elephant, and sitting there would pass the morning in long, long letters to Louise, to Marianna, or to Sara. The rustling dry blue sheets would gather covered with her fine, strong writing. Telling of the smallest detail to be carried out, for the grandchildren, for the stepchildren, for the neighbors, for all the maladies of the season, for the change of clothes, for the preserves, for the garden, for the church. Minute directions in a most commanding manner that were accepted by her daughters and I believe always quite fully carried out. And at home every morning these daughters would sit down and write letters, to their mother and to their sisters. Long dull letters full of concrete and practical facts. So the shuttles of the family life darted back and forth year in and year out, weaving a solid, indestructible tissue.

CHAPTER EIGHT 🐚 OTHER WORLDS

I got out of our house by way of Dorothy and Madeleine Scatcherd and Nina Wilcox. The Scatcherds lived three houses above us on Delaware Avenue in a white wooden frame house that was very small and ordinary on the outside but had a strong particular charm within. They were Canadians and there were two girls and a little boy, Newton, until later, when Emily the baby was born. She was named after Mrs. Scatcherd's sister, who lived with them, Aunty Em Wood. When Dorothy was eight years old and Madeleine and I were ten, Aunty Em came home from Paris.

Aunty Em was very fascinating. She had the small room next to Madeleine's and we children used to gather around her there like flies. Her dressing table was covered with lovely brushes and many combs. Bottles of scents of all kinds were there and powder boxes with downy puffs in them. And on each side of the glass were photographs of strange-looking women, some in fancy dresses with cocked hats or ruffs, some in high bunched curls, and one in trousers. Yes, one in real men's trousers and taken in the act of lifting a high silk hat from her head, from which all the hair had been clipped! This photograph almost frightened us and yet we were fascinated by it. One day Dorothy asked Aunty Em who it was.

"Who is that lady, Aunty Em?" she inquired.

"That is my dearest friend, sweetheart. That is the Baroness Blanc," she answered.

Aunty Em was the first woman who ever smoked a cigarette in Buffalo and she smoked them all the time. She was a being who was full to the brim with a rich liquor of some kind. It must have been hard for her to come back to Buffalo. Almost at once, we knew in the indescribable way by which children know things that people didn't like Aunty Em. They were afraid of her and disapproved of her. She certainly was too different from them. She was full of laughter, twinkling and dimpling with it, but she and the other Buffalo people didn't laugh at the same things. She knew things to laugh at that they had never heard of.

Now Aunty Em had a secret. We always felt she had many secrets but we couldn't imagine what they were. She had reached out around Buffalo for friends when she came back, but she hadn't found any. She hadn't found a single "pal," as she called it. She had two young friends on the stage, Della Fox and Johnstone Bennett, the latter a girl too who with short hair, an eyeglass, and man's clothes always took young men's parts. But they only came to Buffalo once a year. Aunty Em had really no one to play with, so she took to us little girls. And one night when we were having dinner over there, Mr. and Mrs. Scatcherd went to the theater and Aunty Em and we were left together.

"If you girls won't give me away, I'll show you something," she told us. We were thrilled. To be in a secret with this fascinating, strange, foreign Aunty Em!

She told us to wait for her and when she came back after a few minutes she had completely changed! She had on a suit of men's evening clothes. She had a real stiff shirt, a long-tailed coat, and an eyeglass! In one hand a small, high hat, in the other a slender cane! Aunty Em! We had never seen a woman dressed anything like a man. Women wore very full, voluminous clothes in those days. No one even had bloomers. They came eight or ten years later, though, for use in school gymnasiums.

We all felt immediately we had a man there in the room with us. And she felt so too. Clothes are so subtle, so mysterious; their influence has never been quite calculated. "Clothes make the man."

Now Aunty Em had to melt our sudden coolness and reserve. She wooed us gently and tenderly. She had an air of magical attractiveness. She said: "Let us dance. I will teach you to dance a new dance." This was different from dancing school. This was queer. She pressed us to her hard shirtfront and we felt her breath on our faces. We gave way to the sweetness of it and felt rather scared.

She danced with us each in turn, and soon we were pushing each other aside to get into her arms again. She wrinkled her nose at us and laughed a kind of wild laugh and lighted cigarettes one from the other.

And then the telephone rang and my mother told me it was time to come home and said to run right along and she'd be waiting at the front door for me. For it was only a step between our houses.

"Wait. I'll go too. But you must remember now. You're not going to tell about these clothes. Your mother and father would burn them if they knew I had them in the house, girls," she said, turning to Madeleine and Dorothy.

"No, no, never!" we all promised, and she put on a big cape and walked to my gate with me. And as we walked down the gaslit street, past the vacant lot and past the Friars' House, that pompous red brick with turrets with all the windows gleaming behind the sheltering shades, I thrilled through and through at the thought of her legs in those trousers underneath the cape—that secret, that almost frightening secret that we had to keep.

People have always been grateful to me for my ability, since I was a child, to put myself in their places, to sense, without knowing causes, the multitudinous fluctuations of the human psyche. This natural sympathy that I could feel was not voluntary exactly, any more than the changing colors of the chameleon who takes on the tone of whatever he comes in contact with are voluntary. I was just naturally fluctuating and flowing all the time, wherever I found myself, in and out of the people I was with. I have always been myself and at the same time someone else; always able to be the other person, feel with him, think his thoughts, see from the angle in which he found himself. This has caused me many inward conflicts, and it has always drawn people to me in the same degree that I flowed out to them and identified myself with them, and it has always made people want to kiss me, to manifest an actual nearness and union, finding it comforting and consolatory. It is the only genius I have ever had but it has been enough, and these pages are given to recording its progress.

It must have been sometime in the late eighties that Oscar Wilde came to Buffalo and gave a lecture to the ladies upon how to do over their houses. I wish I had heard what he said, but of course I was too young to go to hear him. He stayed in Buffalo two or three days and my father flew the British flag on the lawn all the time he was there. He caused a profound movement, a kind of upheaval, through Buffalo society and everyone was talking about him and trying to get him to visit them.

Mrs. Mortimer was one of those who succeeded. She piloted Mr. Wilde from attic to cellar of her large brick house. It was in her own estimation perfectly satisfactory, and what she really wanted, and one imagines expected, from the "aesthete" was a corroboration of her taste. The house was stuffed with "decorations." All the woodwork in it was twisted and tortured and varnished and everywhere there were "drapes" and bunches of gilded cat-o'-nine-tails tied together with great satin bows of ribbon. Seltzer-water jugs made of red pottery that looked like sausages had paintings of wildflowers upon them and ribbon bows upon their small high handles and they adorned the mantelpieces. In the hall near the front door a life-sized carved bear from Berne held out in its paws a card receiver, where the collection of pasteboard squares was left to increase year by year; at least all the worthwhile ones were left, while the insignificant ones or those that were symbols of visitors whose attentions were not valuable were torn up and thrown into the wastepaper basket, an openwork willow affair with red ribbons run in and out of it.

After she had conducted her guest over the place she halted him before the fireplace in the drawing room, an orifice that was covered with an enormous painted paper fan from Spain with a bullfight depicted upon it, and clasping her little hands together she looked up at him and cried: "Now, Mr. Wilde, what do you really think I should do with my house?" And waited for the seal of his approbation, confident that his answer would be: "Do nothing. It is perfect as it is." But alas! It is reported that he gazed at her in a somber fashion and replied: "Burn it, madam!" and then seized his hat and fled from the scene.

Margaret Strane came to live across the street with her aunt Amelia. She was a silent, rather haughty-looking girl of about sixteen. I knew her when I was about fourteen years old. She wasn't pretty, but she had heavy-looking blue eyes and there was an attraction about her of a dark nature, so that always after I had been with her, after one of our low-voiced, secret times, I felt uncomfortable. I felt dissipated and unstrung and miserable. I used to go across the street hunting her, though, looking for her through the rooms of the old stone house. When I came upon her somewhere in a dark corner of the somber rooms, she rose, and together we made our way to someplace yet more silent, more secret, where we would be undisturbed. And then without preamble I would reach out to her and run my hands over her small breasts that budded out provocative through the thin summer muslin.

A little later, when I was taken to see *Anthony and Cleopatra* with Fanny Davenport in it, all the interest of the play lay for me in the large blond breasts of the languorous queen: round they were and with a deep cleft between them.

The story of the play was woven for me about the cleft between the two full breasts. I identified myself with Anthony and trembled when he drew the mature blond woman close to him so that her bosom was crushed against his gold-bordered tunic.

When *Iris* was played in Buffalo, it was a profound experience for me and set up an inner conflict that was threshed out then and there and gave me the opportunity to decide an important question for my own life. Iris, it will be remembered, succumbs to a young lover in the absence of her violent and unattractive husband. She spends the last night he has in England in his arms—apparently sitting on an upholstered sofa. The second act ends with them sitting there in their evening clothes and the curtain of the last act goes up to find them still sitting there. But the dawn is coming in the window, so they are obviously sinners. Then the young man goes away forever on his long journey. The husband comes back unexpectedly and finds out the truth of things and, after throwing all the valuable bric-a-brac in the room onto the floor and tearing up all the lace curtains, he turns Iris out of the house. When he turned her out on the street we all knew she was ruined—that there was no place on earth for her to go, that there was no chance for her except to find another lover. We knew that because we were supposed to see it that way in those days—in about the year 1895, I think it must have been.

Everyone went out of the theater in a subdued mood. The men were pensive, the women scared. The men felt, "Poor thing! It's a pity . . . a damned shame . . . but that's the way it is." The women were thinking it wasn't worth it, that night on the sofa, and ruin forever after. They looked at each other and smiled foolishly as they filed slowly out through the thronged aisles of the theater.

I was in a tumult myself. I remember very distinctly the confusion of feelings in me—the feelings of shame, of fear, of doom, of the certainty that some such fate would overtake me someday. For I felt as Iris felt. I knew how much she must have hated that old husband and how easy it was to love the young man. Like Iris, I too, it seemed to me, would sometime run close to the wind, would find myself at the mercy of a fool, as so many other women did.

Then, too, I would be flung out—kicked out into the open world . . . alone . . . alone. That word "alone" scared me as it always had, even when I repeated it to myself silently. I saw myself in Iris's place stumbling down the stairs and out into the world—alone. I was appalled for a moment at the vision, but hard upon it came an afterthought, ringing through me like a bugle, clear, cleansing, and reassuring. "It doesn't have to be that way. Iris needn't be lost. Why should she be? Why, for goodness' sake, should she be condemned to be lost forever because that noisy fool of a man kicks her out? It's not the end for Iris if she doesn't feel it is. If she thinks it is, though, maybe she will be destroyed.

Maybe that Iris will be destroyed, but I will never be." I registered it right then and there—joyful, certain, strong. No matter what happened to me, I would never go down and I would never be destroyed.

CHAPTER NINE 🍃 SCHOOL

Spring days when the ground in our yards grew moist and soft and springy and when the air was full of the sweet rich smell of the manure on the flower beds, and the trees began to show buds—and then to have to go to school! Into the close, overwarm rooms across the street to St. Margaret's. How I hated it!

I do not remember learning a single thing at St. Margaret's, where I went to school until I was sixteen years old, except one day in Miss Tuck's Bible class when she told us that "Leah was tender-eyed" meant one of two things: that Leah had either gentle eyes or else sore ones. Beyond that I remember nothing, though I suppose I must have absorbed some other facts. But I remembered that, for I looked at Miss Tuck and wondered about her eyes. They were strange; I couldn't decide whether they were tender or sore. They were very soft and they looked as though they hurt her—as though what she saw with them hurt her.

There is so much that might be told about life at St. Margaret's! The fragrance as well as the nastiness of those days stays strong on me yet. Our yellow-and-white assembly room—St. Margaret's colors—how much happened in it and around it! Our class mottoes were painted on the ceiling. Mine was "He also serves who learns to stand and wait." I used to ponder deeply on those words. I made them answerable for much in my life. They accompanied me, sowed early, and grew into my texture. "He also serves who learns to stand and *wait*." Wait! How hard to wait for what we must have *now!* How easy to wait for what we should do now! I held those words to meet the clamorous call to do something.

I knew (how early?) I must work. Work how? I did not know—at lessons, maybe. But I evaded them always. Work? What was work? I scarcely understood, though they all told me day after day, "You can do anything if you only work." What does it mean to work? No one could tell me. One day Mrs. Bush gave us a theme for composition. "Now, girls, work and try to bring me in something good." That evening I took the theme and in some way I lost myself in it. For an hour I was gone. My pencil flew involuntarily across the page. I was only a messenger for the story that wanted to be told. I finished it breathlessly. I felt tired, empty, negative. The next morning when I woke up I felt happy and lighthearted and I ran to my composition, but when I read it over it seemed perfectly dead to me: it had gushed out of me whole, in what seemed words of fire and water, and now it was lifeless, stupid, dull. I took it to class because I had to take something, but I felt ashamed of it. The next day when Mrs. Bush brought the girls' papers back corrected she said:

"Some of these are fair, though some aren't so good. But there is one here that shows real ability. Miss Ganson's paper is evidence of what she can do if she will work. It is more surprising to me than I can express that a girl who can bring in a paper like this won't take the trouble to apply herself."

So that was work, was it? I couldn't remember the formula! It had happened by accident. It was as though I had known for a moment how to swim and then had forgotten how I had done it. I couldn't do it when I wanted to. I just had to "wait." I learned, then, early to say to myself that I was serving by living: by hearing, seeing, smelling, tasting. By growing and sleeping, by failing and by dying. And all the years through I have said to myself I was serving by waiting. Waiting to work.

Another experience something like that of the composition comes back to me now. At St. Margaret's we all had drawing lessons every Thursday. Miss Rose Clark came from somewhere and on that day every girl in the school spent an hour sitting tangled up with a drawing board and sticks of charcoal and bread crumbs. I enjoyed her special kind of vision. I liked to enter her world and see life through her eyes. She adored beauty. She saw nothing but beauty; all the rest she ignored. She lived completely through seeing and her eyes borrowed the energies of all her other senses, so that she not only saw with them but she heard with them, she tasted with them, she felt with them.

She had a "studio" downtown in an office building and there she used to paint and paint. I fastened onto her, since she was so different from anyone I knew. She was about the only artist in Buffalo. At one corner of the studio were hung a couple of shelves and below them on a table was a copper kettle over a spirit lamp, and on the shelves were the precious scraps of "old blue and white" Miss Clark had collected here and there, and that she had cherished. Sometimes I had a scrap of lunch there with her on Saturdays—bread and butter and tea crackers and jam and an orange. And as we sat there, generally in silence, and Miss Clark held the blue-and-white cup in her long fingers with their long, often dingy nails, I saw her eyes plunged into the color on the cup and I knew she was drinking *blue,* not tea. And I drank it with her. I learned how to see with Rose Clark—and that was all. She could not teach me drawing, for that was having to do something, but she without knowing it or meaning it, being one of those people who were living in some special and intense experience, taught me also her way of life.

CHAPTER TEN 🖎 MISS GRAHAM'S SCHOOL

When I was about sixteen, Grandma Cook, at her switchboard up in her room in New York, persuaded my mother that I needed the firm hand and the disciplined environment of Miss Graham's School. She wrote: "Mabel needs something that she cannot get at home nor in any day school. She is very strong willed and only the supervision and control that a child receives continuously day and night in a boarding school is going to get her under. You will have trouble with that girl if you don't heed what I tell you. She is a mixture of a tomboy (for which she needs the deportment of a New York school) and a sly minx, and she has, as I have frequently told you, a queer look in her eyes. . . ." My mother took me out of St. Margaret's and we went to New York.

The tall narrow house was a prison—that was all it meant to me. I had been accustomed, in Buffalo, to "run wild" all over town. After school until dark, I had galloped my pony, or bicycled, or caught rides from one end of our part of town to the other, full of my own affairs, pursuing my own investigations into life, collecting experience. But in Miss Graham's I shared a room with two other girls, one of whom refused to sleep with the windows open and the other of whom poisoned the air with a decayed tooth. I who had always slept with my head to a wide-opened window even in the dark zero cold of winter at home, so that the snow sometimes fell on my face, really suffered in that confinement. "Plenty of fresh air," as my mother called it, had grown to be my first need. It still is. Waking in that stuffy room in the mornings there with the two girls in the room who had absolutely no quality or interest of any kind— just any two girls from the Middle West or New Jersey—I usually began the day with a feeling of depression, of uneasiness. And it was so colorless, so dull, that I will not take the space to describe it. But from the first I made up my mind that I would not stay there, and I opened up on my mother with a barrage of letters, telling her I couldn't stand it—the shut-in life I had, the stuffy bedroom, the lack of outdoor life.

None of the girls at Miss Graham's made any impression on me except Daisy Davidson and Mary Shillito. Mary Shillito was something new. She had been brought up in Paris with her sister Violet, her father representing there one side of a great firm of Cincinnati merchants. Mary had a completely foreign air. She lapsed into French all the time, and indeed her parents had brought the girls to New York *to learn English*. How strange that seemed to me! They had separated the two girls, who had never been away from each other, and Violet was up at Miss Ely's School on Riverside Drive.

When she came, somewhat later than I did, after school had opened, I approached her, full of curiosity. And because the other girls instantly sized her up as a half-wit and were ready to make her the butt of their jokes about "foreigners" and "Frenchies," she was in a panic in no time, her fingers at her lips with that horrid habit she had of nibbling at her nails, looking like a rabbit driven into a corner. I went up to her and drew her into my room, not with any intention to save or protect her but because I wanted to sample her, to savor her quality—to reach through her to the places where she had been, and to the life she had known.

It was all of Violet that she told me. "Veeolette," she called her. Veeolette was extraordinary—that fact emerged immediately. When Mary talked of her sister she was *all there,* more than most people, really. She conveyed to me by some magic in herself the magical, the transcendent power of Veeolette. She, by words forgotten now, part English and part French, and more than by words by some direct communication of unspeakable things, made known to me that Veeolette was an ineffable being, perhaps the only being on this earth so powerful, so profound, so spiritual. *"Une grande belle âme. Elle sait tout"* ["A large beautiful soul. She knows everything"], Mary said.

"And your father and mother, what are they like?" I asked, absolutely enthralled, my own soul expanding at once to receive Veeolette, whom I felt I must know as soon as possible.

"Un cochon et une vache" ["a pig and a cow"], replied Mary succinctly, with a curious vividly wicked flash in her eyes. *"Les pauvres!* ["The wretched things!"] They don't know what they have in their house! They do not know my sister. To them she shows an obedient child. She knows that they are not of her quality, that they can never *understand.* "

This was the first time I had heard *"la grande vie intérieure"* ["the life of the soul"] mentioned, but it became a familiar phrase to me—part of the code of our subtle, occult, secret feminine existence.

Never was such a glamorous being as Veeolette, both before I ever saw her and afterwards. But all this time I was impatient there at Miss Graham's. My days after all were long and full of restlessness. I continued to write to my mother begging her to let me come home and I grew more and more careless in my "deportment." I didn't care. I wanted to be expelled. I wanted to go home. Mary begged me not to try and go home and leave her there. To her it was even worse than for me, for she felt her soul, her spirit, was starved and imprisoned in that New York school that seemed so barren, so flat, after her life in Paris in the apartment up along the Avenue du Bois where she and Veeolette had their own small suite and their own *gouvernante* [governess], a mademoiselle, who was just there for their use, to take them to beautiful concerts and *conférences* [lectures] and *musées* [museums].

I asked to be allowed to go to the Symphony concerts at Carnegie Hall with

Mary and, sitting together, we held hands—damp hands—convulsively squeezed when the music penetrated our empty places, filling us with rippling thrills. Beethoven became my master. He was the first on my list, as not long ago Bob Rumsey had been! Then Chopin! If I were a practiced writer, I supposed I could tell what Chopin meant to me now. It invaded the secret unopened corners and flooded me throughout.

Mary told me about Wagner. "He is like a god," she said, and then she told me about the *Ring* and about Bayreuth, how people went there as on a pilgrimage and listened in the dark to that music that seemed to unchain all the valiant powers of the soul—as well as its demons. She told me of that world of the Nibelungen, and how, once one knew it, one carried it wide awake in oneself ever afterwards.

"We are going again next summer," she said. "Mamma has promised to take us if we are good this winter and learn *l'anglais* [English]. Cannot you demand your mamma to take you also?" she asked.

A wonderful thought! And immediately I seized upon it. I must go into that Nibelungen world with Mary and Veeolette. One day a letter came from my mother telling Miss Graham that when I went home for the Christmas holidays, I was not coming back.

CHAPTER ELEVEN &> PARIS AND VEEOLETTE

When June came my mother and I sailed for Europe. We landed in France and we went that night to Paris to stay at the old Hotel Meurice on the Rue de Rivoli, because my Cook grandparents had always stayed there on their occasional European voyages, from which they returned with alabaster sculpture and Holy Family paintings reproduced in Italy from old masters.

Mary Shillito came the next morning after breakfast [and] took me in the open carriage to lunch at her house. We drove through the sunny Rue de Rivoli, through the Place de la Concorde, and along the Champs-Elysées, out under the Arc de Triomphe, until we reached the Avenue du Bois, and on the left side of it, behind one of those high walls that secure the desired privacy of French family life, we came to the place where Mary and Veeolette lived, in a neighborhood of silence and green trees.

Violet Shillito did not burst on me all at once: she came into me gradually, opening slowly to my perceptions like a flower that reveals its beauty slowly bit by bit as one looks deeper into it. Violet was vivid and glowing. She did not fluctuate with a rising and falling fire as Mary did. She was one of those who burned forever with "a hard, gemlike flame." She completely understood and understanding, she forgave. I have never known any man or woman with such wisdom and such love as she had. She knew everything intuitively and at the same time she had a very unusual intelligence—teaching herself Italian for her pleasure in order to read Dante in the original when she was sixteen, learning to read Greek in order to read Plato and the dramatists. She was studying higher mathematics at the Sorbonne the first year I knew her, "for the beauty."

The first glimpse we had of each other, I looked at her and knew her, and impulsively felt I would love her best of all the world forever, for I saw her genius and I felt her singular power. And she looked at me and loved me too for whatever she saw in me, and knew me better, too, better than I knew myself— knew that I would love her and leave her behind without a breath of compassion when it came my time to proceed on my way; knew that I would take her and, without pity or imagination, drop her; knew all this, but more than this— knew that that was my destiny, that I could not help myself, that some inner law would always lead me. I did not seem less significant or less lovable to her because I was not the forever kind. She took to me as I did to her and our hearts bounded to each other.

I was enchanted to be really there at last in those rooms of theirs that Mary had told me all about. Their little salon was quiet and cool. It had some small chairs and tables of brown Louis XV, the chairs covered with faded green brocade. There were some bookshelves set into the paneled wall, with many small volumes bound in red and brown and green leather. They looked soft and blurred and as though they had been in and out of those shelves hundreds of times. I came to know them well. I became acquainted with all those enchanting French people: Alfred de Musset and George Sand, Sainte-Beuve, Flaubert, and de Vigny. There I read first their books and incorporated into myself their various poignant savors.

Nothing had ever deepened me or opened such wide gates as Violet and what she gave me. A whole new world of personalities and experiences in the books and music in her little salon. I have named only one or two to note the kind of colorful company I entered. But the range was wide, going back to the Greek classics and forward as far as José Maria. The great lack was humor. The principal motive was pain in all these lives I touched. The words in *Amiel's Journal* that I first found there also sound the weariness of the vision they all celebrated: *"Que vivre est difficile, oh, mon cœur fatigué!"* ["How difficult life is, oh, my tired heart!"] This was the note of the *fin de siècle* [the end of the century]—of more than that, or the end of the great era that had lasted for hundreds of years. Since those days I have seen coming into the world something new, something braver than resignation or sorrow nobly borne. Sorrow has had its day, and weariness too. The world has had a rebirth and a new set of values has taken the place of the old one. I think that Violet knew she would not go on into the new life and that I perhaps might.

Whatever we experienced in the life outside of us was valued only for its inner effect. If one could take it into oneself, as one drew the perfume from a rose, then only it had a significance for one. No one of us three, at the time, cared to fare forth on the stream of life. The Shillitos were turned inwards and I turned with them. *La grande vie intérieure*—therein we met and studied the secret motions of the soul. We took very little pleasure in anything for its own sake. A walk in the Bois was a very different thing for us than for most of the *jeunes filles* [young girls] we met there with their demoiselles. For us it was to feel more vivid inside from the motion and the sweet air among the trees: it was to feel our souls expand as we walked arm linked in arm, slowly, along those *allées* [paths] and talked of our latest observations in the deep sea of the psyche.

How I wish I could remember some of our wonderful talks! But alas! All the detail of it is gone and I remember only the feeling of it, the rich, sufficing, mysterious flow of emotion and ideas between us that so charmed us with ourselves and each other and gave us such a sense of significance and superiority that it made us feel ourselves more interesting and more valuable to the invisible life of the earth than anyone we knew! We really considered ourselves special individuals. We really felt aloof from the rest of the world, Violet from her inner conviction of high evolution, we from our association with her.

Sometimes when I stopped to think of myself (*my* self) irrevocably bound by blood and necessity to the common, insensitive person I supposed my mother to be, and when I realized that she ruled my days, my habits, my life, she who was at the opposite pole in the power of understanding—well, I felt the muscles of my soul strengthen; I felt how I was singled out by the deputies of God for the visitation of torments far greater than those that other people were able to bear. I felt my importance as a soul corroborated by the burden I had been given to carry!

We were all to meet at Bayreuth in a short time, but meanwhile Mrs. Shillito had taken a place at Pierrefonds for the summer and they went down there for a few weeks before the pilgrimage. They begged their mother to ask me down for a little visit and she did so.

I saw Violet against the dark immovable mass of the château as she walked knee-deep in the grasses already yellowing, for it was July. She had on a soft blue batiste dress open at the neck, and a coarse straw hat trimmed with black velvet bows and a wreath of poppies and wheat. Her arms were bare to the elbow and there was such an expression of something in their soft pink curves, in her substantial wrists and padded, intelligent hands. I could not think what it was they expressed so fluently, but it was something vital and feminine and even matronly.

I thought that [Violet] looked as though she had come out of the round turrets to meet us, leaving her tapestry frame when she saw us on the road. She was always like that; she belonged to all ages, she was like a synthesis of the past. Sometimes she seemed to be a little Chinese Kwannon with her slanting eyes and the faint patient smile and her hanging, clasped hands. In memory of that look she had and that I always wanted to see again, I bought one after another whenever I ran across one of them, my white Chinese porcelain Kwannons. They stood in a row on a long carved walnut chest in the Villa Curonia, all sizes and all serene—all looking like Violet.

The picture comes back to me clearly: Violet and Mary and I standing on the old stone floor that had a few strips of rush matting on it, standing in our little flannel peignoirs, brushing our hair, while two candles on the muslin-covered dresser threw great shadows of us over the whitewashed walls.

When we blew out our candles and lay down together in the bed, the moon slanted in a long beam of white through the oblong of window high up on the wall. Violet and I lay in the quiet stone room, and I let it all drift into myself, all the past of that place. I turned in my dreams to Violet where she lay beside me, a long, stiff effigy in the white light from the moon shining on the wall. I saw her smile gleaming still and sweet and subtle. She knew me and could read my imaginings as though they unfurled before me in scrolls of thought from behind my brow.

"What?" I asked her tenderly, more to let her know by the tone of my voice that I loved her than that she should tell me what I knew already. I reached out my hand and laid it shyly upon her left breast, cupping it with my palm. Instantly it was attuned to a music of the finest vibration. From between her young breast and the sensitive palm of my hand there arose all about us, it seemed, a high, sweet singing. This response we made to each other as the contact of our flesh ran from hand and breast along the shining passages of our blood until in every cell we felt each other's presence. This was to awaken from sleep and sing like morning stars. We lay in silence that yet was full of shrill, sweet sound, and all that stone room became vital with the overflow of our increased life, for we passed it out of us in rapid, singing waves—an emanation more fine and powerful than that from radium.

We needed no more than to be in touch like that with each other, just hand and breast, to make our way into a new world together. *"Je t'aime"* ["I love you"], murmured Violet, and I answered, *"Et je t'aime."*

"Je ne savais pas que je sois sensuelle," she whispered, *"mais il parait que je le suis."* ["I did not know that I was so sensual, but it seems that I am."]

"Et pourquoi pas?" ["And why not?"] I asked, for it seemed to me if that was what was meant by *sensualité* it was exquisite and commendable and should be cultivated. It was a more delicious life I felt in me than I had ever felt before. I thought it was a superior kind of living too. She gave a tiny little sigh and continued to smile, but a deeper, a different meaning had come into it now. Something incredibly antique and compassionate, like an unaging goddess fresh and unfaded, yet of the most ancient days, seemed to gaze at me from under her drooping lids.

I saw again in her the Kwannon look—Kwannon, the goddess of mercy who knows the meaning of everything and still smiles her small smile, the merciful goddess who has reached the end of her long evolution and who forfeits Nirvana to come back to earth and help men complete their destiny. I felt my own childhood comforted and assuaged when I saw that look on her face. I felt someone there ahead of me in the invisible distance, someone who would be there before me and wait, no matter how slowly I came on behind her, and who would show me the way. As a child I had felt no one in front of me—an unopened space with no paths in it had encircled me; my parents had seemed like dim, dull figures far, far behind. I could not make them a part of my journey. I had to set off alone by myself and I was always alone. But now I knew there was someone on beyond me, that she, not I, knew loneliness.

CHAPTER TWELVE 🕮 AT BAYREUTH

We were strolling again a few weeks later, arms linked together, about the grounds outside of the Wagner theater in Bayreuth. On a hill stood the Opera House, and out of it, in great waves, arose the new music of the nerves and the blood of man. Musical history is the history of the race, showing it in its different stages. We were assisting at Bayreuth at the spectacle of the demolition of form, of the disintegration of the persistent classical pattern that had lived itself out. When the musicians of the orchestra pressed themselves forth, in those herculean sounds, irresistible, magical, and not to be withstood, it was as though we saw, falling all about us in cascades of broken beauty, the perished forms of Bach, Mozart, and Beethoven. This music blew that other music to pieces. Indomitable, willful, and rich in its virile anarchy, it came into the world not to change it but to tell about the change that inwardly had already begun to take place.

Leaving Bayreuth after hearing that music, people were filtered out into the world with their old half-dead classical loyalties and faiths permanently, almost consciously, abandoned. They carried away and disseminated a new virus into the thought stream of the world. Wagner was the disorganizer of this time that marks the end of what has been called the Aryan civilization. Wagner voiced for the white race its desire for annihilation, its need to destroy and to be destroyed—the triumphant and despairing cry of imminent natural decadence.

CHAPTER THIRTEEN 🍃 CHEVY CHASE SCHOOL

When we returned to Buffalo my mother sent me for a final year of education to the Chevy Chase School in Chevy Chase, outside of Washington. It was chosen for two reasons, first because it was a country boarding school and I would not have the excuse of being shut up that I had brought against Miss Graham's School for Young Ladies, and also because the principal was Mlle. Bouligny, a Frenchwoman from New Orleans, and as it was the rule to speak only French there, it was hoped I would develop the good beginning I had made in learning that language through my friendship with the Shillitos.

The teachers I looked over, or rather felt my way over, for new flavors of additional experience. Two of them seemed to possess qualities that I wanted to explore. One was Miss Murrey, the piano teacher. Her face had a remote resemblance to the Mona Lisa's subtly molded countenance. Particularly in her photographs. She had a small photograph of herself taken at a picnic; she was seated on the ground with a number of nondescript people about her; her tiny features, in the snapshot, seemed to bear upon them the mysterious, knowing look of [Leonardo] Da Vinci's women. For this alone I applied myself to cultivating her and winning her attention. I succeeded so well that she made a confidante of me and told me she was going through a terrible struggle between her feeling for a man, the (to my thinking) coarse-visaged person who stood directly behind her in the little picture of the picnic, and her love for music. He wanted her to marry him and she wanted to go to Munich and study and give her whole life up to the piano. Of course I could see no choice! I told her what I thought: that between the man—what if he was good-looking and had some money; he was just a man in a bank!—between him and music in Munich there could be no question which would give her the deepest, most spiritual life.

A southern girl named Beatrice, a girl with dark smooth skin, huge black melancholy eyes, and heavy silken black hair, sent me a note one day in study hour. Another girl handed it along to me—the small three-cornered stiff note. I opened it and read the simple words: *"Je vous aime.* Beatrice." That night I stole into her room and into her bed after the last prowl of the dormitory teacher through the corridor. She was waiting for me, though no words more had passed between us.

Beatrice lay in her bed like a sacrifice, straight and relaxed. Her black hair against the pillow was all I could see of her, but I found a sweet flowery odor all about her. She lay there undemonstrative but yielding. I kissed her and caressed her body in the tentative, delicate way of girls—with the tips of my fingers in her hair and about her little breasts that were soft and without tension. I loved her warm, sluggish, slow life. There was no fire there—just a warm dark drifting perfume in the night. We lay with our bodies' length together and we breathed the new aroma that came from the blend of our so different natures, and each of us added something to ourselves that we had not had before. And then we fell asleep so and slept all night, until dawn, when I must rouse myself out of that deep, silent, southern spell and hasten back to my own room where the air was cool and without savor and the bed without any life in which to bathe my limbs.

There were many little happenings in the Chevy Chase world that year, but only two that count for much in my memory: two strange people who came into our environment and left an impression. One was a biologist named Reed. He and his wife had rooms in our large school building and they ate with us. And sometimes they invited a group of girls into their sitting room at night and he would talk to them and tell them things. From him I first learned that in our nine months' imprisonment in the womb we pass rapidly through every phase of animal life from amoeba to man, so that we carry in our very texture the firsthand experience of all life that moves on the earth. And he told us things that were the early findings of the science of behaviorism—the origin of fear in humanity coming from ignorant training of children.

I remember how he told us that a baby has no fear and that it has the strength and the faculty of monkeys that would enable it to swing from its fingers on the limb of a tree, supporting its own weight, if we would only cultivate it instead of impregnating the child from birth with the idea of helplessness and the idea of falling. He showed us how from the time a child is born we pass on to it the illusion of fear; that we have fostered fear in the world as though it were some valuable quality. As time went on it leaked out to Mlle. Bouligny's ears that Dr. Reed was filling the girls with dangerous radical ideas, and we weren't allowed to go and listen to him anymore, to the one room in that house where we would really have learned something.

CHAPTER FOURTEEN 🙝 COMING OUT

The summer after I left Chevy Chase School, which was the last summer before I came out at a formal ball, I spent a good deal of my energy in making conquests. My interest in men was in discovering my effect upon them, instead of in responding to their feeling for me. I saw that I did have a strange power over them, but I had no imaginative insight about it: I did not understand what the effect was—nor how they felt. We girls used to talk about men and say:

"My dear! He was so excited, you should have seen him!" But I didn't quite realize what this meant.

Boys didn't interest me much. Bob Rumsey had been the only one who had caught my imagination and that hadn't lasted very long. What we called "older men" seemed much more interesting and they, too, were more taken with me than people of my own age. I had several mild flirtations with these "older men." I wouldn't do anything, but I would look at them in a way I knew how to do that seemed to make them nervous or upset. I wouldn't let anyone kiss me; the very most would be the slight touch of knees during an evening at the theater or hands clasped a moment in the darkness of the carriage.

With Frank Wiley I went further. I had grown fond of him in Richfield Springs one summer; he was Canadian and lived now with his mother and his stepfather, the Colonel, and since his wife, neglected and suspected, had finally left him, she had "gone to the bowwows," as they used to say in Buffalo. Frank Wiley had clear-cut features and cold blue eyes, and a finely chiseled mouth. He was very good-looking indeed. And he took me driving in his little runabout, around the park and around the cemetery, and little by little he aroused a feeling of emotion, a nervous thrill, in me. I felt well when I was near him. He began to kiss me that summer before I came out and I liked it.

One night Frank Wiley grew rougher with me. He changed in a twinkling of an eye from an attractive manly, vibrant influence into something unfamiliar, unknown, unwanted. It was as though he had passed out of my world and left me alone in the garden. I never cared for him in the same way again.

When the time came for my ball, I determined not to have one of the usual kind that all the girls in Buffalo had. We all "came out" at the Twentieth Century Club, a women's club a few doors below our house on Delaware Avenue.

I consulted Rose Clark, who was the most "artistic" person I knew, and she

agreed to decorate the ballroom. She got Nanny Patterson to help her. Together they turned that characterless room into a "Baronial Hall." They painted
great family portraits by Rembrandt, and Velásquez, and God knows who else,
framed in wide somber black frames. They hung banners and coats of arms,
escutcheons, and garlands of holly and enclosed the lights in rude lanterns.
They had carpenters make old settles and huge seats and tables stained black.
In fact, they removed the curse of refined mediocrity from the place and instead of it they produced, I supposed, the most "artistic" setting it has ever
been my doom to adorn.

Nearly everyone who had been invited to the ball had sent me flowers, and
several hundred dozens of roses, mostly pink and white, and pounds and pounds
of violets were banked up behind us where we stood at the top of the stairs of
the little reception room that led down into the Baronial Hall. My mother and
I received there all the thousand guests as they poured in at about ten o'clock.
The musicians were concealed in a little balcony behind some medieval banners. They were not playing medieval music, however. They played at that
time, "There'll Be a Hot Time in The Old Town Tonight," and other period
selections.

Soon the ball was under way. The incongruous scene melted together—*fin
de siècle* clothes of the nineteenth century blended, with the help of punch and
champagne ("that flowed like water, my dear!"), into the background of the
Middle Ages.

I refused to dance. Four or five hundred polite inviters who had to ask me
did ask me and were refused. I sat and sat and sat. People began to look more
and more disheveled. They ate, they drank, they danced the night through. I
was never so bored in my life. I smiled and smiled—and sat; sometimes I took
a turn about the room, strolling slowly on someone's arm, and was bumped
and pushed about. I caught a glimpse, from time to time, of my father's face,
growing darker as the hours dragged on. He didn't dance either.

It grew intolerably hot and the ice was melted in the wassail bowl, but the
party was going on perfectly, everybody seemed to think. Towards morning,
when I felt my face stiffened from smiling, and I could hardly keep my eyes
open anymore, I saw my father prance out in one of his furious, stamping moods
to the middle of the ballroom floor. Raising his calamitous eyes to the musicians' balcony, he began to hiss at them in a burst of anger. Instantly they caught
his order and his rage, and in a flash they were playing "Home, Sweet Home."
My father turned, his eyes glued to the floor, and stamped away and up the
broad stairs, and everyone smiled and clapped their hands good-naturedly.
They all knew Charley Ganson and his ways.

My mother and I drove up the street the few yards to our house. We didn't say anything. When we got in, my father was already upstairs. We both climbed to our rooms. The three ships rocked madly back and forth on the angry sea above the face of the tall clock on the landing, whose hands pointed to ten minutes past five.

"Well, that's over with," sighed my mother as she sailed into her room and left me to mount up one more flight. I was "out."

VOLUME TWO

European Experiences

(1898–1912)

FOREWORD

The following pages are taken from a number of volumes called *Intimate Memories* that were written in the hope of giving a picture of the world I have known for the last fifty years. They were not written for publication nor intended to be seen until I and all those others who figure in them were dead. But I finally agreed to publish the first volume called *Background,* and since it appeared, so many people have asked me for a further account of my life that I have finally gone through the succeeding books and drawn from them what I felt I could print now without hurting anyone's feelings, while still presenting a true and coherent story. But it must be understood by anyone who reads it that it is not the whole story. That would seem to belong to others as much as to myself.

In the original foreword to the books are written these words:

Here I begin, as they say, to give myself away. But this is what anyone must do who writes a true history of himself—and I feel a gladness rising in me at the thought of it—of giving myself away whole, all of me, to the world— to my world. Giving back to life and all that life brought to me early and late, showing the crude and unflattering aspects of the past, the influences and the changes as the years move along. But what a delicacy one needs to tell all these so seldom recorded things!

I shall have to say here: "What a delicacy one needs to tell a story and at the same time not to tell it! I hope I may be forgiven where I fail."

CHAPTER ONE ✦ GREEN HORSES

Emily Scatcherd and Seward Cary were the first bride and groom I ever saw. One day in June, a friend of mind, Nina, and I were sitting over at her place on the grassy bank that rolled down to the sidewalk. Two doors below us we saw a girl, all covered in a mist of white, come out of the house with a dark young man—and some vaguer other people. They all got into the closed carriage waiting for them and drove away. It was Emily going off to marry Seward, and Nina and I were thrilled to see her in her shapeless, shrouded white.

Emily and Seward went off to be married and Nina and I waited to watch them come back, and not long afterwards, the bride, as in dreams, turned into a real person. Emily and Seward had always known each other. The Carys and the Rumseys and the Scatcherds—they all married each other, and there must have been some affiliations of business that brought them together. The Carys were the real autocrats of Buffalo. I cannot think of any reason why they thought they were better than anyone else except that they actually were so. Why they were so I don't know unless they were of a better blood than the rest of us, though of no better lineage. By a better blood I mean they were really better human creatures, not strictly in the biological sense, but socially. They were more amusing. They had more flavor to them. And as for virtue, they were fearless in all things. They weren't afraid of anything. They laughed at life, at pain, at each other, and at the town. Six sons, the sons of old Dr. Cary and Julia Love—adopted daughter of the Iroquois Indians in Batavia.

Seward caught my imagination when I was seventeen or eighteen. He was lean and dark and he looked like pictures I had seen of Indians. He was not very tall nor broad. His face was thin-skinned, his eyes were like onyx. They had a dark, direct, smiling look in them, a following, ruthless look. He had deep, gashy grooves down his cheeks, and he walked light and true on his small feet, a beautiful dancer. When the Indians came, years later, to our Pan-American Exhibition, he loved to tell of how, when he walked up to the old Chief Geronimo with hand out and said, "How!" Geronimo accepted him for another Indian like himself.

I did whatever he told me. He taught me to ride. He used to send to Canada for green horses and he trained them for the foxhunt down in the Genesee Val-

47

ley and sold them to his friends, and I used to help him break them. That is
how I learned to ride. A rough way. The attraction between us was psychic
rather than physical. I mean I was drawn by his magnetism, I was aroused and
alive to him whenever he was near, but I wasn't longing for the consummation
that grown-up men and women want. Nor, I think, was he, though I am not
certain. Anyway, we never came to the time when all we wanted was to be in
each other's arms. I never wanted him physically in my life. But I wanted terribly to be with him.

After I learned to drive four-in-hand, Seward gave me my whip, a small,
light, long-lashed one, and I've never had more pride in anything since. This
was something I had won by my own power, I thought. I didn't realize that
the man's force had galvanized me until fear had been as nothing beside my
wish to show off to him, and that it had been won by his power, not mine. I
wonder, I really do, if any woman can ever do anything that is not drawn out
of her by the man. It seems to me that the function of the male principle is to
give impetus to the feminine life. (Perhaps if I can write a wholly honest record
in these books, it will reveal itself that this is true, or maybe that it is not. At
this moment I do not know.)

Every summer Emily and Seward went "down to the Valley," where the riding was the attraction, for in the Genesee Valley the Buffalo families lived somewhat in the English country-life fashion. Arthur Brisbane used to go there to
hunt, too. He was a Cary cousin. Arthur's father, the elder Brisbane, had been
the greatest journalist of his time; an original-minded man, he had lived in
France, the friend of Fournier [Fourier] and the exponent of Karl Marx. When
slavery was still unquestioned in the South, he bought the column on the front
page of Charles Dana's newspaper, the *Sun,* and set himself out to oppose the
ownership of Negroes. One of the most fearless and self-inspired men of his
day, he initiated reforms and fought unfairness, never relenting.

And now, Arthur has his "Today" column, emulating his father. But the
elder Brisbane was more of an initiator, more of a reformer, while Arthur has
a way of instructing and interpreting through his pointed, sardonic observations. Old Brisbane wanted to hasten what was to come. Single-minded and
idealistic, he had less patience and acceptance than his son.

In those days, I always felt our true existence was in the minds and hearts
of other people. If one could become *real* to others, then one *was* real to oneself. So from babyhood, aloneness in a room was a terrible feeling, one was not
existing! "Nothing takes place save in the eye of the beholder" was true for me
then. I was not much to look at, ever, I am sorry to say. (Really sorry.) But I
was alive and had always a forward stride in my petticoats. And after the first
plunge I knew how to make myself wanted as much as I wished, to be wanted

and appreciated. The Cary family were amused at me and their house was just what I needed at that time in my life, that old house where Seward had been born.

That year Emily invited me to come and stay at the seashore near New York in a house they had taken there for the summer. My family let me go. Emily had a new baby girl and a little boy two years old. Her daughters, Eleanor and Phoebe, were very shy, pretty little girls of ten and twelve. Arthur used to chaff them and play with them, and several times I heard him say to them he was going to marry one of them when they grew up, but he didn't know which one it would be. Arthur talked to me a little while and tried to draw me out, but I was shy and silent—on my good behavior. I, who was so wild and turbulent inside, I am sure I did seem, often, to strangers, a self-contained, reserved thing. But the quieter I was, the more wide awake I felt towards life.

Arthur asked me at this time what I wanted to do in life, what I liked, what I felt. And he was friendly, understanding, and sympathetic. I told him I wouldn't marry and I wouldn't stay in Buffalo like the other girls, but that I would like to live and try to understand more and feel life itself.

"All those people there in Buffalo seem asleep to me," I said.

"Do you want to work?" he asked.

"I don't know. I don't know what I could work at," I answered. "I don't know how to do anything. But would you give me something to do on your paper?" I asked him hopefully.

He laughed a little, I suppose at the idea of this girl trying to leave Buffalo and all the chains holding her back, and coming, unprepared and undisciplined, to work on his paper. Women didn't do that sort of thing then. We talked a while and he drew me out further and I felt he was my friend. Nothing more was said of work on a newspaper, but later I was content when someone told me he said, "Mabel has brains. She has *brains.*" Many years later, still believing in me, he gave me my first impetus to write and my opportunity to do so, and since then I have been at it with few interruptions.

CHAPTER TWO   REAL LIFE

The first serious thing that ever happened to me from without was a trick that was played on me by Karl Evans. Karl had seen me riding and driving with Seward. He had seen me at the country club bouncing off green hunting horses at the time I had had eyes for none but Seward.

Karl's parents, the Edward Evanses, lived over on North Street in a big, plain, comfortable redbrick house. Mr. Evans was the president of the Anchor Line Steamboat Company and he tried to make all his sons go into that business with him, but only Jamie, the oldest, did so. Ellicott wouldn't go near the waterfront office, and Karl went, but only to play, not to work. He was a rugged-faced boy with the long Welsh upper lip of his family and a crooked smile. He had small, deep-set blue eyes and crinkly hair. He was unmanageable because you couldn't make any impression on him. He didn't reason about anything. He just trusted to his feelings and did what he pleased. He had no principles, not any more than a child has, but he was gentle and kind and had a certain lovable quality that always got him through tight places.

[Karl] seemed amusing to me, but not important. Rather like a nice dog. I drove with him once or twice in his little light runabout, for he loved horses and smart harnesses and he had a couple of polo ponies and played a good deal out at the country club. He told me he thought that we would make a wonderful pair together and could have a great time because we both liked the same things. Yes, we did like the same things, but he didn't like all the things I did. He didn't even know how I loved reading, and strange, beautiful things for houses, or that I had many far thoughts of a life he could never touch.

I didn't tell him, either. I learned very early to talk to people only of the things they knew about and liked and never to try to tell them all that I carried locked up in me. In this way, from the first, I always seemed a different person to all the different people I ever knew. It made a curious confusion in the minds of those who have tried to talk me over among themselves, for they couldn't ever compare notes—they seemed to be, each of them, talking of different women.

With Karl, I lived into the fun of outdoor life, houses and dogs and motorboats and all that kind of thing. I liked all that. He talked to me about shooting, of hunting ducks and rabbits, and he fascinated me with stories of the Indians. He had been out in what was then called the Indian Territory and stayed with the Indians for months at a time. He told me how they took him in like one of themselves, how he loved them because they knew how to live, not the stupid, shut-in life of people in Buffalo, but a true, easy life of hunting and singing.

But all this time he was engaged to a beautiful girl, the youngest one of the three Uebellhoer girls, who were all beautiful and noble looking—and of whom it had been said, "They never came out; they just came over." Their father was a German who had made money in a brewery, and he migrated from the East Side and bought a big house on North Street a few doors from Karl's house. Karl had been fond of Elsie. He didn't love her, he told me, but she had grown to look on him as her own, and they had expected to marry some time. In fact, Elsie's father had, with some misgivings, decided he would support Karl for Elsie.

Now I had absolutely no compunctions about people's claims on each other. I never had any feelings of the validity of personal claims and anything I wanted and could get seemed to be mine. Since I could get it, it became mine. This made people feel I was an outlaw of love and they started early enough to call me a pirate and a "home breaker." This never troubled me, for it only seemed to testify to my power, which I was forever feeding. To strengthen it was my dearest, my deepest wish, the exercise of it my most profound enjoyment. That Karl was engaged and yet attracted to me constituted his attraction for me. I wasn't in the least attracted to him physically, though I appreciated his winning, charming, careless way.

Soon he talked a little more of our becoming engaged. But I only laughed and put him off and when he tried to kiss me and put his arms around me, I held him off still more, for I was unallured. But then one night I called him on the telephone because I knew he was at Elsie's house. He came running to me where I waited for him at the iron gate at the foot of our front walk. It was a dusky summer evening and he ran to me, breathless.

"When the telephone rang, I knew it was you, and I started for it and Elsie stood across the stairs to prevent me. I pushed her out of the way so hard she fell, and as I ran out of the house, she was crying and saying I had thrown her downstairs. But I had to come."

"*I* want you," I said in a hard, low voice, without any love, just with power. I became engaged to him at that moment, but truth to say, I had no thought of marrying him, but only of keeping him from Elsie. That night when I went into the house my father, with some inscrutable intuition such as even unloving fathers have, called me to him and said to me darkly:

"Now see here, I won't have you carrying on with that Evans boy. He's no good." The full-grown rebel in me answered him instantly.

"I am engaged to him!"

"What! I won't have it! I forbid you to see him again! I won't have him in the house. If I catch you speaking to him again, I'll lock you up. Do you understand me?"

"I understand you," I answered, "but I'm engaged to him all the same." He leaned toward me menacingly.

"You get out of here! Go to your room."

My mother had been watching us with a curious detached mixture of amusement and triumph on her face. When he came towards me, she gave a warning look and made a gesture to me to go. I walked out quiet and slow, but with a wild joy in my breast. I had never felt so complete till then. I went up to my room and to bed, but I couldn't sleep because I felt so full of surging, wild life.

I felt like singing or riding a fast horse, but my thoughts were not of Karl or of my father; they were all intent upon the deepened, thrilling life I felt filling me full like a strong tide. I felt I could do anything.

Karl and I used to meet secretly after that. I told him what my father had said. And I told him that since my father had forbidden me to see him, that I would see him. We used to meet at the club or over at Charlotte's, my best friend then, who always was interested in my affairs and liked to help me. He talked to me of all his plans. How we would go all over the world to the wild places hunting and shooting. He had been taught to shoot when he was nine years old by a guide named Jack Piper. Jack was his best friend, he said, and the most wonderful shot. When Jack had grown hard up because he didn't know how to do any work except hunt, Karl had persuaded his father to get him a job as motorman on the little trolley car that ran the two miles between Youngstown and Queenstown, two tiny villages along the Niagara River.

The Evanses had a big country house down there at Youngstown named Penjerrick, after their legendary place in Wales, and Mr. Evans had influence in that county. Jack Piper had ranged all about there with Karl and they had acquaintances among the few Indians left, and there wasn't a hole or corner hidden away in Niagara County that they didn't know. They had slept out in many a cranny and crevice together since Karl had been a little boy—and now he was twenty-five years old, but as much a little boy as ever to Jack.

One day late in July, Karl came and told me of a plan he had made. He couldn't wait any longer for me to see Penjerrick and Jack, he said. He asked Charlotte and me to see if we couldn't get off on Sunday morning early and go down to Youngstown in the train and he would meet us there. Then we would get into Jack's trolley to Lewiston and ride the two miles and back and maybe something would fly across the track and we would see how funny Jack looked, hunting from the platform.

Charlotte and I agreed and we left quite early in the morning on the train that took us down to Niagara Falls. Karl met us at the station and he had a kind of lilt in him and a kind of steady shine that was new. He took us in a train to the small car that Jack drove up to Lewiston. "We'll ride up with him when he goes to fetch the people down from the little church up there. You'll like to see that church, Peg [Mabel], it's so old and it has a pretty window in it that's been there for ages."

[Jack] ushered us into the empty trolley and got up in front and started it off down its two-mile run. It wasn't long before we reached the end of the line and there at the right side of the road, up a little hill, stood the small stone church we had come to see. A few people were coming out the door and down the winding path to the road, and the church bell was ringing.

"Come on, Peg," said Karl. "Come and see it while the people are coming down to the car." We got out, Charlotte and Karl and I, and climbed up to the little church.

The bell kept on ringing as we went in the door, and the last few people passed us and went on down. We entered the little building and sure enough, it was very lovely. Small, but of fine proportions and a rich stained-glass window above the simple white altar. We walked down the aisle to the chancel rail to see it better and as we reached the step, the minister—still in his robes— came toward us from a little door at the left. He came right up to us and he had a book in his hand.

Karl was standing by me on my right side and the minister said, smiling kindly: "Good morning, Mr. Evans. Is this the young lady?"

A movement of assent came from Karl, and the minister looked at me and said in a more premeditated, serious voice: "Will you please kneel down, Miss Ganson?" Only then did I realize what was happening.

I began to tremble and looked desperately behind me, looking for escape. But directly back of me stood Jack Piper, that guide, philosopher, and friend of Karl's. He had his eyes fixed upon me with the most ruthless and determined look I had ever yet had brought to bear on me. Oh, hunting was good that morning, after all! I could no more have managed to escape past that determined, dangerous man than the casual rabbit that might, all unaware, try to make a dash past his trolley as he sped down the track.

My knees shook violently, so violently, indeed, that I sank upon them with an involuntary motion. Karl, too, sank sanctimoniously down beside me and produced from his pocket a gold ring. Jack Piper continued to stand like a policeman just behind me. I looked at the shining crimson-and-sapphire window and said to myself: "I am being married!" I had never thought about it at all. All my thoughts had been given to not marrying. I want to say right here that this experience was one of the very few things I have ever *had done to me* in my life. Most things I have done consciously, knowing what I was doing even when I was actuated by foolish or mistaken or self-deceived impulses. But when I was twenty-one, I *was married*—the passive, the truly female experience!

When we turned to walk out of the church, Karl stopped and went through the customary ritual of rewarding the old man who had linked us forever together. Jack Piper still stood facing me, portentous, and at last his solemnity was able to match the moment. He bent his big body over to me and said in a low voice: "Now you've got the finest lad on earth and you be straight with him or you'll be answerable to me."

I was all myself now, and at his words I gave him a haughty look, for any note of authority stirred at once the rebellious spirit watchful in me. I belonged to myself only and my own law was the only one I could admit.

Neither of us told our families. I don't remember why we didn't. Maybe we didn't know how to face the consternation or the responsibility we had incurred of living together. I know that we were really very inexperienced up to that time and we didn't have, at the first, the slightest idea of how to live or where.

Most young couples have their families to counsel them about houses and help them to get settled. But I knew my family would be furious, so furious that they wouldn't want to do a thing; neither would they let me bring Karl home to live because he was the last choice in the world anyone's parents would have made for a son-in-law! And he didn't think his father and mother would take us in, for they had succeeded in emptying their house and had settled down to an old age, undisturbed by the demands of the young. They were perfectly satisfied with each other. All they asked of their children was that they go and get houses and families for themselves, quick.

But naturally enough, we began to think at once of building a nest. I told Karl of a small white house I remembered. We went to the agent and Karl rented it for a very small sum and then we surreptitiously had it painted and papered and Karl moved all this things up there secretly. And up there, working together whenever we could get away, we slipped by degrees into the marriage relation. To me, at first, it was only a necessary concession I must make to Karl, for now he took it for granted that I should let him do as he pleased. But it was a blind, passive, unsurprised, and unmoving experience to which I submitted myself without either pleasure or pain. Until one evening something happened. And, strangely enough, in the house of my parents. My father and mother were out for dinner and I had taken Karl into the house to wait for me while I ran up to get an evening wrap, for we were going to the theater with Charlotte.

The gas was turned rather low in the rooms and the hall, as it always was when the family were out, and the house was very quiet. I ran upstairs to fetch my cloak and came down again running and caught Karl's hand to hasten him out—but he put his arm around me and said in a whisper:

"Wait, Peg. . . ."

And, good-natured, I made no opposition. He bent me over backwards until he put me on the floor on the thick rug. And there in the room that reverberated forever for me with my father's furious impotent angers and chilled me with my mother's aloof indifference, there for the first time I experienced the amazing explosion of the internal fireworks.

I had never heard of that gentle transformation that is, in sensation, as though the nerves expressed themselves in the manner of silent, fiery fountains falling on black velvet. My body had burned with high fires but had never penetrated this far, strange other world. No one had ever told me about this definite, so definite and surprising thing. And I had never read of it. For it so happens that until one has experienced it, nothing in any words can make one know it. *Passion* is an equivocal word to the unawakened girl, making her dream and wonder, but telling her nothing. And none of the French books I had read had told me anything, it seemed to me now. *"Plaisir d'amour!"* ["The pleasure of love!"] It came as a complete surprise to me when I was twenty-one.

But my limited friendly marriage with Karl was so inarticulate in expression— I had so little to say to him about my inner life and thoughts and feelings— that this, too, seemed something separate and of my own experience, of no earthly use to speak of or to tell him. I was so much too old for him. I was always thinking, analyzing, dissecting, while he lived only in action. So I said nothing to him at all.

With just this central marvel to life, everything fell into its own place, and people I saw now in relation to it, and their beauty and their truth seemed revealed in exact proportion to their sharing of this fiery heart of life. I saw my father lost away out in the darkness of another dreary world that had no inner sun to liven his dark spaces, no fountain of white fire to turn his blood into purity and music. At the instant I thought of him, in this new illumination I experienced, he became to my perception tragically repulsive and lost beyond hope. My mother! A pang went through me when I thought of her—a new more tender feeling. I felt she was nearer me than my father was.

All through the evening, sitting there in the theater in the darkness, my young thoughts thrilled back and forth across the world and space into the past and forward to the future. All the people I had known came back to be placed in my new cosmos in the order determined for them by their share in the vital mystery of love. My body sang and my heart sang and I was full of a humble and melting gratitude for being alive and for being awake at last after the long dark sleep of my youth with my parents.

It is curious that my thoughts did not particularly include Karl in this new adventure of my *vie intérieure*. He sat there near me and he had been the prince of the fairy tale who comes to deliver the sleeping princess. But I did not remember him as a vivid part of my new experience, nor take him with me on the long, internal exploration I was making of life by the light of the new lantern I held within me. No, he was the accident in all this. The casual stranger whose passing lit a light that would burn as long as life lasted in me, long after he himself had gone on.

The next day I knew I could no longer go on drifting in my father's environment. I wanted to be gone from there. I wanted to live in my own little house. And I told this to Karl and we debated how it would be best to break the news. We were really scared. But Karl had a splendid idea. He said, "I know! We'll get Dr. John to tell your mother. You know him, don't you?"

But I said, no, I didn't, though I'd heard of him. He was the Evanses' doctor.

"Oh, Peg, he's the bulliest man! You'll love him. He's able to handle your mother, I bet."

Dr. John, whose name was John Parmenter, met us there that afternoon. I'd seen him around before and knew he was of importance in the community, but I hadn't noticed him more than casually. Now, as I looked at him, he seemed a fine man to me. He was big and broad, with deep blue eyes, one of which swerved off to the outside, making his gaze seem very wide. He looked strong, healthy, alert, handsome, sensitive, and bold. He was not at all nervous or even ill at ease. He had the kind of health that makes people feel perfectly secure wherever they find themselves.

Well, we told him all about it, how we were married and how we had a house and how we wanted to go and live in it and didn't dare tell my mother— and we asked him if he'd go and tell her. "Yes," he agreed, "I'll go, but I don't think you're considering your mother at all in this. Don't you know she'll be more than angry? She's going to be very sorry you didn't tell her, that you went off like that and got a house ready and everything behind her back."

My mother wasn't angry. She was melted and she had somehow liked what had happened. It looked as though she had been smoothed out a little by the doctor. "Well, you've got to do this thing right if you're going to do it," she said. "No one will believe you're married at all. You've got to be really married. We'll have the wedding at Trinity and then we'll see what plan we can make."

The next day she began to make plans and on the third of October [1900] she staged a real wedding at Trinity Church. My father, upon hearing the news, had given a whoop and gone to bed with a terrible attack of gout, so my grandfather came up from New York to give me away.

We went that night to the tiny white cottage on Bryant Street and it seemed natural because we had been there so often getting it ready, for we had possessed it for two months. And the next day we went on our wedding trip. For a wedding present, Karl had given me a silver mounted gun and I had given him a beautiful pair of hunting dogs. We went to the Adirondacks to hunt deer for a fortnight.

The second day we were there, Karl told me to wait in the woods in a spot where the deer had their runway, and he posted me there and left me with my gun while he went to another place below with the dogs. A strange thing happened to me there in the woods. The familiar trees and rocks were changed under my eyes; they slowly slid away out of their habitual appearance and became unreal to my eyes. It was terrifying because I did not change with it. I sat there with my gun on my corduroy clothes and I felt my heart turn faint and my blood change. And from that time I did not feel like myself anymore. In the morning when I woke up I could not raise my head from the pillow for an hour or two and when I dressed I was nervous and depressed. The honeymoon was over.

So we went back to Buffalo to our little house where I went to bed with weary indifference as to who I was or where I was. Karl called Dr. Parmenter to come and see me and he found me listless and ill. He didn't like the little house at all and said I mustn't stay there. I didn't care. He went to my mother again and told her I was pregnant and the cottage was too damp to be safe for me, built as it was on the ground without any cellar. I stayed in bed a good many days until there appeared to be "unmistakable signs," said Dr. Parmenter, "of a miscarriage." He waited a short time and then had a specialist come in and hasten the whole thing.

Karl returned now to the Anchor Line office and, I presume, to his motorboat. Dr. Parmenter came to see me every day and I received him with red camellias stuck sideways into the mass of lively brown hair I wore piled high on my head.

The next time I knew that I was going to have a baby, there began for me the most contented months I have ever known. Like an interlude between the gusty, stormy spring days when quite suddenly the winds die down and the sun shines quietly and steadily over the drenched earth, and you forget, in those mild hours, the dark wrenching and bendings of the rooted world under the streaming skies.

Maybe the reason is plain for, biologically, at that moment I myself was of the greatest value to this fruitful earth that I have ever been before or since: I contributed then the maximum of service. I did what was most wanted of me. All the rest of it, the passions and the storms, even the wisdom and the courage, the beauty, the pleasure and the pain—all of that was nothing to nature, who first and last claims us only for her simple reproductive design. She lets us play and wander and lose ourselves psychologically to the God who is the Father of the psyche, but when *she* wants us, she summons us firmly and like a kind, firm mother says: "Now, no more nonsense. Time to get down to the real job." That was what Parmenter had said, and it was really the way he felt. He was very near the source in his true, uncomplicated, natural living.

And this, I suppose, is maternity. All in the womb. There we possess and are possessed by our own. Ever after birth there is the tug and the pull: but in the reciprocity of the womb, there is unity and peace and the only legitimate contentment we are ever allowed to know in this world. We are centered. Let us be glad and know that we are glad for the months that nature binds us. They are the best of all. I believe I would give up all of the psychological life for the nine months of the biological claim.

One morning when I left my bath a warm stream of fluid poured from my womb and I knew my time had come. Dr. Parmenter came over after breakfast and reassured me. [He] came in and out during the morning, and after lunch he came with his bag and remained. I was walking the floor when he came into the room, and after the clutch of the iron hand released me, I strode up to him and seized him by the shoulders. "You help me!" I commanded him, my teeth clenched. "Do you hear me? You *help* me!" And I shook him hard, back and forth. Immediately he was in command, his mastery flashed up in him at my dominating touch upon him.

He led me to my big bed and helped me up on it. But the next pain that seized me was too much—just beyond endurance. The roof seemed to rise above the universe—the earth seemed to rend itself. This was an outrageous pain. Parmenter hastened to me with the chloroform. I was out in a minute.

Before I opened my eyes I knew there was a change of consciousness. The baby was gone and my soul had returned to my body. Ah! Melancholy awakening! Before I opened my eyes, I tasted the bitterness of that return to knowledge and feeling and the estimations of the psyche. I didn't want to meet the new life. There were a few sounds in the room. Slowly I returned to the life of the soul. I lifted my eyes with an effort of the will, saw the doctor putting his instruments into his bag. He came to me with a merry look on his face.

"Well, you've outdone yourself! A thirteen-pound boy!" he said. "Miss Ganue will bring him in soon."

The attentive nurse exclaimed in wonder and delight. She had never before seen a baby so strong at birth, nor so beautiful. But I didn't feel the baby. I didn't feel anything for it. I saw it was a nice baby, but it didn't seem to be mine. I felt sorry for myself and wounded all over my life. The tears came into my eyes and scalded them behind closed lids. It seemed to me I didn't want a baby after all.

My father was ailing more and more. One day, some weeks after the baby had been born, I wandered into the old house of my parents. The house was quiet downstairs. Upstairs (my mother was out and so was my father's nurse)

I heard a sound of regular moans coming out of my father's room, and I went in. He was lying in the darkened room, his head low on the pillow, his chin covered with a dark stubble, his fleshy nose pendulous over the querulous mouth. He turned as I came in.

"I'm awfully sick," he moaned, as his breath came faster. "I wish I had a cross. Do you think you could find me a cross in this house?"

Cold as ice, without a single throb of response in me anywhere, I said, "I'll look." I didn't feel anything.

At three o'clock that morning, after a night of delirium, my father died. Two days later we drove, an uninspiring procession, to the crematory in the cemetery. The whole dreary, lifeless performance seemed infinitely boring and rather disgusting to me. I had no other feelings. It has taken a lifetime to be able to have the right feelings at the right time.

I remember with what surprise I saw my mother, hidden under yards of dark veils, step forward in the chapel, out of the group before the coffin that stood on three raised steps, and kneel suddenly with outstretched arms flung out protectively or imploringly over the dumb wooden box. It seemed to me the freest gesture I had ever seen her make and most tragic.

Yes, these were dark, tragic days, one tragic thing after another. I had been ill in bed for ten days from an operation that had been necessary ever since the baby's birth, and I felt very weak and broken. It seemed incredible that once I should have been so happy, breaking green horses with Seward, driving about with him in the coach, all of us whooping merrily, full of joy and youth.

The morning returns to my memory when Dr. Parmenter arrived at nine o'clock. He had never come to see me so early while the nurse was there—and we were shocked at his face.

"Mabel," he said, coming up and taking my hand. "There's been an accident. Karl. I'm afraid you must try and come to the hospital."

"What? What is it?" I demanded.

"Shot. This morning, early, out after ducks."

"Is it bad?" I asked.

"I'm afraid so," he answered. "He wants you."

I sat up then, and tried to stand. I was still weak; I felt floppy and light-headed, and the soles of my feet pricked as I put my weight on them. Somehow they put some clothes on me and a long cloak, and Parmenter carried me down to his car and drove over to the General Hospital. On the way he told me a little. Karl and Bristoe had gone out at daylight after ducks. Karl was walking ahead, and Bristoe had snapped his gun shut, and in doing so had emptied the whole charge directly at Karl—into Karl's back, and had broken it.

And they were alone. Bristoe hadn't known what to do. He had half dragged, half carried Karl to the nearest house and had gone for a wagon, anything to get Karl back to the city, where he would have some care. Lying on straw in the farm wagon, Karl had bumped over the country ruts to the hospital, conscious, unconscious, conscious again. Parmenter urged his car faster. I felt, as always at terrible moments in life, perfectly numb. Very clearheaded, but everything else muffled.

We finally reached the threshold of his room, Parmenter trying to support me, for I tottered a great deal from weakness. With infinite kindness and sadness in his voice, he said: "Easy now, dear. Be as strong as you know how."

I went in, and Karl's face, gray-green instead of ruddy, faced me from the pillow. The strange doctor and nurse looked eagerly towards me and motioned me over. I saw him catch sight of me as I neared him, and a kind of queer, smashed gaiety was in him still.

"Hello, Karl," I said.

He raised up his head a trifle and gasped: "Peg! Tell Bris it's all right—" and fell back dead.

There followed the horrible detail of the burial, the smother of funeral flowers. All Karl's brothers and brothers-in-law and cousins were his pallbearers as they had been his ushers. Only one stranger among them: Bristoe, the friend who had shot him. That I insisted upon. It was the only detail of the proceedings that I raised my voice about. Bristoe must be asked to be a pallbearer, too.

So now my mother and I were both widows. And John was nearly a year old. And I was about twenty-two. Life went on, in a way, there in my rented house on Delaware Avenue, but a year or two after, I had a nervous breakdown and my mother sent us to Europe for a change, with a trained nurse for me and one for John. [In July 1904] I set out rather sadly and without interest.

CHAPTER THREE ❧ FRANCE

The week on the steamer passed like a blank, a white banner unfolding idly against a blue sky. I stayed on deck all day, lying on a long chair—listless, tired. John made friends with all the other passengers. He looked charming in his little white piqué suit of knickers and blouse. He was a large, noble-looking child and very friendly with everyone. At two and a half years he was talking fluently. The two trained nurses and he went down to the dining room for their meals, but I had mine brought up on trays to the sunny deck—and I lay and watched the great summer clouds piled up in mountain ranges. The July air was balmy and sweet, the ocean a deeper blue than the sky, and it was all very pleasant. But the depression that lay on me like a soft, dark blanket weighted me down so that I could scarcely lift my limbs.

The night before we were to land, my nurse begged me to come down with them for my final dinner. "Come on. It's jolly. You'll like it. And there's such a nice young man in tweeds at our table, just opposite us."

I went to please her, dressed in one of my white China-silk dresses with a full skirt, the waist gathered into the belt, and the neck cut round. The lighted dining room with waiters hastening about it with loaded trays, the long captain's table down the center, and the smaller tables on each side of it, filled with laughing, careless people, gave me a sudden pang, for I knew of the dreadful depths below appearances.

"Is it always as gay as this?" I inquired of the nurse in a languid, satirical tone as I sank into my revolving chair.

"Sometimes it's even gayer," came a merry rejoinder from the other side of the table. I looked across and saw the "nice young man in tweeds." He was smiling brightly at me, and he had a red face, kind blue eyes, and short curls surrounded his large, open brow. His head was round with rather small features grouped together in the center, leaving a great deal of forehead above and a mass of chin to balance the lower part. He had a good face; his blue eyes were full of fun.

Later, he sat next to me on deck, talking about architecture. He was an architect, he lived in Boston, and he was returning to Paris for a couple months' vacation. Like all [École de] Beaux Arts men, he ran back to the old scene whenever he got a chance. He told me I seemed to know a lot about architecture and I answered that I'd always had a great many ideas and feelings about houses, and then I made a remark that he brought up to me later, but that he received at the time with composure, though it caused him to "sit up." He said I told him that I could always talk to men on their own subjects better than they could.

The next morning he was on hand as we stood at the ship's rail watching the green shore of Havre. John, knee-high in the eager crowd that waited there, clamored to be raised so he could see too, and the young man, whose name was Edwin Dodge, lifted him to his shoulder and held him. John was content and gazed benignly down upon everyone with a sort of superior condescension. And in this manner they preceded me and the nurses along the gangplank and safely onto land.

Then, from the confusion of that arrival, two black figures emerged and greeted us: Mary Shillito and her father—in deep mourning for Mrs. Shillito and Violet. Violet had died the winter before in Cannes of typhoid fever and Mrs. Shillito had died in the spring.

My mother had cabled Mary of my arrival, telling her I had been ill, and when they met me there, the past three years fell away and I was awake to the loss of Violet, whose death had left me unmoved when I heard of it—so shut in I had been in the little circle of my life.

The year I came out, Violet and Mary had been taken back to Cincinnati to make their debut—and that winter Violet came and spent a fortnight with me in Buffalo, but it had been a time of changes and new interests for me. The old intimacy I had had with her had been submerged beneath the attentions of young men and the conquest of them. Together we had gone to dinners and dances. I was at the center of a whirling twister of hot magnetism then and entirely cut off from Violet. I could scarcely give her a thought.

It all flashed back in a swift review. My heart turned over in me, dislodging the years. Ah! Where was our *"grande vie intérieure"?* Violet was gone and I was left to find my way alone. Here in France I wanted her back. Terribly.

The next morning, after breakfast, I ran out of the old Hotel Meurice, where my mother had cabled for our rooms, and around the corner in the Rue Castiglione. I secured a new hat for myself, a broad-brimmed, black transparent one with two black ostrich feathers, and I found a little short cape of frilled yellow-green changeable taffeta [that] looked very pretty over my full white silk dress with the black hat above it. As I hurried back to the Meurice, who should be coming out from the dark square opening into the sunny courtyard but Edwin Dodge. We met there in the bright sunshine of the morning and he stopped in amazement upon seeing me, and so did I, for I had forgotten all about him.

"Are you staying here?" he cried, lifting his eyebrows in a mockery of despair and recognition. "Well, so am I." And he gave a short laugh, whirling his slender cane. At this moment, up drove Mary, and her expression upon finding us together was unmistakable. His presence there gave her pause and was a source of grave conjecture.

I turned from him abruptly and went into the hotel with her. When we were in the sitting room she gave me a bunch of lilies of the valley that she carried and then we had a long talk. She told me of Violet's illness and wept as she told it. *"Elle voulait partir de ce monde"* ["She wished to leave this world"], said Mary. *"Mais elle disait toujours à Marcelle: 'Prend garde à Mary—et attends Mabel. Elle arrivera un de ces jours.'"* ["But she always told Marcelle: 'Take care of Mary—and wait for Mabel. She will come one of these days.'"]

"Who is Marcelle?" I asked eagerly, and Mary told me she was a young French girl Violet had met at the Sorbonne, and with whom she had made great friends. Marcelle was a girl with a strong, independent character, the kind

of character that a man is supposed to have, and she had become so attached
to Violet that she had lived only for her.

After Mary and I had lunched together, I returned to my room and found
a note from the young man, a gay, debonair scrawl, telling me that the very
best thing I could do would be to dine with him that evening, and that he
would come for me at seven o'clock. I was ready when he came and I had on
a fresh, white silk dress. Together we left the hotel in the summer evening.
The sun hadn't set and as we drove out along the Champs-Elysées in the mellow light, with the wide and sumptuous sky above us, the city seemed at once
serene and animated. He took me to Armenonville and we sat in the garden
with a green tree drooping overhead and ordered *sole au vin blanc* [sole with
white wine] and other lovely things.

"Where *did* you get the little cape thing?" he asked me as soon as our dinner was under way. He asked it with the characteristic, exaggerated emphasis
Boston people often use to cover up their self-consciousness.

"This morning—around the corner," I told him. We sat bathed in the fe-
licitous Parisian atmosphere, mild, suave and secure, and while we waited for
our dinner we drank little glasses of Quinquina Dubonnet. The small orchestra agonized sweetly a short distance from us . . . *"Plaisir d'amour . . . dure un
jour . . . chagrin d'amour dure toute une vie-e . . ."* ["The pleasure of love lasts
only a day . . . the pain of love lasts a lifetime . . ."]

"Rubbish," I thought to myself, and threw up my head to look at this young
man from Boston, who, I found, was examining me very intently. He liked
me—I couldn't help seeing that.

I didn't talk much, but it didn't seem to be necessary. We chatted a little;
he joked a good deal and said funny things in a way that made me laugh. He
didn't say personal things after that one question about the silk cape; he talked
about what he had done that day, about going back to his old atelier, about
seeing his old friends. He told me of his days at the Beaux Arts, which he'd
left two years ago to return to Boston to start practicing architecture, of how
different the life was, how much more attractive it was in Paris. I agreed with
him that it must be. I was not silent, nor was I communicative, but I was permeated through and through with the charm of the moment, and I must have
breathed out some of the *bien-être* [well-being] that I felt.

The evening passed as it had begun, serene and animated. We smoked a
great many cigarettes and then we jogged back to the hotel in a little dark blue
fiacre under a large, amiable moon. When I got out at the Meurice, after he
handed some change to the *cocher* [driver], he turned, lifted his hat, and exclaimed in his mannered Boston way:

"Well, I consider that was a perfectly good evening—and the thing for us to do is to repeat again, soon." I smiled a goodnight and turned to go in. He swung his slender bamboo cane in the air once or twice and then hastened across the street to enter the Tuileries, evidently bound for the Rive Gauche [Left Bank]. I went to my room, and opening the long windows that faced the Rue de Rivoli, let in the moonlight; then, with never a conscious thought, I went quickly to bed and sank into a dreamless sleep.

The next morning while I was eating *croissants* and drinking coffee in bed, [there came] a note from Edwin Dodge. "Don't you consider it would be a mistake if we didn't dine together this evening? Shall I call for you at seven?"

I dressed and went to find Edwin Dodge. "I can't go tonight," I said at once, standing before him. "I've asked those friends of mine, the Shillitos, to come and dine here with me."

"Oh, that's impossible. It's much more important that you come with me. These nights with the moon and everything. Now you send them a *bleu* [telegram] and I'll be back for you this evening at the same time as last night."

At seven o'clock I met my new friend and we were embarked on a little boat and went up the Seine together in a perfect delight at the escapade. He was cheerful and ruddy and full of witty sarcasm at the expense of the Shillitos who, he said, were probably celebrating their release with a bottle of champagne.

Mary arrived early [the next morning]. Hatted and gloved and all in black except for the high white ruche in the collar of her severe and nunlike gown, she advanced trembling. The tears quickly suffused her blue eyes when she saw me and I knew she was more hurt than angry, though she wanted to appear dignified and strong, the better to achieve the victory she had set out to win.

"I'm awfully sorry, Mary," I began—but could not go on. There really was nothing for me to say. Then she told me, trying to be calm and with her voice shaking, that in "Papa's eyes" I was fatally compromised.

"What shall I do?" I asked her wearily. The only thing for me to do, she told me quickly, was to go *at once* to Marcelle, who awaited me down in Burgundy. I agreed to go.

Marcelle gathered me up and swept me along into her life without considering anything. She collected us all at the station with a great display of force and we were bowled along the dusty, flat country road between vines until we reached her home. In the twinkling of an eye, we were deposited in our neat, adequate rooms. Everything went smoothly, unemotionally, practically. Life ran along like a big oiled machine without thought and without feeling, and there we were—in a château in Burgundy.

Almost at once, Marcelle began to lay plans for us to pass the remainder of the summer together. We would go to a cool, high place that she and Mary had been to before, somewhere in Switzerland, and there I would rest and grow stronger. And because I had at that moment no will of my own left, no wishes, even no grief, I was willing to let whoever would detain me and plan for me. I floated easily on the current.

The second morning, when the mail was brought in, Marcelle, distributing it, scanned a letter with open curiosity before handing it to me. It bore a Paris postmark—and was in a handwriting I had seen before. Edwin Dodge, sitting in the Paris café near the station, buoyed up by excitement and a couple of drinks, insisted upon my return. He begged me to come back to Paris. He had things he must tell me, he had things he must show me, places he must take me. Why did I not return immediately? Might he expect me? Soon?

This letter seemed to quiver like something alive in the quiet, slow decorum of the château. It fluttered and palpitated there like a bird. Marcelle was on the *qui-vive* [alert] as I read it. I saw, when I looked up at her, that she had had an instantaneous warning of danger. Danger of what? The letter did stir me a little and make me wonder why I was here in this dull château when somebody wanted me so much to be in Paris. The château with its sluggish life suffered in contrast with the thought of Paris. I wanted to go. I would go.

Only a faint recollection comes back to me now of Edwin springing on the train to join me at some small country station, his face red from a number of Pernods, consumed during his nervous waiting. He struggled to maintain the facetious note and his gay, light touch, but his hands were trembling. . . .

The facts were briefly these: Edwin asked me to marry him and I told him I would. Why? I do not remember why. Maybe for John, maybe in an attempt to build up a new form of life, maybe urged to it by something very practical in me. I told him I wasn't in love with him and I felt nothing for him except a desire for him to be about, to help me, and to enable me to make something new and beautiful. He was blind and deaf to everything since the bolt had fallen upon him. I told him if I married him I would always be faithful to him.

All I realize of it now is that I had turned to beauty and the pleasures of delicate food and wine for my sustenance, and my thoughts were of a life made up of beautiful things, of art, of color, of noble forms, and of ideas and perceptions about these that had been waiting, asleep, within me, and that now allured me by the untried, uncreated images.

On the third of October [1904], Edwin and I were married in the *mairie* [town hall] of St. Sulpice by a person with a silver chain around his neck with the bust of La République over his head upon the wall. Grandma Ganson, beaming and smiling, accompanied by her favorite clergyman, Dr. Jessup, was in the small group of Americans, mostly friends of Edwin's. I cannot remember the name of his best man any more than I remember much else of all this time. One thing, though: as the man in the silver chain spoke his words over us, John's voice rose a little distance away, from the arms of his nurse. He leaned out to me and, stretching his hands, he cried: "I don't want to be married! I don't want to be married!"

Edwin and I found ourselves in a large "Palace" hotel in Biarritz somewhat late in the season. We had a salon where we dined alone on the first night by the light of a wood fire and candles. Later, when it came time to sleep, I undressed in the bedroom and came back to the fire in a lace negligee to warm myself and to try to summon back to my benumbed body a feeling of comfort and of life. But in vain. I sat on the floor close to the small, cheerful blaze, hugging my knees and wiggling my bare toes. It was no good. I felt no ease, no pleasure, no response in myself to anything outside of me. In fact, it was as though I were not there at all and I did not know where my self had gone.

I awakened the next day with the first warning of a long sadness that lay over me for many months. Depression. Like a burden on the heart each new day came heavily forward. The burden of love undelivered is the ultimate load. I'm afraid that I did not even try to be cheerful with poor Edwin. In the bleak negative state I was in I must have been terribly hard to put up with.

At this time I began to buy things. With love unsatisfied, some people turn to food, others to drink, still others will add pearls to pearls, turning frantically here and there to satisfy the basic craving, but it is difficult to find a substitute, and Edwin told me once that all men look at a woman's face and instantly size her up. Either "she has it" or "she wants it." That is the chief question men ask themselves about women, apparently. Well, I didn't have it, so I tried to appease myself with silk.

The rapid change in me since we had married finally, I think, worked upon Edwin. He himself could not account for it. One morning, as we drove silently along the magnificent border of the sea where the great waves roll in like gigantic ostrich plumes unfurling, he said some trivial thing to me and I did not answer. Wrapped in my silence, I carried on a scathing conversation with him in my mind, wherein I annihilated him and put him where he belonged.

He repeated his remark, good-natured and kind, always, and I exclaimed: "Oh, why do I have to listen to things like that?"

He was hurt, then angry, and he, in his turn, rejoined: "Well, if this is marriage, excuse me!"

To which I replied nothing at all.

He was adorable with John, who had joined us with his nurse. He went in bathing with him every day in the ocean, where the big waves buffeted them and made them laugh. They became great friends and allies. When I saw them walking in from the water, both dripping, dressed in striped bathing suits with high necks and knee-length trousers, I was furious at their unalluring appearance and decided that really I hated men anyway.

The end of Biarritz came finally. We were going to the Riviera for the winter, so we left in November to look for a villa. And that was all there was of honeymooning that time.

We ended by taking the Villa Wentworth on Cap Martin, away from the main road and the resorts. Our world was a garden as was Adam's and Eve's before us. The land dropped away from the house straight down to the sea in curves and billows of thick bloom. Flowers were banked above each other on either side of the tortuous paths that were planned to go as far as they could before they reached their goal—that rocky shore with the blue water dinging forever at the sharp boulders jutting out of it.

My life was completely inactive. I rarely left the place and then only in a carriage the few times I went shopping or to call for Edwin at the tennis court, for I had to do this occasionally to make sure that he was not playing with some woman or girl, but only with men, as I had made him promise me.

I went to meet him once on foot, and this was a great mistake. Teetering along in my high-heeled slippers at the hour he was to come, I encountered him hurrying home between the trees of the roadside, racket in hand. He caught sight of me at a little distance coming toward him, and he did not know me. His mouth dropped open when he recognized me, and he exclaimed: "My God, Mabel! You're short! I always thought you were tall."

My secret, guarded quite carefully, was out. I had not wanted Edwin to realize I was short. I presume because it made my hauteur and authority less convincing. I had never, till then, let him see me walking at a distance from him. It took me quite a while to build up my transcendence again, for so much depends upon proportion in this world. If I had not been a little too broad for my inches, had been the small type all over, I could have queened it just as well as a tall, imperious woman. But something a little squeegee in proportion always dims one's authority. We are made powerless by the ludicrous.

Over beyond Mentone, far away in the distance, we could see from our garden the blue peaks of a mountain range, the mountains separating us from Italy, where we had determined to go and live for a year as soon as I was stronger.

These mountains became a symbol to me of the separation between myself
and life. I used to stare at them and imagine a wonderful existence beyond
them, and I made John learn to look in that direction until he, too, began to
invest that barrier of peaks with great significance.

So the months passed. When spring was gone and the lacerating heat of summer began to strike the villa walls, we left the garden where we had capitulated
to melancholy [and] repaired to a small place in the Alps called Villars-sur-Aigle,
and lived until fall in a small wooden chalet that clung to the side of a hill. In this
high altitude my sadness crept away out of me and I began to be happy at last.

CHAPTER FOUR 🕮 ITALY

The first evening in Florence, I leaned over the deep embrasure of the window
in our *salone* in the hotel on the Arno that had once been a palace belonging
to an old Florentine family. The city lay dark and quiet and the river flowed
soundlessly just below the bank across the street. The curving row of gas lamps,
following the bend along the parapet, lighted the massive facades of the palaces
across the way. The light had not entirely left the sky and across the river one
saw the land mounting swiftly in a procession of hills, and these were dotted
here and there with faint lights from villa windows and open doorways. Far
away to the east there was a hill with a faint glow in the clouds above it and a
pale tower showed against the sky, "Giotto's Tower."

As I leaned there, the strange odor of Florence mounted to me—a smell of
damp, old stone, of damp box and laurel from dark garden corners where the
roots are never dry, and of cypress trees soaked in sunshine, cypresses that have
known only air and light. And mixed with these, the odor of dust and roses.
A queer smell it was, made of strong contrasts and delicious to my senses, but
not a part of me. Its unfamiliarity made a kind of arrogant anger rise in my
heart, and I found myself saying to the indifferent old city, lying there, its two
parts bound together by a dark ribbon of river: "I will make you mine." After
which challenge, I withdrew to the patient, enduring room behind me. I felt
very contented there in that room in Florence on that first night. I felt that I
could sink down into its past and it would support me. We soon found how
everyone played with the past in Florence. It was the material of their days.

I met the first Florentines I knew through Eva and Charlie Eyre. They had
lived there for so long that they knew everybody: Italians, English, Russians;
even those with whom they had feuds, for there were always some people who
were cutting somebody else. Unless one lived in a remote castle too far to move
in and out of the society there, or unless one chose to remain perfectly aloof
and indifferent, one had to become embroiled in unending, bickering intrigues,

take a side, be converted to the opposite one, carry tales, repeat secrets, constantly hear horrors about one's friends, and, in fact, live in a very highly charged human atmosphere.

I had heard Eva talk about Bindo, and I had seen him come out of the Palazzo Peruzzi. He was tall and large and lean and he had the long flowing lines from the tips of his fingers to his shoulders, from his smooth curly head to his slender feet, that are seen in the early Italian paintings. His full name was Bindo Peruzzi di Medici; his title, Marchese; and he was of the last generation of his family, those powerful Florentines whose coat of arms—three balls upon a shield—is to be found all over Italy. The last of the Medici! The last of those soldiers, bankers, and art patrons—Lorenzo, Catherine, Juliano; the blood of them all ran in his veins and mingled curiously with the New England blood of his mother. She was the daughter of a sculptor and had lived in Rome and been a friend of the Brownings, and in New England of all the Brook Farm group.

Peruzzi became Chamberlain to the King and when Bindo was born, the King offered himself for godfather. The King, with whom he was always a great favorite, gave him his beautiful mare when he entered the smart Roman cavalry regiment, and he was one of the most conspicuous of that band of young nobles who were considered the most daring horsemen in Italy. He had all things save one—money. The family had palaces, villas, and old family retainers, but the sign of the three balls had become for them the last hope of their desperate efforts to raise money, instead of being their arrogant emblem proclaiming they could lend it, as in the days of the great cinquecento banker. Bindo was extravagant. He had to have all the extreme paraphernalia of a fashionable, sporting young officer, and one heard gruesome stories of the visits his redoubtable mother made to the pawnbroker to sell the old silver, laces, jewels. . . .

When Bindo was twenty-one or -two, along came the inevitable older woman. When he was lost to her, she became a fury. She swore she would ruin him and, with all her thwarted feeling turned to poison in her, she schemed until she was able to produce some letters Bindo had written to a young soldier. These she sent to his general. Court-martial and a trial were inevitable. The letters were proven to be forgeries and Bindo was declared innocent. But still that unappeasable woman plotted until the day came when, a year later, she sent other letters to Bindo's general. Once more he was summoned to appear before a court-marital—but this time he refused to come and, instead, sent his resignation, together with his sword, to the old soldier. He returned his beautiful Arabian mare to the King and left Rome immediately to join his mother in Florence.

As soon as I saw Bindo driving—eyes straight ahead of him and a stoical smile on his face—I wanted to know him. He was the most attractive person I had seen since I had been in Florence. I had met a number of odd people, and many interesting ones. But Bindo seemed much more of a person than anyone I knew. I asked Eva to introduce me and she hesitated, saying that maybe Dodge wouldn't like her to, but I assured her that idea was nonsense and that I did as I pleased. She spoke to Edwin about it and he said, without hesitation, of course, to bring Bindo to see us.

So it came about that I met him, and it ended by a great friendship that grew rapidly between us, between Bindo and me, I mean, for by this time we had bought the Villa Curonia and Edwin was always over there. Bindo liked me and I liked him immediately. He was gentle, humorous, and full of whimsical fantasy—a perfect companion. He used to come out to the Villa to tea with me sometimes. He would sit by the fire in the twilighted high room and he told me things. He grew very intimate, for he loved me—I knew that—but it was without any need in it save for friendship, sympathy, understanding. These I gave him. I loved him too immensely, I think. He was so dear, so appealing, so magnetic in some almost unnatural way.

He told me all about the Roman crash, and about his feelings for Lady S. And the other fatal feeling that arose in him and suddenly submerged him. "The first time, when they declared me innocent, I was guilty. But the second time I was perfectly guiltless and I could have proved it very simply. But what was the use? It was all the same. . . . And I would not go through that again."

One afternoon, Bindo came to tea, and he seemed particularly overclouded and absentminded. He did not come out of his mood as we sat there. Usually we were both quite happy after we'd been together awhile, but this time he couldn't manage it. Finally I asked him what it was. He hesitated and then he said: "Oh, money as usual. Mamma has to pay a note in three days and we've not a thing to raise it with so far as I can see."

Suddenly I remembered my string of pearls that Grandpa Cook had given me when I came out in Buffalo. I told Bindo to wait a moment and I ran to my bedroom, which was next to the salon, and drew the pearls out of my bureau drawer. I returned to him, and I ran and plumped myself down beside him on the couch. I was in a breathless hurry to relieve him of his anxiety. "Look, Bindo," I exclaimed. "I can help you. Here are some pearls. Take them and sell them. I don't want them."

"You are such a dear, *carina mia*" ["my darling"], he said, and kissed my hand. His eyes shone with tears, but he went on smiling. I pressed the box into his hands.

I saw him oftener now than ever, and liked him better all the time. And he grew to depend upon me more as the weeks passed, I think, and seemed less strained and showed less bravado. One day I took Bindo and we went over [to the Villa Curonia] together. Edwin was drawing on the table inside. He looked very New England and nice, as men go. But graceful, adequate, seigniorial Bindo seemed to fit the grand lines of the old country house so much better than anyone else.

"It will be a beautiful place," said Bindo admiringly. "I wish we could live here together," I cried on an impulse. He smiled at me affectionately. "We would have a good time together, wouldn't we?" he went on, as though humoring a fancy of mine in which there was no harm, only playfulness.

How soon after that I don't know, but people must have been fussing about Bindo and me. Maybe Eva Eyre heard things people said and told Edwin something of it. Maybe the Marchesa had boasted of her son's attachment to a young married woman. It would have been like her to use the chance to whitewash him and prove that the horrible things people said about him were not true. Anyway, Edwin began to grow very irritable about Bindo. He said things against him, like: "It's all very well, but really, I don't like that fellow. . . . I wish you wouldn't spend so much time with him; people are talking about it."

"There's no harm in seeing him," I said. "And I'm not going to alter my life for a lot of old cats." And I invited Bindo and the Marchesa to dinner the very next night. I wanted to talk to Bindo alone and could scarcely wait until the coffee had been served before I dragged him into the next room on the pretext of trying a new song that I had just found.

"Listen, Edwin's worried about us."

"What can we do?" he asked anxiously.

"I don't know. Why don't you try and have a talk with Edwin and make him understand? It's so silly! We aren't making love or anything!"

Suddenly he said, very low, "If they take you away from me now, they may as well put a knife in me."

I wheeled around, forgetting the piano, and saw his face—pale and sad. And I caught his two hands in mine. "Bindo! I am your friend, and I will *always* be . . . I promise you, I will not let them separate us, no matter what happens!" Edwin heard my passionate voice unaccompanied by the piano, although he couldn't have heard the words. He got up and came into the small room in time to see Bindo drop my hands as though they burned him. The remainder of the evening was very difficult.

Sometime in the middle of the night something awakened me. I opened my eyes and saw Edwin standing at the foot of the bed in his pajamas, with a lighted candle in his hand. After a moment he spoke, and his voice was short and snapped at the ends of the words. He looked flushed and worried.

"I'm tired of what's going on," he said.

"What *is* going on?" I asked sarcastically.

"I don't know, but whatever it is, I don't like it," he answered. "And I'm going away. You can come with me if you want to, but if you don't you'll never see me again."

I knew he meant it when he said he was going. I had seen a certain decision and obstinacy in him before when he took me away from Marcelle. And though I cared for Bindo and felt I understood him, I didn't want the dreadful confusion that would ensue if I remained in Florence and allowed Edwin to leave me. I had gone through so much already! I wanted, now, a house with a husband in it, a father for John, and some kind of peace. I couldn't face chaos again.

We went to America. All the way over, on the boat, I stayed in my cabin and quivered at the idea of going back to Buffalo—to Buffalo, that I had hoped never to see again. Then we landed and we went at once to Buffalo and I began to have a very good time! People were glad to see me again and I them; my absence abroad had passed so quickly everything seemed the same, with a few more babies added.

I thought less and less of Bindo. After a while we got ready to return to Italy. It was almost summer now, and I faced the change with delight. I wanted, deeply now, to be at work myself on the Villa Curonia. We had never spoken Bindo's name since we had left Florence, but before we came into the city [Edwin] turned to me and said again, with that short, sharp utterance he had used in the early morning when he had stood by the foot of my bed: "I want you to remember one thing. We're not going to have anything further to do with the Peruzzis. If you see him in the street, I don't want you to recognize him. We don't know them."

Hearing Bindo's name again struck a pang, like a knife wound, into my side. I remembered and I loved him again, but I was silent and unprotesting.

We went directly to the Villa Curonia. I was thrilled when I walked into the great, stark house, clean and garnished with spring flowers. It seemed more beautiful to me that night than it ever did again, though it grew in grace and charm all through the following years. The next morning I was eating my breakfast on a tray in bed and Edwin came into the room with a strange, stern, rather excited expression on his face. "Some man has just telephoned me and says the Marchesa Peruzzi wishes me to know that the Marchese Bindo shot and killed himself in the night. And a good thing, too," he added with his unregenerate puritanical cruelty.

Ever since then, for Bindo's sake, I have liked and been a friend to those others like him, who have been driven by some fatality, uncontrollable and blind, from the path over which they were intended to pass.

CHAPTER FIVE ✍ MAKING A HOME

We wanted—I wanted—a sunny house. Nearly all the villas were built facing north or east for coolness in the summer, and we wanted a house to live in in the winter. At Fiesole and at Settignano they faced south, but there they were so close together, the walls of one often constituting the walls of another, and all looking down on each other's red-tiled roofs and terraces and gardens from where they perched on the steep hillside. I wanted space around me—an *ampleur* [fullness] of airy space and no neighbors. Besides, I wanted *grandeur*. Not the formal grandeur that one would have had in the Medici villa at Settignano, where the severity and rigid symmetry, the proportion of height to length and breadth prohibited grace and ease in spite of its stately elegance— no, I knew quite well the kind of queen I wanted to be and the type of royal residence in which I would immolate myself. It must be very spacious, with the nobility and the dignity of ample spaces, but it must also have the poetic and tender charms of unexpected corners and adaptations to small, shy moods, twilight moods. It would allow one to be both majestic and careless, spontaneous and picturesque, and yet always framed and supported by a secure and beautiful authenticity of background.

After looking far and wide, we finally found the Villa Curonia in Arcetri. The house was perched, as it were, on a raised dais with the round, gray Italian hills falling away on every side, and then the land, after a few spacious leagues, curved up again to form a horizon like a bowl. A high, special hill of its own in the bottom of a green bowl—that was the lay of the land around the Villa Curonia. The curving roof, in fact the general appearance of the house, resembled somewhat the imperial villa below it, and we were told that it had been built at the same time and had belonged to the grand dukes, who had given it to their family doctor.

Starting at the foot of the hill, a drive ran steeply halfway up to the house, and then turned abruptly and proceeded to the top. Edwin had cypresses, as large as would bear transplant, placed along the outer edge of it, and I had May roses, the small, pink, single rose that blooms nearly all the year around, planted at their feet, and a thick band of iris inside these. They grew beautifully; in some months there was a firm line of pink and lavender all along the base of the warm, dark cypress green.

Edwin had charge of the reconstruction of the place; I was to do the furnishing. He was to make the shell; I to line it. That is the way we decided to divide our attention to the place. Recently turned out by the Beaux Arts in Paris, it was a plum of an occupation for Edwin to have the old house to think over, to add to, and to restore.

Which way shall I take you? The North Salon, as Edwin always called it, was a long, wide room—perhaps it was fifty feet long. It had three high windows deeply embrasured, and one went up a stone step to look out of them through the iron grills onto the north terrace. This room was as aloof as it is possible to make a room in a dwelling house. The proportions were stately, and yet gracious. The ceiling was vaulted and the walls whitewashed. There was a thick rug woven in Austria of dull gold color. On the walls, which, in their long, white spaces would otherwise be repellent, there was a thick stuff hanging in folds caught and looped onto large iron-headed nails at the base of each pilaster that supported a vault.

In the center of the wall opposite the windows, we placed a beautiful old intricately carved doorframe, painted in golds and blues, its fruits and flowers crushed into a pattern of complicated reserve, the swoop of the top containing a painting of the Madonna, an embroidered gold-and-gray curtain hanging in the entrance of it. This door was a very fair symbol of myself at that time, for it led nowhere. Like the fireplace in the hall, it was only for effect.

There were six really admirable cinquecento tapestry chairs in the North Salon, and a gold-framed tapestry fire screen that went with them. Tapestry in golds and blues as fine as needlework, designs of long-limbed people and hounds and fruits and cornucopias. They were a fabulous extravagance of ours, but we had to have them. Each chair cost a thousand francs (two hundred dollars in those days), which was a most unusually large sum to lay out on a piece of furniture. But Edwin especially had to have them, and there they sat against the wall, and one beside each round table at the two ends of the room.

It was almost inevitable for one to become seriously involved with *things* over there, emotionally so, I mean. There is so much thought and feeling given to them. To their discovery, their attainment, their disposition in one's house. It's almost like a love affair, the drama over an antique.

[The Gran' Salone] was the big room Edwin had built across the whole west end of the villa. It was ninety feet long and had three high French windows opposite the door and they opened onto a high, serene loggia that ran the length of it, and was lofty over the formal garden we built below. It was not a twilight place. It was warm and sumptuous and full of ruby color. It was re-assuring and bolstered one up. I found the perfect tone of red damask to cover the walls here. In Italy, to say "red damask" does not tell anything exact. There are a hundred shades, each with a different feeling to it. This one was a yellow-red, not a blue-red or a violet-tinted one, as on the chairs and curtains in the white dining room. It was not *framboise* [raspberry] or rose red or old rose—it was a golden red. It had a great glowing pattern climbing up it, of satin on silk, and it was stretched flat against the walls.

The way the light came in past the full golden red curtains, the way the logs burning behind the grill threw golden light on the dark oak floor, the glimpses of the Italian hills one caught from outside the loggia, framed between the pale stone columns . . . like the backgrounds in early Florentine paintings . . . fire-light flickerings on silver and bronze, somnolent great masses of flowers from the garden, the green dying eastern sky from the high east windows, the crimson glow from the western sky over towards Pisa—and then, in a while, Domenico coming in with a waxen taper to light the oil wicks of the six tall Florentine lamps whose lighted flames brought the whole place into one crimson dusk, with little, flashing flames at regular intervals . . . there was a soothing magic in all this.

In the morning it was brilliant from the sun shining in on tiger skin and roses, on golden red damask and red-gold carving. It was in these hours that Jacques Blanche painted his large canvas of me, sitting to face the somewhat malicious morning light and shimmering in apricot and orange silk, with the long string of amber beads like frozen honey, John kneeling beside me on the tiger in a dark blue sweater and an expression both deprecating and impatient on his irregular face.

On summer nights before going to bed, Domenico would bring enormous platters of sliced watermelon and bunches of grapes to us here—and the groups of shadowy women eating the ripe fruit in the dim light were as sumptuous as ever Sheba was, surrounded with her maids.

The *Gran' Salone!* How achieved it was! How many remember it now? To me it is so dim and far away it is only with an effort I can recall it at all. It satisfied something in me I had to have, to cover up the old ache of that Buffalo house I grew up in. As I record this, I remember breaking into an exasperated rueful anger one day and exclaiming, hardly knowing what I meant, but trying somehow to express the inherent injustice of life: "How can I be expected to permeate this place with a fictitious personality! It's a miracle, what I *am* doing!"

And now, deep, deep into the dream of blues and faded gold [of the first bedroom] that drew one into a soft medieval hush as soon as the portiere fell across the door. Vaulted ceiling of thick gold that has almost forgotten how to shine—and dark blue stars sprinkled over it, the heavy porous gold coming down to the flat corbels that supported the arches of the vaults, and below it the walls hung in blue damask so faded, so tender, so blue-gray pale like twilight. From the four green-and-gold curving consoles that ended in snubbed carved lions' heads gilded over vermilion, a bed was created, wide and low: two gold lions at the head, facing out on each side, two gold lions at the foot. Over this deep couch a heavy somber silken spread of brocade. Blue, but deep and foggy like a midnight without a moon.

Dressing in the morning! What a flurry of soft colors and perfumes, all the confusion at the end! *Never* the right one—never till seven times seven were tried. One after another snatched and dropped to the floor. All the order gone, the bed a sea of soft fabrics, the floor ankle deep in abandoned essays! Why is one never satisfied? Blue is right one day and all wrong the next. Why? Why? Oh, the nerve-racking effort to *succeed!* Never attained!

Lots of very smart things from Paris. The same little white silk dresses, the full skirted for mornings. But for the evenings! Oh, then the Renaissance coats hanging from the shoulders with huge full sleeves slashed open from shoulder to wristband so that the underarms will show through. The stiff brocades, old and worn, but the colors of Titian and Tintoretto, that hang with heavy angles from the nape of the neck to the floor and drag behind, making one stately. Golden braids and silver, old ones from churches, to edge the long, straight opening in front and around the wrists. And beneath the solemn stuff, the softest crepe underdress, next the skin, always white or cream, full gathered, flattering, becoming . . . ("She is very Renaissance. . . .")

The brown hair parted and wound into two fat coils over the ears and a turban wound round and round over the smooth head. Turbans of chiffon, of gold-and-white fabric, of orange-and-white-striped oriental silk . . . ("She is the first woman in Europe to wear turbans, you know.")

Sweep, sweep the thick carpets with stiff brocades! Soft little satin slippers, pink, blue, green, and white. Rows of them on the shelf in the bathroom next door. Like bibelots. Sweep the graveled terrace, forget the dew and the dust. Sweep the long terrace, making a long line from shoulder to earth. Head back and eyebrows so disdainful! (Weltschmerz!) [world weariness] Pour the Chianti . . . pour it, Domenico, from the gold Venetian glass decanters into tall, gold-and-white goblets. The dead Florentines are thick in the dusk all about on nights like these.

[In bed in the mornings] it's rather delicious to lie in the center of that blue damask float, against three or four big pillows, and smell the smells of one's life: jasmine, coffee, cigarette smoke, powder. Lie flaccid for a while, letting it be. Not for long. Edwin's step overhead; into the room, stepping facetiously. How Bostonian! (*"She* is very Renaissance!")

"Heavens! I can't stand this. I'm going to dress. I'm going down to town. I'm going . . . I'm going. . . ."

In the bathroom the huge bath is set down three big steps lower than the floor. Tiles. White tiles with old pictures on them. Gay! One can almost swim in this tub. Hurry! Hurry! In an anguish of haste. Why? To go somewhere. Where? This is haste. Pure haste without incentive. Without goal. Haste for its own sake, barren, barren.

Overhead in the ceiling there is a square opening large enough for a man to come through, but he never comes through. Why should he? This bathroom is right below Edwin's. In his floor there is a trapdoor. Medieval. When he opens it, if he ever should, he would find a long silken ladder coiled, hanging on a golden hook. This was a whim. Edwin's and my whim one day. (Very Renaissance, really.) It was for Edwin to come down on instead of going along the long corridor to the stairs far away in the *cortile* [courtyard], or even down the narrow stone stairs from the bedroom next to his own, down into the library and back to my room through the "little yellow *salone*." This silken ladder was also for haste, lover's haste. But Edwin never hastened down it except once to see if it would work, and it did, perfectly.

But this Boston man, in his superficial way making everything commonplace! How his coat rode up between his shoulder blades when his arms reached up on the silken cord—and his unaccustomed feet in calfskin oxfords groped for the next rung! (What a universe between him and me! I so deep, so fatal, and so glamorous—and he so ordinary and matter-of-fact! Little does he guess of the layers upon layers of perceptions of understanding, of feeling for things, that I carry locked in me. The things I know!)

Through the shadowy, perfumed, blue bedroom, then, into the Little Yellow Salon that I intended to be my very own sitting room, but that was as much anyone else's as mine—for I was rarely alone. This room was extremely piquant. It had long brocade curtains of small intricate design in pale gray and light yellow—a close in-and-out pattern of satiny stuff that was used in other places in the room on pads for the cane-bottomed old French chairs, and cushions on the deep low couch that was covered with butter-colored moiré silk.

In this intimate, eighteenth-century room, where so many whimsies gave a sense of ease and elegant ennui, all was delicate and pale toned. The intertwined yellow and grays were like an exquisite female version of the strong austerity of those same colors in the great North Salon so close—but separated by the thick wall.

We usually sat here on winter evenings, for it was warmer than the *Gran' Salone,* whose great interior was hard to heat even with the furnace and the fireplace, where we burned great logs. No, the little salon was, after all, the most comfortable, the most intimate room in the villa. It had a cheerful, smiling, reassuring air, and it was always crowded with fantastic, feminine oddments. It was here I wrote all my letters except when I wrote them in bed after breakfast—on thick, white paper with a violet monogram inside a silver circle around which Whitman's words pursued each other: "Do I contradict myself? Very well, then, I contradict myself."

All the rooms upstairs were high ceilinged and with big windows. John's room, shared by his nurse and later his governess, was at the right-hand side of the stairs facing over the south terrace, and he had a playroom adjoining it, with a cupboard in the wall, shelves just like the one I had loved so much in the Scatcherd nursery years before, only his was filled with toy soldiers, trains, and bears instead of the dear little cotillion favors that had allured us, above our heads.

But John had no fun in these rooms. He hated his governess, Miss DeFries, and used to watch her from his little bed in the morning spending, "hours, Mother," he would say, "just hours brushing her hair." He was lonesome in his rooms. I know it now, but never thought of it in those days. One night as we sat at dinner on the terrace, I saw a small flash of white across the library door— and I knew it was John, who was, by that hour, supposed to be in bed. I left the table and hastened in. He had bolted from his bed and lay panting in his little pajamas in the middle of my own blue bed with the gold lions at the corners. In the dim light his eyes looked huge and troubled.

"What are you doing here?" I asked him, angrily hating to be disturbed or upset by anything queer or worrying.

"I don't know. I went crazy," he said. I bundled him back in a hurry. Hateful!

[On the terrace] people had their breakfast, one by one, on a little table under the roses: Domenico hovering; coffee so strong and the milk steaming hot. Each one his tray—the women having theirs in bed. Still farther down the graveled terrace the wide branches of a large old ilex tree hung rather low over the table when we had dinner there on summer evenings.

The dinner table was long and narrow and covered with a coarse, handwoven cloth that hung to the ground. In the twilight with the flagons of wine and a round loaf at each plate and the blossoms sprinkled here and there, it was like a picture of the Last Supper before the disciples sat down. But after we had all flocked out and taken our places, I do not know what it looked like. Mixed, with sometimes [Eleanora] Duse and her "jeune créature" ["sweet little thing"]; sometimes Arthur Rubinstein and Carl Van Vechten and Paul [Draper]. Sometimes Gertrude Stein is there, spreading through the openings in her chair, and always seeming to be dressed in brown corduroy, and Alice is with her. And other times Leo [Stein] is there, the moon shining on his bald spot and he chewing absently with a swift rotating motion like a goat's, as he peers down the table seeing nothing but his own thoughts. The Actons, Ducie Haweis and Stephen—how beautiful she is and how dried out, no sap! Pen Browning, Janet Scudder, Mary Foote, Mary and Marcelle, André Gide. . .

An unending procession, different every time, fantastic and unsubstantial like a dream. All a-making and an aping of pictures and talking about them. People always being told they had "character," which did not at all mean that they had virtues—quite often the contrary. But that they had *genre:* strange form, or "interesting color," or they were very "period" or picturesque. The only people who counted, who were visible to the trained eyes of the Florentine world, were those who resembled works of art of a bygone day, so that everyone did his best, often unconsciously, to revert. Everybody looked like somebody of the past or some painting of the past. The farther past, the better, too.

The Villa Curonia loomed sumptuously about me, heavy, golden—carried so far towards perfection, it seemed important to me—a career in itself. I had given so much thought to it—so much time. I was a part of every room in it, of every strip of silk and velvet. I had lived desperately and in despair into every nuance and every glint, seeking to lose my desire in them. In a lack of love I had tried to pass out of longing into materials—and out of my passion I had built my house. Now I was caught and entangled in it—inseparable from it—now it was too powerful for me to tear myself out of, to go seeking mere stark delight. I sometimes lay in my green-and-gold bed guarded by the four crusty lions, and I thought: "Myself and another just lying on the bare earth—instead of this. Would it be worth it?" and some part of me leaped—pressing against the barriers, yearning outward towards the world, crying, "Let's go!" but another part sank deeper into feathers—allaying itself with form—decreeing I should stay in my beautiful shell. So to protect and comfort ourselves do we build our prisons.

CHAPTER SIX ✥ WALBURGA, LADY PAGET

Lady Paget came to live, in the early nineties, up at Bellosguardo in a beautiful old villa that she restored and filled with her romantic personality. She was a Theosophist and she had plenty to do, for her belief was that everything she learned in this life was a saving of labor in the following ones. If she learned to make shoes here, she would never have to be a shoemaker. So she made her own shoes, rather clumsily, to be sure, but with an inevitable, medieval quality about them; the fanciful velvet and silk slippers embroidered with beads, edged with fur, had the character of the woman who lives in a tower.

She grew very affectionate with me but always there was in her the unconscious certitude of my America outlandishness. There was always, between us, the feeling that she took one on in spite of one's race, and she would even try to help me overcome it or make the best of it. It was perhaps for that reason, walking through the villa in the first early days when it was about completed, that she said: "Now you must give a reception."

I knew how to do it if it had to be done: almost Renaissance, the wide doors open, the dining-room table laden with fruit and flowers and luxurious things to eat—a Medicean feast, and the guests strolling in a poetic twilight against the garlanded background of a spacious *fête*; music and soft light and roses in the midst of the damask and velvet hangings. Tintorretish.

As the pale green evening sky shone into the *Gran' Salone* from between the columns on the loggia, and the great white sparkling star popped over the faraway hill, a beautiful voice arose singing the "Evening Star" song from *Tannhäuser* and there was a murmur of delight for it was thought very *ben trovato* [well chosen]; such songs were still able to awaken a response in those old days.

As the light faded out of the rooms, the tall brass Florentine lamps were lighted. The roses began to droop and smell more fragrant. As they dropped their petals the guests began to go, lighted at the doors of the *cortile* by servants holding flaring torches; at intervals all down the avenue the wavering flames of the burning pitch lighted the carriages and the few automobiles.

It had been a dramatic success. But above all I felt a fatigue from straining myself to fill an empty form that could be blown into a fullness for a while, but that would always collapse when one ceased to blow it up. There was always that to be done over again. Life did not stay created. However, there came, very faintly to my tired mind, a little satisfaction at the presence of those figures who had animated the rooms for an hour: at the friendship of Lady Paget, the head of the English society in Florence (because of her marriage to Sir Augustus, greatly her inferior as a human being), and at those atoms named Princess de Rohan, the Count and Countess Pourtales, and all the others nearly forgotten now, who had by some chemistry been summoned to my side.

CHAPTER SEVEN ✎ AESTHETIC

When it was completed, the villa, resting in its gardens, was at ease. It settled upon the round hilltop in perfect serenity, bathed in a gracious light, luminous and at leisure. Waiting. In the quiet splendor of the rooms there seemed to be a patient eternity of waiting attention. Every crouching fold of damask or crunched angular shape of velvet, steady glowing gold, or shadowy forms of ancient polished wood, the million billion organized glints and sparkles, the layer upon layer of textures that passed from rose petal all the way to hand-wrought iron . . . every assembled atom in that stately treasure house agreed together in a community of waiting.

And I? As I walked through the rooms, over and over again I felt I was made for noble love, not for art, not for work, not for the life of the worldly world, but for the fire of love in the body, for the great furnace of love in the flesh, lighted in the eyes and flowing, volatile, between the poles. Not lust, not merely appetite or hunger, not ambitious ladder love, not love with any intention beyond itself, but love the element like fire or wind or water. *So* I wanted life to make use of me, of my cellular intelligence, of my whole attentive being, and I had prepared the setting for my own predestined life, the life my nerves and heart and inmost essence wanted.

I had not carried out this design consciously but from deep within, and Edwin had helped me. I think no one could have entered that place without feeling it was spread for life, a sumptuous and protecting preparation for romance. It had a noble luxury, deep, deep and subtle, made poignant and precious by its exclusion of banality. Ah, yes! A house for Love. . . .

One day, waiting in the motor outside the French Lemon Bank, I saw Gino. When I say I saw him, I mean that I saw him for the first time as he really was. His torso balanced lightly and spread rapidly to wide shoulders. His head was small and round with the features held close to the circumference like a chunky sculpture by Maillol. The short blond curls crept from under the visor and turned up about the edges of his cap.

He was looking full at me the instant I perceived him and his look had the simple, direct intensity of a bullet. The present fell away and I recognized him for a knight, a page, a courtier—he might have been any one of a hundred figures I had seen in the Florentine paintings. How he came to us, I don't know. How long he had been driving for us, I cannot recall. I only remember seeing him that day, and henceforward, never *seeing* him otherwise. Not a word passed between us, not a sign. But that my life grew richer and truer there was no doubt, and that he shared my life there was no doubt, either.

I could think, now, of nothing but Gino's face, of his manner of standing, of his round, classical head with its long upper lip, short blunt nose, and curling blond lashes. It seems incredible now—but it was a strong thing I experienced, and, had there not been one thing stronger in me that is nameless, it would have put an end to me. For the delight became a misery, quite soon a torment, for it demanded fuel. This fire wanted fuel. I wanted, or thought I wanted, Gino, or I wanted some life from him. Also, I did not want him. Certainly I did not want to want him so. He was nothing to me. Nothing. But to the furnace I had become, he was everything.

"I will put an end to it," I thought one night. And, taking a glass bottle, I pounded it between two stones in my bathroom and buried the bits of it, broken, in figs and swallowed a great deal of it, waiting for hemorrhages. But for some miraculous reason, none came. I did not understand why not.

CHAPTER EIGHT 🍥 MARCELLE AGAIN

Of course Mary, Marcelle, Edwin, and I came together again after a while in spite of the ebullition of feeling between Edwin and Marcelle when we left them in Switzerland. Although Marcelle had prophesied evil things to Edwin upon that foggy morning, and Edwin had put up a screen that prevented her poisoned steel from reaching him at all, he had laughed as we drove off to the train, and he called Marcelle a witch woman, and we had both forgotten what she said.

But things had come to pass somewhat as she had foretold. Between Edwin and me there never was a deep marriage relationship, although there was a great friendship, for it was impossible not to respond to his even-tempered generous nature and his gaiety. My particular criticism of him was of his avoidance of the deeper undercurrents. He seemed to me to live entirely upon the surface of consciousness, and I thought he never attempted to analyze experience as it touched him; he seemed to prefer the superficies of living, the externals, to the inwardness of things. At that time I was so self-centered that I could not see any *raison d'être* [reason for being] in any other type but my own, and I have thought many times since then that Edwin was a veritable saint to put up with me as he did. Doubtless his ability to do so came from that easygoing acceptance of things as they were, without questioning them or defining them too closely, that I deplored in him!

So I went along beside him in the shut-in loneliness of a self-imprisoned and inhibited young married woman, but I always guarded my behavior very carefully and sometimes, with stoical self-control, for there was that never-forgotten promise I had made when I told him I would marry him—the promise to be "faithful" to him, that promise to which he had paid so little attention but that really became the central fact in my pleasure-seeking days.

So when we went up to Paris I used to see Mary and Marcelle. When I went to visit them in the château later on, I felt at first a little low-spirited. Everything was so regulated, so exactly ordained. I suppose I had to start something moving. Anyway, I did. So I began to try to throw a little net around Marcelle. I believed if I could be near people I could convey something of myself across to them, something that drew them back to me, and by putting my attention upon Marcelle, by giving over something of myself to her, sure enough, I lighted a little fire in her and gradually of itself it burned higher and higher until the stony casing she had built around herself fell away and there she was, a glowing lamp, all heat and languor and a good deal of light.

She became lovely all at once, opening like a marvelous unexpected flower, and then, once awakened, she became almost terrible. In her room long after midnight, a candle threw long, wavery beams across her narrow bed that had hitherto been so cool and unperturbed, and they fell upon Marcelle's streaming, loosened energy that poured out of her at last in unresisting delight. Just to lie there and be alive, in love, was enough. Her face was grown rosy, her lips were crimson and unbound. Dark red rose petals were tangled in her hair, and some lay fluttering upon her breast. Night after night Marcelle gave herself up to the luxury of streaming love that passed out of her across to me from the eyes and the handclasp. Each day she went about imbued with a new graciousness; laughter fell upon her face, and a different movement spread and stirred all through that rigid stone château.

[After a short trip to Aix-les Bains] we returned to the château. I stayed only a little while because Edwin sent for me to meet him earlier than we had planned. I missed Marcelle and I suppose she missed me. I missed the warmth we made for each other and I hated to grow cold again. It was hard for me to feel all my invisible feathers sink softly down once more—to feel myself grow dim. It was hard for me, but after all I was still myself—burning dimmer. But what of Marcelle? She would have to learn to live in a new way for she had lost her "character." She had just become herself. I wondered about it, but I felt sure she would know how to create a life for herself.

CHAPTER NINE 🖎 FLORENTINE VIGNETTES

Gladys Deacon. How beautiful, really, and how [Bernard] Berenson admired her for her art value. Her mother, living in the Roman Villa Carparola lent her by the Roman duke, outlawed, no where left to be but in an upholsterer's heaven because the only world she knew was already inhabited by the Duchess, how sad that was, and silly but *de l'époque* [of the period], and how it handicapped Gladys!

When she was little she went to school with Consuelo Vanderbilt and the other girls of that New York group. Then the life was broken up, because her father and mother were divorced and her mother came abroad and brought her daughters. To Rome. A divorce in Rome! How foolish to go there and find that of all one's kind, only the men are nice to one! Nothing for the mother to do but accept the situation . . . and take the Duke for a lover.

This made Gladys a freelance. She was beautiful, as Judith was beautiful, or like Salome, and she loved only herself so she was not bothered about lovers. Nothing really counted, *au fond* [in reality], for Gladys, I believe, but to recover the ground her mother had lost. All the life in Florence was just marking time. Did she actually know, one wonders, what it meant, the task she set herself? Colossal! She will marry the Duke of Marlborough, Consuelo's husband. She will play for that, and she played.

Rumors reached Berenson from Oxford, where the scholars of the world congregated, telling him about Gladys and the Duke of Marlborough. . . . She will . . . she won't . . . finally she did! It took time, but Gladys became the Duchess of Marlborough. She had to do it, one sees that, after the Roman Duchess cut her mother. Certainly.

John [George] D. Herron was a professor at a middle-western college; he had broad economic principles and tried to teach them. He was married and had several children when the destiny of his life became clear to him. He fell in love with Miss Rand, who, I was told, was the dean of the college. I hope I may arrive at the true spirit of their story even if the facts are inaccurate.

She was the daughter of the man who endowed the Rand School in New York, a school of socialism, very advanced in those days, and they came together through the communion of their ideas. He left his family and together they went to live in Florence in a villa in Settignano. They were neither of them young and they were deeply in love with each other; they suffered for their love and it made them very serious. They were overclouded by their situation and could not altogether pierce the cloud.

They had a little boy about two years old who seemed to be the core of their life. He was the fruit as well. The fruit of their difficult sacrifice of convention and duty and good opinion. It was he, perhaps, who inspired the sort of unconscious, special pleading they expressed . . . one did not know to whom it was addressed, perhaps to the world at large, but it emanated from them all the time in their surroundings. The house, the clothes they wore, the dinners they gave, the things they said, were all a kind of special pleading for the right to live, to love and to be happy.

People experienced life more deeply thirty years ago, I suppose. They acted, and their acts had deeper consequences, more effect upon them than seems the case now. They suffered more for their happiness, and perhaps, too, their happiness was greater. It is difficult to know.

CHAPTER TEN   MURIEL

I remember noticing how perfectly certain of herself Muriel was the first time she came down the stone steps on the *Gran' Salone,* Paul behind her, she in her cherry-colored broadcloth gown with jabots of lace, Paul forever in cutaway coat and gray-striped trousers.

Bending slightly backwards, she was like a hard, slender, polished ivory figure carved from an elephant's tusk; she seemed to have been produced complete from that curving, unyielding form and ever afterwards to have retained, like a special destiny, the arbitrary character of the material from whence she had emerged. Muriel came from Haverhill in Massachusetts, from a spacious house set in a large property, called Birchbrow, and she was born into a family named Saunders, and Paul, at Harvard, went to visit her with a college friend.

He was musical and endowed with a fine tenor. He had a long, rectangular head with hair in porcupine quills brushed straight back from his high, square forehead, and his eyes were like a pale blue and as though painted under his motionless brows. He had no mobility, no flexibility in his physique, and his profile had the straight, inanimate plumb line of a not very good Greek statue.

They took a small villa a little way below in the Via San Leonardo, and later on, while Muriel was in the nursing home having her baby, I don't know how it began but Paul thought he fell in love with me. I suppose I must admit I tried to attract his attention for it was a compulsion with me in those days. I had been storing up my own unattached energy for the expected visit of Mary and Marcelle, and then I turned it all on Paul, so by the time the two girls came, he was well installed in the magical hollow dream I used to create around people, and in which they drew delighted breath for a little while.

Paul was always dressed then in white flannels and he was always at the piano. All my memories of him and what he said are either of him at the piano, talking about Bach and Beethoven (for his musical taste was austere), or from the front seat in the Renault when he sat driving eighty, ninety miles an hour and leaning down to me to whisper: "God! Mabel! You are life. . . ."

And I see the disconsolate backs of Marcelle and Edwin as, drawn together by a shared abandonment, they disappear down the road, scuffling the autumn leaves under their feet, off on a walk to talk it over.

Paul *would* have me. I wouldn't give in. I continued to be "virtuous" while keeping my environment on tenterhooks. The villa grew full of a tenser life as Paul stalked through it, stiff-necked and tight browed, his immobile blue eyes fixed upon some inner picture of how to win his way, his chin drawn into his collar as he hummed unconsciously the Schumann lieder [songs] that at the moment best expressed his feeling.

When Muriel came back from the nursing home, he told her he had to have a "grand passion" in his life on account of his music and that I was it. This was not an original idea on Paul's part; it was the musical convention of the period. I had a feeling at the time that it was hard on Muriel when she frankly told me what he had said, for she really loved Paul. She yearned over him, he pulled at her heart, she felt him. But I said to myself: "Well, life is like this. Paul says he has to have a grand passion; maybe he does." It did not seem to matter much who the object of it was. I had happened to be there ready for him to throw his light upon and he had thrown it. I felt myself illumined by it, and I sunned myself in it and felt I was being used by the demands of musical life. Paul broadened and swung into turbulent César Franck compositions as a result. . . .

As for me, I didn't think of it at all in terms of love. I wanted a strong draught of human fire blowing upon me and I found I was drawing it out of Paul, who happened to be there for me as I, merely, happened to be there for him. That he called it a "grand passion" did not matter much except that I accepted the conception, having read all about Chopin and George Sand.

That it drew him away from Muriel I was too ignorant to realize. Besides, I thought, trying to be worldly, he was over his desire for her, and it would probably have happened with another if not with me. Muriel's misfortune was having given herself into his keeping. She was constituted for love, for devotion, and for the creative role of family life. Had it been another man whom she had fallen for, with stronger fiber, she would have made a great success of marriage. She could not any longer spend herself upon Paul. This was a tragedy. She had had bad luck. . . . But Paul's attention turning to someone else so soon proved the turning point in her destiny. For a long time after that she lived for the satisfactions of the ego and made a success of that.

After a while, the Drapers moved to London. Muriel had a transfiguration there. From almost poverty, a bare little *villino* [small villa] down the road, and her cherry broadcloth dress growing less and less proud except for the pride with which she wore it, they became rich and fashionable. How? With Paul betting on the races with almost uncanny luck. Soon they appeared to have several hundred thousands, a large house, and Muriel was sitting in a box at the opera in ivory satin with an entire pair of jet-black raven's wings found upon her small, pale head. One heard fantastic tales of her triumphs in London. She was so brilliant, so polished, and so hard, so much more than ever ivory hard. And Paul kept on winning with the horses and spending money freely and singing the German lieder with great success.

She triumphed in London while the money lasted, though the way to her large drawing room was difficult to find, they said. I remember Henry James's baffled description of his first excursion there as, unable to resist satisfying his curiosity about this unique and surprising figure from his own Massachusetts, he accompanied her home from a dinner party in Sloane Street.

> The bewildering girl drew me into a motorcar and out again and down a dark pathway that had ever so narrow a margin; then through a passage to a doorway that quite remarkably opened at our approach, through a corridor, down some steps until we were standing unexpectedly in a noble Italian *salone* where candles burned against tapestries.
>
> And all this time she was pouring out a variety of phrases that I will admit both tickled and affrighted me—an alarming young woman—amazing. . . .

CHAPTER THIRTEEN ❧ THE STEINS

I like to write of them together since I first knew them so—though later they were far apart. They lived in Paris at 27 Rue de Fleurus, and when I first knew them, people were beginning to go to their apartment to hear Leo talk about two new painters he had "discovered" at the "Independents" exhibition—Matisse and Picasso. Earlier still, he had come about the Cézannes—and holding forth night after night in his big living room, he had forced people to see their value. Then he bought all those funny ones and started talking about *them* and people used to go just for the laugh they got out of it—and there we found ourselves one evening. A large, rather bare room and a few good chairs and tables and *those pictures* on the walls.

Leo was always standing up before the canvases, his eyeglasses shining and with an obstinate look on his face that so strongly resembled an old ram. In one of my visits I met Picasso and again later Matisse there. With whatever was essential in Leo's vision, he had seen the intensity in the work of the small Spaniard the first time it hung in the wild Salon des Independents. Buying those distorted compositions and hanging them in his apartment, he felt the need for making others see what he found in them, and this turned him eloquent.

I don't remember his words now, but with a fire no one would have suspected in the thoughtful, ramish scholar, he sought in every way to interpret the intention in them. I do remember that from the earliest time I knew him he fulminated against any art expression that was merely the running of water downhill. Music for instance that sang itself, the clichés of melody whose bars followed one another in an automatic fashion in one's mind after one heard the opening notes and phrases.

Leo seemed to be an enemy of gravitation; he required more than just the natural laws when it was a question of art forms. The conventions of sound or painting were unutterably wearisome, always proceeding along the lines of least resistance, to drop from the known to the still better known.

"Tension," he used to say, "is the requisite for a living work of art." By "tension" he meant looking beyond, to what we call the *au de la* [the other world], for further vision; he found it in unaccustomed places. Later he expounded his aesthetic theories in a remarkable and original volume called The *A B C of Aesthetics*. If it is necessary to him who would go onwards to overcome gravitation, Picasso was the man Leo craved. Picasso, I suppose, more than any other painter carried the faculty of seeing farther than natural sight usually allowed.

Most people see as far as the eye permits—Picasso came along and used his optic nerve as an instrument that seemed to overcome the natural boundary and brought new experience to the psyche. Seeing freshly, and putting down on his canvases what he saw, he actually extended the field of vision for the whole world. A new vision captured is a gift of a god. It is a victory over the natural law of gravitation. Since people have seen Picasso's pictures they have been able to see everything a little differently. He is one of the men who have made a difference, and the more difference there is, the more life there is.

So, it is easily seen how Leo took him to his heart rejoicing. In those early days when everyone laughed, and went to the Steins' for the fun of it, and half angrily, half jestingly giggled and scoffed after they left (not knowing that all the same they were changed by seeing those pictures), Leo stood patiently night after night wrestling with the inertia of his guests, expounding, teaching, interpreting, always the advocate of tension in art! Always the enemy of gravitation. And if it had not been for him perhaps Picasso could not have overcome the world, which always means overcoming the magnetism of the world, the great inertia, the drop along the line of least resistance, like water flowing downhill. So to Leo, too, we must give credit for a gift.

Picasso was a small, compact man, and the most remarkable things about him were his eyes. They were far apart and of a burning black. He had a most lambent, penetrating, burning look in them. Somehow, I believe that if we all used all of our faculties as Picasso used sight, they would be many times magnified and strengthened.

Matisse was another element altogether. A watery element. Large, pale blue and coral tones—blond—fresh and clear. One thinks of the sea, and bright fish. His canvases were all painted with light. Where his predecessors, Monet and those, had merely decomposed light—Matisse went much further and *saw through matter.* He saw that everything is vibrating at a different rate and that everything sparkles and radiates—is in a state of translucence, is more or less loosely bound together by inertias. He painted nature with an increased vision, and he too made a difference to the world—because he too overcame gravitation and pressed onwards into the beyond.

I felt the excitement of new experience in these men and what they were doing, and I tried to carry on to Jacques Blanche, when he was painting me, something of their intention. "They are going to teach the world to *see,*" I reiterated over and over. But he was up against middle age, past his zenith, past the growing period. Sadly obdurate, puzzled, and discomfited, he continued his portrait, shaking his head.

Gertrude Stein was prodigious. Pounds and pounds and pounds piled up on her skeleton—not the billowing kind, but massive, heavy fat. She wore some covering of corduroy or velvet and her crinkly hair was brushed back and twisted up high behind her jolly, intelligent face. She intellectualized her fat, and her body seemed to be the large machine that her large nature required to carry it. Gertrude was hearty. She used to roar with laughter, out loud. She had a laugh like a beefsteak. She loved beef, and I used to like to see her sit down in front of five pounds of rare meat three inches thick and, with strong wrists wielding knife and fork, finish it with gusto, while Alice ate a little slice, daintily, like a cat.

Gertrude had direct firsthand reactions of her own about life just as Leo did about paintings. He had taught her this secret. I remember she was the first one—of all those sophisticated, cultured people I had grown accustomed to—who made me realize how nothing is anything more than it is to oneself. For instance, Gertrude didn't care whether a thing was *bon goût* [good taste] or not, or whether it was quattrocento [fourteenth century] or not, unless it affected *her* pleasantly, and if it did please her she loved it for that reason. This is the theory that Leo bases his aesthetics upon and she was his first disciple.

[In the summer of 1912] Gertrude and Alice came to stay at the villa. The year before, Gertrude had lived in Fiesole—and she had trudged down one hill and across town and up another to see us. She used to wear a sort of kimono made of brown corduroy in the hot Tuscan summertime, and arrive just sweating, her face parboiled. And when she sat down, fanning herself with her broad-brimmed hat with its wilted, dark brown ribbon, she exhaled a vivid steam all around her. When she got up she frankly used to pull her clothes off from where they stuck to her great legs. Yet with all this she was not at all repulsive. On the contrary, she was positively, richly attractive in her grand *ampleur*. She always seemed to like her own fat anyway and that usually helps other people to accept it. She had none of the funny embarrassment Anglo-Saxons have about flesh. She gloried in hers. She was a wonderful companion and I missed her after the silence came between us.

Edwin was, seemingly, off somewhere, probably in America, and that summer there was a young man there tutoring John. He was in love with me just as a matter of course, and his blond, fresh, blue-eyed youthfulness had a great allure for me. Merely of the flesh it was—but so it was. I was young too. But bound as I was, as though in irons, by that promise to Edwin, I didn't dare take him. This was fear—not morality. In fact, I suppose it was really immorality, though I remember I felt very virtuous at the time!

Gertrude always worked at night. After everyone was asleep she used to sit at Edwin's table next door writing automatically in a long weak handwriting— four or five lines to the page—letting it ooze up from deep down inside her, down onto the paper with the least possible physical effort; she would cover a few pages so and leave them there and go to bed, and in the morning Alice would gather them up the first thing and take them off and type them. Then she and Gertrude would always be so surprised and delighted at what she had written, for it had been done so unconsciously she'd have no idea what she'd said the night before!

She began the "Portrait of Mabel Dodge at the Villa Curonia" and by this time the symbolism had become so obscure that only by feeling it could anyone get the key to what she was saying. This is what she said about me as she sat in the midnight silence:

The days are wonderful and the nights are wonderful and the life is pleasant. . . .

Bargaining is something and there is not that success. The intention is what if application has that accident results are appearing. They did not darken. That was not an adulteration.

So much breathing has not the same place when there is so much beginning. So much breathing has not the same place when the ending is lessening. So much breathing has the same place and there must not be so much suggestion. There can be there the habit that there is if there is not need of resting. The absence is not alternative.

Any time is the half of all the noise and there is not that disappointment. There is no distraction. An argument is clear.

Packing is not the same when the place which has all that is not emptied. There came there the hall and this was not the establishment. It had not all the meaning.

Blankets are warmer in the summer and the winter is not lonely. This does not assure the forgetting of the intention when there has been done and there is every way to send some. There does not happen to be a dislike for water. This is not heartening.

As the expedition is without the participation of the question there will be nicely all that energy. They can arrange that the little color is not bestowed. They can leave it in regaining that intention. It is mostly repaid. There can be an irrigation. They have the whole paper and they send it in some package. It is not inundated.

A bottle that has all the time to stand open is not so clearly shown when there is green color there. This is not the only way to change it. A little raw potato and then all that softer does happen to show that there has been enough. It changes the expression.

It is not darker and the present time is the best time to agree. This which has been feeling is what has the appetite and the patience and the time to say. This is not collaborating.

All the attention is when there is not enough to do. This does not determine a question. The only reason that there is not that pressure is that there is a suggestion. There are many going. A delight is not bent. There has been that little wagon. There is that precision when here has not been an imagination. There has not been that kind of abandonment. Nobody is alone.

If the spread that is not a piece removed from the bed is likely to be whiter then certainly the sprinkling is not drying. There can be the message where the print is pasted and this does not mean that there is that esteem. There can be the likelihood of all the days not coming later and this will not deepen the collected dim version.

A sap that is that adaptation is the drinking that is not increasing. There can be that lack of any quivering. That does not originate every invitation. There is not wedding instruction. There is not all that filling. There is the climate that is not existing. There is that plainer. There is the likeness, lying of liking likely likeness. There is that dispensation. There is the paling that is not reddening, there is the reddening that is not reddening, there is that protection, there is that destruction, there is not the present lessening there is the argument of increasing. There is that that is not that which is resting. There is not that occupation. There is that particular half of directing that there is that particular whole direction that is not all the meaning of any combination. Gliding is not heavily moving. Looking is not vanishing. Laughing is not evaporating. There can be that climax. There can be the same dress. There can be an old dress. There can be the way there is that way there is that which is not that charging what is a regular way of paying. There has been William. All the time is likely. There is the condition. There has been admitting. There is not the print. There is that smiling. There is the season. There is that where there is not that which is where there is where there is what there is which is beguiling. There is a paste.

Abandon a garden and the house is bigger. This is not smiling. This is comfortable. There is the comforting of predilection. An open object is establishing the loss that there was when the vase was not inside the place. It was not wandering.

There was not that velvet spread when there was a pleasant head. The color was paler. The moving regulating is not a distinction. The place is there.

Likely there is not that departure when the whole place that has that texture is so much in the way. It is not there to stay. It does not change that way. A pressure is not later. There is the same. There is not the shame. There is that pleasure.

There is that desire and there is not pleasure and the place is filling the only space that is placed where all the piling is not adjoining. There is not that distraction.

Praying has intention and relieving that situation is not solemn. There comes that way.

The time that is the smell of the plain season is not showing that the water is running. There is not all that breath. There is the use of the stone and there is the place of the stuff and there is the practice of expending questioning. There is not that differentiation. There is that which is in time. There is the room that is the largest place when there is all that is where there is space. There is not that perturbation. The legs that show are not the certain ones that have been used. All legs are used. There is no action meant.

The particular space is not beguiling. There is that participation. It is not passing any way. It has that to show. It is why there is no exhalation.

There is all there is when there has all there has where there is what there is. That is what is done when there is done what is done and the union is won and the division is the explicit visit. There is not all of any visit.

The third night that she wrote, a hot August moon was shining in from the loggia across my bed—and that young man crept along the red-tiled passage and breathed my name against my door. My heart beat flutteringly as I opened it with an extreme of caution. The walls between Gertrude and me were thick but the doors were just ordinary ones. . . . He and I clung together in the moon-light with no whispers. We grew tired standing together and swayed towards the wide, white-hung bed—until we were lying, arms about each other—white moonlight—white linen—and the blond white boy I found sweet like fresh hay and honey and milk.

My natural desire for him was so strong that it passed over me in deep waves like light shaking out of clouds—yet I only clung to him and began to babble: "I can't—I can't—I can't. . . ." And so we remained, for heaven knows how long—while Gertrude wrote on the other side of the wall, sitting in candlelight like a great Sibyl dim against the red and gold damask that hung loosely on the walls.

Finally the moon slid away and it was black dark on the bed, and I told my companion to go back to his room at the far other end of the house. I went tiptoe to the door with him to let him out and he covered me with a last, fresh fire—and breathed in my ear: "I love you so—and the wonderful thing about you is that you're *good.*"All this so that Edwin—away in America—could have his trust in me!

As Gertrude went on with the "Portrait of Mabel Dodge," writing her un-conscious lines, she seemed to grow warmer to me, to which I responded in a sort of flirtatious way though I didn't feel anything for her now because my fire was drawn to another, and my eyes to his long limbs and his swaying shoulders. But one day at lunch, Gertrude, sitting opposite me in Edwin's chair, sent me such a strong look over the table that it seemed to cut across the air

to me in a band of electrified steel—a smile traveling across on it—powerful—
Heavens! I remember it *now* so keenly!

At that Alice arose hastily and ran out of the room onto the terrace. From
that time on Alice began to separate Gertrude and me—*poco-poco* [little by
little]—but the real break came later on when I wrote the first thing that was
ever published in America about her writing. It was an article for *Arts and
Decorations* in the number of the magazine that was sold at the Big, First, International, Independent Show that we got up in New York when I went there
to live. But the tale of that comes later.

Gertrude—for some obscure reason—was angry. Leo told me it was because it appeared to her that here was some doubt as to which was the more
important, the bear or the one leading the bear, but I felt that it was Alice's
final and successful effort in turning Gertrude from me—her influencing and
her wish, and I missed my jolly fat friend very much.

CHAPTER FIFTEEN ✒ GORDON CRAIG
AND A GREAT IDEA

I saw a strange figure pushing a baby carriage along the river one day. He had
long, fine brown hair waving under a low, broad-brimmed hat—and a long
cape flapping in the wind. He peered out through shining glasses and the thin-
lipped, flexible mouth with its pointed chin under a delicate, long nose had
something womanish, and, yes, something old-maidish and witchlike about it.
This was Gordon Craig and he looked like Mother Goose drawn by Arthur
Rackham. The baby was Isadora's [Duncan] and his, and he called it his little
Snowdrop.

Craig had ideas but they didn't include any notion of time or space, nor
could he understand the usual conformities, for he seemed to be without a
sense of relativity. When he made the beautiful stage set for his mother, Ellen
Terry, to give *Hamlet* in London, it wouldn't go inside the proscenium arch unless they took the roof off the theater, which was irritating to the management—
and he annoyed [Carlo] Loeser, who had rented him a *villino*—by walking in
his garden stark naked until the neighbors complained and made Carlo speak
to him about it. When the latter went to remonstrate with him, Craig threw
off his trousers and shirt, flung out his arms, and with his pointed chin up exclaimed: "But is it not *beautiful?*"

Craig flapped through the villa once, talking of light, of space, and the need
for a new world, but that was all I saw of him until one day we met on a train;
he was on his way to London, Edwin and I to San Moritz for the winter sports.

Since we were thrown together for a few hours, a sudden wave of mischief seized me and I began to improvise for his benefit as I had heard him do.

"Why not do something on a grand scale?" I began passionately. "Why not take Florence up in both hands and re-create it? Show these deaf and dumb, half-dead people what Florence was once upon a time!"

"How splendid! It might be the beginning of another renaissance if one could light the spark. . . ."

"Yes, turn all Florence back to the cinquecento—an immersion in the past in which everyone would participate—where there would be no audience but only actors . . . revive the old costumes, and the old customs. . . ."

"People would be ashamed to continue living in the ugliness of industrialism after days like I could show them. . . ."

Edwin sat reading the *Herald* and let us rave on. I was having a fine time—wholly given over to the plan, in which I lived imaginatively with Craig, yet all the while preserving some part of myself back with Edwin and industrialism.

"With you behind me I feel I can do anything," he exclaimed with enthusiasm. "This idea is the idea of a genius! A pageant such as the world has never known—the Florentines filling their streets dressed like men and women. If you do this with me I will give you my little Dionysius [his son]!" he cried, at one moment.

He wrote to me from the train on the way to London, and he wrote me from London. Would I see it through? And then the questions!!!

1. Will you give all your time to the idea for one year?
2. Will you give up every other interest for it?
3. Will you feel yourself dedicated with me to the creation of a great work of art—and forsake all other claims for it until it is completed?
4. Will you refuse to listen to those who may draw you from it: husband—family—friends?
5. Will you consecrate all your available income and try to raise money from your influential friends for it?
6. Will you—in toto—give yourself, with me, to this Great Idea so that Florence may live again?
One—two—three—Off we go—

Gordon Craig

I just numbered the answers and wrote "No" [to each] and closed the sheet with:

One—two—three—Off you go!

Mabel Dodge

After a few days I received his answer, written as usual on lovely rice paper with a black India ink mask engraved at the top, and his black, black handwriting:

I have passed the last days attending the death of a great idea and giving it as decent a burial as possible. . . .

A mountain was in travail . . . brought forth a mouse.

Sincerely yours,
Gordon Craig

CHAPTER EIGHTEEN &? HOW THE GREAT
COLLECTIONS ARE MADE

[Arthur] Acton had the great Villa Incontri upon the Via Bolognese, where he lived with his wife and his two small boys. She was "petite," Dresden china—gowned by Worth, and the boys were never much in evidence. Instead, there were countless *putti*—madonnas and children, pairs of angels, and a surprising collection of genuine, antique, terra-cotta bas-reliefs.

The villa was crammed full of *objets d'art,* of old velvets, damasks, cinquecento furniture, glass, carven mirrors, everything in profusion, crowding the great rooms and hanging thick on the high walls. The marble hall had a fountain playing in a holy-water fount and Acton tried goldfish in it once, but they all jumped out one night, or were tossed out by the *jet d'eau* [water jet] and were found in the morning stuck fast to the shining marble floor and had to be scraped off with a knife, he said. There were always new things in Acton's villa and the old ones must have made way for them, though there were so many things that one couldn't really keep track of them.

Carlo Loeser was an art critic. He was the middle-aged, tormented son of the Brooklyn department store man far, far away from the grim palace in Florence where Charles lived with the Cézannes. His Cézannes were the first ones I ever saw, and it took a great deal of silent observation on my part before I understood those sliding apples, those crumpled linen cloths.

Loeser lived in a studious discomfort. His rooms were meagerly furnished with a few *perfect* pieces of quattrocento noce [walnut]; cinquecento was far too ornate for him after a youth in Brooklyn. "Vulgar," he called it. Himself—he looked like a terrier, with one ear up and the other down, so cocked was one eyebrow and so snapping his red-brown canine eyes. Head on one side, his long face creased into deep lines, he often laughed spasmodically and satirically with rarely a genial laughter. It was more like a suspicious kind of mirthful bark. His voice had a timbre like catgut scraping the strings of a bass viol, but his speech was very scholarly. He was an aesthetic student and a very good judge of painting.

Up in the Viale dei Colli, beyond San Miniato, he had a little villa that he had been restoring, building, and unbuilding for years. With the woeful lack of genius often noted in critics, he foolishly thought to arrive at perfect dimension by rule and order, so that he passed the years in a scrupulous and careful search for authenticity, and never understood why the thing never came off. It was correct, yet it just wasn't right and never lived. His poor little villa! How he struggled over it! It was the same with his bitter enemy Berenson, when he "did over" the garden of I Tatti and killed it—having in the place of its poetic, irregular intimacy nothing but a graveyard. Somebody should restrain these art critics.

We saw each other continually, Loeser and Edwin and Acton and I and others. We were always talking trecento, quattrocento, cinquecento or discussing values—(Berenson's "tactile values"), lines, dimensions, or nuances in knowing phrases. Everybody in Florence was like that. The life was built up around the productions of the dead. At the Berensons' they played a guessing game that consisted of spreading a lot of photographs of paintings on a table and then, taking one, somebody would cover it with a piece of paper out of which a little hole was cut, so that only a fold of a cloak, or a part of a hand or face would be seen, and everybody would guess, by the "treatment," who had painted it. That was considered the way to pass a really gay evening up at I Tatti!

CHAPTER NINETEEN   EDWIN

I associate Edwin most clearly with motoring about Italy, for we went everywhere, to all the provinces, to all the walled towns not only once but over and over again. Edwin always went to *see* things and know about them but I went only to feel them. I suppose I have been inside nearly every church in Italy once, but the following times I would sit alone outside in the motor, just sinking into the countryside and trying to feel my way into its life. While Edwin, and any others who happened to be along, would get out of the car in the blinding sunlight, and be swallowed up by the cool damp churches, I would sit, sometimes on the ground under a shade tree, and imagine the life going on around me, becoming identified with it, understanding it or believing I did. When he would reappear into the bright, silent foreground of the piazza in his gray tweeds and with the brim of his Panama turned down over his cheerful red face so that he peered up from under it, he would seem like a considerate relation—so rare in this world—neither welcome nor unwelcome, but indifferently kind. He never infringed upon my thoughts nor invaded my imagination. He seemed incurious most of the time about my silences, so I pursued my fantasies undisturbed.

At lunch I used to eat with great intensity the nutty, coarse bread, rubbing it in salt as one does radishes, and I consumed great dishes of pasta, washing it down with goblets of the good wine, and the food had its own special imaginative quality that it derived, for me, from the simple modes that had produced it: the women, baking, were richly happy, and lively with true life; the men, pressing the grapes, were quickened with the sap. I felt the warm stream, magnetic and alluring, that flowed from the Italian peasants into the bread and wine they set before us. When I ate it I gathered their life into myself, and identified still further with them; I felt I was one with them. So I thought I took the Holy Communion of Italy and Italianized myself. Thus every hour and every *fiasco* [flask] of wine widened the distance between Edwin and me, until the inner separation was pretty complete, made so by my selfish ego, long before I left him.

CHAPTER TWENTY-THREE ✒ THE END OF THAT

I am afraid I gave less and less to Edwin as time went on and I grew more and more unaware of him. He was only the figurehead on my ship. Sometimes when I was really interested in something or caught in some illusion, however, his attention seemed to me to increase and he would get on my nerves. I felt he was incapable of realizing the stiff struggles of my life. I was a Nietzschean, I thought, beyond good and evil, indomitable, unbreakable.

It was a situation without a solution. He did not understand me, or approve of me, or like the people I was always collecting, after I had finished collecting things for the villa, but he couldn't get his attention off me and turn to someone else. We were both honest in our own different ways. I wanted of him nothing except to be a husband and make a part of the background, and I wanted it for John as well as for myself; I did not want to face a divorce and all the talk that that would make, as well as my family's disapproval.

Yet as the years went by—five—six—eight—ten—I became more and more irritated. He always seemed to laugh at instead of with people, and in the wrong place. He was a wet blanket. I felt that the talk at our table when he was there was limited by his inferior sophistication, and that he seemed to keep things at a commonplace level with his facetious, Boston humor.

As John grew older and the time was approaching for him to go away to school, I began to have sly, darting impulses towards divorce that all through the years I had suppressed, although for long Dr. Giarre had been urging me to leave him, for he saw that Edwin seemed to make me ill. There was no one to counsel me; I had not found my way alone, and we both suffered from the ignorance of our epoch.

I didn't know where to send John to school. I thought of a preparatory school in England, and got him put up at one with Oxford to follow. But I was full of doubts of the "system" after reading H. G. Wells, and the *New Age,* and I never acted in anything unless I felt a certain assurance.

Finally I wrote a long letter to Mr. Wells in England. I didn't know him but he seemed to me to be very advanced. I told him about our life in Florence, and that I was, myself, in sympathy with socialism as an idea: that John would have a lot of money someday, and that I wanted him to know what to do with it, yet I hardly dared withhold from him the conventional education of the majority of boys or to reject it for him. It seemed as though I should let him have it all, and then reject it for himself if he wanted to. However, at the end, I asked Wells if he knew any good school where boys were given an education that embodied socialistic thinking.

He replied, rather briefly, that my problem was his own: that he didn't know what to do with his own boys! But he supposed that the place for a rich young American was America! This dashed me a great deal for I hated the thought of going back to America to stay. I couldn't imagine myself there after living in the glow of Italy. With my teeth clenched I had made a lovely setting to live in, and though I never really lived in it, and the frame had become more important than the picture, I still clung to it wistfully. The picture never was painted. . . .

I had learned to live in a place where it was of more importance to have authentic works of art, particularly Italian ones, than to have one's favorite college win the autumn football game, or to have the right president elected. The values of life were centered in the perpetuity of the grand epochs, and a scrap of genuine primitive painting on a worm-eaten board, found in a dingy, cavernous cellar in Sienna or Perugia, meant more to me and my Florentine friends than the tallest skyscraper on earth.

I often used to go down to the Pitti Palace, to walk across the Ponte Vecchio through the picture gallery above the little shops. Nearly always it would be empty, and one could pass alone through the queer place, from one side of the Arno to the other. Yet it was always extremely full of people for me, the people of the past quietly staring out at one, while the river flowed beneath us. It was full of fascination and made one imagine things. I used to go into their lives and sense and understand them. One could enter it like going into a dream.

And it was much in this way that I took the people I knew in Florence. They were like portraits in a picture gallery to me. I liked going into their houses and gardens and *experiencing* them, really going *into* them, and by observing them, to become identified with each in turn. It was really each in turn, for they, too, were separate from each other, artificially grouped into their small cliques or living in a solitary manner.

It was a picture gallery, of different lives, where each in its own way was complete in itself. Even the homosexuals had a completeness about them, though they were generally unhappy at being cut out of the picture. They had a completeness that came from the everlasting need to balance their lives, to cultivate friends who would cancel others, to cultivate an appearance of ease that would cover their furtiveness, to create the eternal alibi that would deceive the biological minded in a world they had, after all, to live in, too, with more than a merely legal status! The worst element about them was the tragic one, and they knew it. I never knew one of them who really sanctioned his own life except the ones who were celibate, and few of them had a vocation for that. Their inverted love turned negative in them . . . they hated themselves and others. . . .

So taken altogether, this Florentine collection of people were like the Ponte Vecchio collection of paintings; they were not, perhaps the best in the world. They were just the casual figures of Florentine life in the early days of the twentieth century. Finally I said to myself: "I have *seen* them."

I was not so sorry to make up my mind to leave Italy for (as I said to myself) John's sake, as I was horrified at the thought of living in New York, for that was, of course, the only place to live in if one went back. My imagination refused to work on the idea of New York. Any way in which I imagined it seemed just too dreary and unattractive for words, with Edwin in and out of the house at regular hours, and those Americans one knew so well, for one's sole amusement. How could one ever possibly dip into their lives? One knew them all too well already. One had it all, all, inside one, too. And the only way I was able to live was vicariously—imagining myself into other forms than my own. The one thing that I simply could not do was to imagine the future. I could imagine the past, and imagine myself into the present. But the future has always remained a blank for me, so that I have never been able to know beyond the day or the hour what life would be like.

I simply revolted inside myself when I thought of New York, yet I found myself making preparations to go there, and as I look back now I find that the decisive actions throughout life have been impelled by a deeper self than the one who thought or wished for definite things. So I selected things from the villa for an unknown house in America. I bought new things that I felt would be lovely over there. I made the arrangements for the school for John in the autumn of, I think, 1912, and one day in the fall we were all on the steamer, with Italy behind us.

It was actually one of the worst experiences I had ever been through, was that voyage. I did not feel torn up by the roots; it was not that I was sorry to leave all the people I knew and have written of here, and many, many more I have not told of because these pages only try to make a picture of the kind of life one had in those days—not to show up every detail of it. The trouble was that I did not care to look back, and I could not look forward. The sea was all there was, and I did not like the sea. I felt nowhere—suspended "between two worlds. . . ."

All through that voyage I sat at the rear of the ship with my back turned to the bow, facing back, towards Europe, for that, at least, I knew. I rebelled against the idea of starting all over again. I rebelled against a new life and a new world, for I couldn't conceive of it save in the drabbest of tones. I sat weeping there, day after day, with Edwin perfunctorily solicitous, and John running back and forth quite excited, and wondering about America and school over there.

We brought Domenico with us and the familiar figure with the smooth-shaved, clerical face above his decent, black overcoat came from time to time to try to make me eat some fruit or drink a cup of broth. He was genuinely sympathetic and probably somewhat shared my apprehensions about our new house. I saw him hovering near, quite often discreetly watching me, with raised and worried eyebrows, and the corners of this thin mouth turned down.

Finally we neared land and one morning there was the Statue of Liberty frozen into its pedestal—there were the tall buildings of New York with dark mists shading them from our vision. My hopelessness and despair broke out afresh at the sight, and I ran to my old place at the far end of the boat, dragging John by the hand. Not in all the Florentine years had I been so maternal as I was that morning! Never so anxious to mold him to the right way of thinking and feeling. I drew him down beside me and we were the only ones left there, looking backward to the Old World.

"Remember, it is *ugly* in America," I sobbed to him, holding on to his hand.

"We have left everything worthwhile behind us. America is all machinery and moneymaking and factories—it is ugly, ugly, ugly! Never forget that!"

John listened till I had finished, his hand in mine, and then I saw him turn his head and look over his shoulder towards the shore. After a minute he said, in a small, firm voice: "I don't think it's so ugly."

And that was the end of that.

Movers and Shakers

(1912–1917)

Part One

CHAPTER ONE ❧ AT 23 FIFTH AVENUE

There I was, settled in the apartment. It was on the corner of Ninth Street and Fifth Avenue, and the four ample rooms faced south so there was always sunshine in them. I liked the somber impressive house as soon as I saw it. It was square and built of brown-painted brick, and it seemed to be planted deep in the ground as though it would stand there forever. The front of it had a blank look like a face that hides its thoughts and it gave one a feeling of immense security. It seemed a refuge from the street.

I had had every single bit of the woodwork painted white, and had all the walls papered with thick, white paper. In the corner room that looked out both on Fifth Avenue and Ninth Street there was a carved white marble mantelpiece, and at the three high windows I hung straight, white, handwoven linen curtains made at Pen Browning's school in Asolo, each of them bearing his little device in one corner. They hung from their cornices all the way down to the floor, and were drawn at night.

In my bedroom, which glistened down beyond this front room and beyond the recreation room and the dining room, I had finally found a use for the yards and yards of white Chinese embroidered shawls and silk I had bought on my honeymoon with Edwin in Biarritz. The pale gray French bed I had had sent from Paris had a canopy over it, and from this four white silk curtains hung, drawn back at each corner and with their heavy fringes hanging flaccid. Behind the bed a great, glimmering white shawl, thickly embroidered with odd birds and reeds, hung faintly visible upon the white wall. Over the bed lay another with fringes to the floor. At the windows, yards and yards more of white silk. The room was dazzling with all this white on white, *plusieurs nuances de blanc* [many shades of white]. It seemed to me I couldn't get enough white into that apartment. I suppose it was a repudiation of grimy New York. It diminished New York; it made New York stay outside in the street.

When I was putting the new apartment together I was occupied and engrossed by it, but when it was finished, all fresh and sparkling, I grew melancholy. More and more I began to hate the thought that I'd been forced back to America, to put John in school, and that Edwin was about to sally forth and rent an office and begin "to practice architecture," as it was so strangely called. It made it no better when he came in one day and laughed at the sight of me sitting there in one of my Renaissance Villa costumes, looking very cross. He infuriated me.

I remember one weekend that John came to stay with us. He was still very Italian looking, though later he outgrew it as the Italian influence faded out of him. Everything interested him, and Edwin and he used to go off together to football games up at the Polo Grounds, the two of them very cheerful and energetic together. I hated to see them so cheerful. I hated to see them set off for that American Saturday afternoon, full of interest in that American sport. I bade my two Americans goodbye in a very aloof fashion, trying to seem cold and contemptuous though my thoughts were hot and angry. I was persuaded that all these years I had been living abroad had been to give John the most recherché and lovely experience; of what use was it all, then, if he was to come back and have it all covered over with mediocrity and commonness? Common associations and companions until he too was of the dead low level of the average American boy? I felt betrayed as I watched them from the window, saw them hail a bus and climb to the top and go sailing away from me.

"Nothing to do" again! The same old recurrent dilemma. There was no life in anything about me. A rumble-rumble-rumble on the streets outside, and inside a deathly stillness wherein one could hear oneself draw every breath. It was from that day on that I began to fall quite definitely ill. Edwin was solicitous and sorry for me, as he always was, but I told him mournfully that it was he who was the cause of my ambiguous malaise. "I don't know . . .," I faltered, "but I think you must go away. Let us separate for a while and see if it won't help." Dear, kind, amusing Edwin! Why did I have to land my trouble upon him, blame him for it?

It took time and increasing depths of melancholy and several nervous crises before our real separation came to pass. Edwin would go and return, go and return again; to Boston and back, to Buffalo and back. Although I was terribly lonely when he went, whenever I saw him again after an absence, when he would come rapidly into the apartment, ruddy and smiling and endlessly patient and hopeful, something would rise up from the bottom to repel him, a sort of nausea at the sight of his persistently debonair, hard-shelled, American aplomb.

This made me wish him away. I persuaded myself that he stood between me and real life, and I decided that his way of thinking was commonplace, for I grew more and more intellectually snobbish, which is a kind of negativeness that always ruled me when I had no feeling for anything. Away, away, away, I pushed, further each week, and behind the compulsion to do this, there was always something crying deep down in me, something simple and faithful and affectionate that reached out after him, and his loving, loyal care that had come to me at a time in my life when I had needed it very much, and that had never wavered or failed me. But I could not go on holding him and driving him from me at the same time; the thing in me that had to adventure into new worlds was ruling me completely. If I wanted to go ahead and *live* mentally, I had to send Edwin away—that was all there was to it. If I were to escape from such afternoons as I had passed the day he and John went off so happily to the football game, then he must go away from me and stay away.

One of the places Edwin and I had dined together was at the Armstrongs'. At dinner a funny-looking man sat opposite me. He was about thirty-five years old and his evening clothes looked a little queer to me, maybe because of his shirt, which was frilly, full of little tucks. He had nice brown eyes, full of twinkling, good-natured malice, and there was a squareness in his face, for his brow seemed square and his jowls were square. He had finely textured, red skin, and though the lower part of his face was heavy and unmodeled, he had a very delicate, small nose. His mouth was his most difficult feature, because of the large teeth with slits showing between them that jutted out and made him look like a wild boar, though the rest of him looked quite domesticated.

His name was Carl Van Vechten and he came of Dutch parentage; this, perhaps, explained the porcine texture of his skin and the suggestion of the wild boar in him, for many Hollanders have that quality. He seemed amused at everything; there wasn't a hint of boredom in him. "A young soul," I thought to myself in my superior way as I smiled across at him. He was the first person who animated my lifeless rooms. He entered the exquisitely ordered and prepared apartment and he enjoyed it so much that he seemed to give it a gently vibrating awareness of itself. He never realized that the lovely objects all gathered together in a perfect pattern had no life of their own nor even any borrowed life from me, and he gave them such an appreciation of the cozy living world they made, soft in firelight and sunshine, drenched with the smell of tea roses and heliotrope, and fine cigarette smoke, that there was an instant response from all those inanimate things and the place became alive for us and for all others who ever afterwards entered there. He set it going on its changing round of appearances.

With him "amusing" things were essential things; whimsicality was the note they must sound to have significance. Life was perceived to be a fastidious circus, and strange conjunctions were more prized than the ordinary relationships rooted in eternity. After Carl's visit, Edwin seemed to belong there less than before it, so that my vital organs produced, accommodatingly, a rapid crescendo of obscure symptoms that sought to remove him instanter. Much of the time I lay listless on the pale French gray couch, dangling a languid arm, eyes closed before the recurrent death of the sweet antiquities about me that lapsed lifeless betweenwhiles. It seemed to me I could no longer explore people with Edwin near at hand as it had been at the villa.

During the deep depression of those first months at 23 Fifth Avenue, although I was amused some of the time by Carl and others, I was really very let down and filled with hopelessness. I was so depleted in vitality that I was continually catching cold and finally contracted tonsillitis very badly. The doctors recommended having the tonsils removed, so I had an operation there in the apartment.

It was later on that Dr. Jelliffe told me his fascinating theories on disease and his belief that nearly all bodily illness is a failure of the spirit expressing itself at the physical level, just as disorders of the brain represent, at the symbolic level, the inabilities of the psyche. Any illness of the respiratory organs, the throat, bronchial tubes, and lungs represented, according to Dr. Jelliffe's findings, a failure in aspiration—the breath of God gone wrong. Tumors, cancers, and so on appeared to him to be manifestations in the flesh of one's unsublimated hatreds for people or situations outside oneself whom one regarded as parasites and whom one was unable to successfully deal with. Most of the insanities that were not of organic origin were, he thought, due to one's own inability to cope with oneself. Be it all as it may! Certainly my throat was testimony either to some lack of aspiration or of failure to achieve. I was poisoned by it and very ill after they removed the infected tissue.

Edwin, so sorry for all this conflict in me, tried to find diversions to take me out of myself. He longed to find the elements that would mitigate his negative effect upon me and to bring them in to bolster up his claim to life in that place. One day, he ran into Jo Davidson at the Brevoort Hotel, across the street. He often went in there to look about, for that was the locale where most anything from Europe might be picked up, and he hoped that something from the Old World environment introduced over here would perhaps be the right tonic once again. Jo brought others, like a child trailing strange bright rags of seaweed gathered on some shore whose waters spread to far neighborhoods. Hutch [Hapgood] was one of the first of these and he, in his turn, brought his affinities. In time there came [Lincoln] Steffens and Emma Goldman and [Alexander] Berkman, that group of earnest naive anarchists; [John] Reed, Walter Lippmann, Bobby Jones, Bobby Rogers, and Lee Simonson, these but lately out of college; Max Eastman and Ida [Rauh], Frances Perkins, Gertrude Light, Mary Heaton Vorse, and the Sangers [Margaret and Bill]; and all the labor leaders, poets, journalists, editors, and actors.

It was ironic that Edwin, in his effort to help me, launched the boat that sailed away and left him behind. With the most profound unconsciousness of my selfish ingenuity, I persuaded good Dr. Sachs, the psychiatrist who was attending me, that Edwin was the cause of my weakness and depression, so he procured that excellent Hebe, Miss Galvin, as a nurse-companion to stay with me, counseled me to eat a great many beefsteaks and to take long walks, and explained to Edwin that it would be better for him to stay away until I was stronger.

CHAPTER TWO ⟨⟩ REVOLUTIONS IN ART

"Here, Lady Mabel! Gregg wants to tell you about our exhibition," cried Mrs. Davidge, bustling into my front room one day. James Gregg was the principal publicity man for the big International Show. What he told me was that he and Arthur Davies, with others helping, were arranging a mammoth show of modern art from Europe, to be brought to the Sixty-ninth Regiment Armory early in 1913. The public had never seen any really modern painting and sculpture and it was time they did, he said.

I knew that only one man in America had ever done anything for the young artists who were trying to break away from the academic conventions, and that was Alfred Stieglitz. At 291 Fifth Avenue, upstairs, he had a couple of rooms where he exhibited modern artists and it took courage in those days. He had plenty. He showed John Marin, [Andrew] Dasburg, Arthur Dove, and others there and people came and gaped, or looked impressed, or wiped smiles off their faces. The American public was still strongly protected twenty-five years ago, and only a comparative few saw these rebel painters. Kenyon Cox and Royal Cortissoz were the outstanding art critics of the day, and they were poised at the Gate of Free Painting with flaming swords. Winslow Homer and George Inness had been the idols of the art columns and still were.

Gregg found me listless—Ariadne with the tide low. "You know Gertrude Stein," he said, announcing it. "Couldn't you try an article about her? It will fit in with the exhibition."

I soon found they talked about that exhibition with creepy feelings of terror and delight. It was an escapade, an adventure. I, grown familiar in Florence and Paris with Cézanne—whose apples and things were met with in a reassuring friendly way on Loeser's walls—and Picasso and Matisse, familiars at Leo Stein's apartment, perceived that here in this other world they were accounted dynamite. These gentle men like James Gregg and Arthur Davies proposed to dynamite America, so they evidently believed. Revolution—that was what they felt they were destined to provide for these States—and one saw them shuddering and giggling like high-spirited boys daring each other.

Edwin was away and I was alone in my apartment and I was glad to see a mood of any kind so that I might enter it and live. I liked to live. But I didn't feel much like doing anything about it. I couldn't turn on action even if I wanted to, for I was never a self-starter. Gregg must work harder. He did. He became more eager and more inarticulate, pressing me to try my hand. He would get it published in one of the art magazines that proposed to reproduce the pictures in the show and it would be sold there at the Armory during those days the exhibition lasted.

I got up a little steam, took out the "Portrait of Mabel Dodge" by Gertrude Stein, and made a slow dive into it—presently emerging with a kind of article. What I said then, was: God help me!

SPECULATIONS, OR POSTIMPRESSION IN PROSE

BY MABEL DODGE

[*Arts and Decorations,* March 1913]

Many roads are being broken today, and along these roads consciousness is pursuing truth to eternity. This is an age of communication, and the human being who is not a communicant is in the sad plight that the dogmatist defines as a condition of spiritual nonreceptivity.

Some of these newly open roads lie parallel and almost touch.

In a large studio in Paris, hung with paintings by Renoir, Matisse, and Picasso, Gertrude Stein is doing with words what Picasso is doing with paint. She is impelling language to induce new states of consciousness, and in doing so language becomes with her a creative art, rather than a mirror of history.

In her impressionistic writing, she uses familiar words to create perceptions, conditions, and states of being never before quite consciously experienced. She does this by using words that appeal to her as having the meaning that they *seem* to have. She has taken the English language and, according to many people, has misused it, or has used it roughly, uncouthly, and brutally, or madly, stupidly, hideously, but by her method she is finding the hidden and inner nature of nature.

After the International Show opened the noise began. "Well, who is Mabel Dodge?" they exclaimed. And thousands of copies of *Arts and Decoration* were sold, for Gertrude Stein's "Portrait" of her, serving as an example of her style, was in it, and she had signed that article—and there was something new under the sun and everybody's blood ran quicker for it! A chance to laugh, to curse, to run cold from *words!* Oh! Look at the letters that poured in. People were struck by the thing and they tingled.

I suddenly found myself in a whirlpool of new, unfamiliar life and if Gertrude Stein was born at the Armory show, so was "Mabel Dodge." The way it happened was that as soon as I had written the article and given it to

Gregg, he showed it to Arthur Davies and told people about it. Long before it was printed, they came after me and got me into the exhibition part of it; asked me to help collect any examples of modern art bought in Europe, in New York, from people who would loan them; asked me to help with the money.

I had an automobile, with a smug chauffeur named Albert driving it in bearskins, and I had a small bank account with nothing much to buy except flowers and cigarettes. As soon as I collected a few pictures from here and there, feeling dignified in people's drawing rooms designating what I wanted, and had written a check for five hundred dollars and sent it to Davies, I felt as though the exhibition were mine. I really did. It became, overnight, my own little revolution. *I* would upset America; I would, with fatal, irrevocable disaster to the old order of things. It was tragic—I was able to admit that—but the old ways must go and with them their priests. I felt a large, kindly compassion for the artists and writers who had held the fort heretofore, but I would be firm. My hand would not shake nor could I allow my personal feelings of pity to halt me. *I* was going to dynamite New York and nothing would stop me. Well, nothing did; I moved forward in my role of fate's chosen instrument, and the show certainly did gain by my propulsion. The force was there in me—directed now.

Things, then, were flowing in and out of the apartment. Edwin had flowed out and stayed out. He shook his head and intimated I would go to the bad but when he read the article in *Arts and Decoration,* and then immediately afterwards kept seeing things in magazines and newspaper about Mabel Dodge, he had a "can-I-believe-my-eyes" sensation and wrote a nice letter in which he said that he was thrilled by a certainty of my "approaching recognition" at last, and that he was sorry this had been so long delayed by his blundering interference. He told me I had been right all the past years—he had not understood me. It was a generous, appreciative letter and I was glad he wrote it.

CHAPTER THREE 🐲 CHARACTERS

Looking back upon it now, it seems as though everywhere, in that year of 1913, barriers went down and people reached each other who had never been in touch before; there were all sorts of new ways to communicate, as well as new communications. The new spirit was abroad and swept us all together. My own part in it was involuntary. The share I had in bringing people together was inspired not at all by any conscious realization in me, for I was at that time really more essentially an instrument of the times than ever before. Freed from Edwin's conservative habit, I thought, I was able to move as the spirit dictated. It was only afterwards that I rationalized the impulses that had urged me to act.

The International Exhibition of Modern Art was the opening indication of this new impetus. That is natural, for it is always the artists and poets who swoop ahead like heralds. One saw the same thing happening in Europe when the Russian dancers, actors, and artists cut an opening for the Orient to pass into Europe, which immediately afterwards became orientalized in clothes and in thinking. Women began to wear turbans and for the first time, then, trousers. For Russia was the last great closed gate between the East and the West. Men began to talk and write about the fourth dimension, interchangeability of the senses, telepathy, and many other occult phenomena without their former scoffing bashfulness, only they did it with what they were pleased to call a scientific spirit.

The essence of it all was communication. It was as if men said to other men: "Look, here is a new way to see things . . . and a new way of saying things. Also new things to say." As Hutchins Hapgood, always the ideal journalist, said: "This is news!" Gertrude Stein's writing had the same effect. It caused an inner upheaval.

From the moment I wakened and drank my coffee in the white bed, embraced by the silken curtains depicting reeds and roosters, the stirring within me began. I felt as though I had the works of clocks in my body instead of a heart and bowels. The dynamic whir and buzzing increased in rapidity and volume until it reached my head, and there it continued an accompaniment to the charivari between my ribs that was fit to burst my brain with its reverberating din—like the thousand devils beating a tattoo against the walls of an impregnable hell. It was necessary to find an escape for these dynamos—so I would reach for the telephone, invite someone to go somewhere, call Miss Galvin and give her a dozen errands, call the automobile and hasten away full steam ahead.

Once as I left the lunch table for a moment to fetch something from my bedroom, I heard Carl say to Hutch in a low mockery of fright: "That woman will drive me crazy, Hutch. She accelerates the tempo so!" "Yes," Hutch agreed, "it's her vibration." While I couldn't rest for the crepitations within me, yet I was gratified at this evidence of my influence on others. That at least was, for me, a reward of virtue, for, I believed, this is my body holding within it all my power instead of spilling it in love.

I thought that power left my neglected womb and ascended to my brain, and from that questionable point of vantage it could challenge other brains. It seemed to me that had it stayed in its proper place men might have really loved me, but that at this particular time the pole was pulsating higher up. This caught men between the eyes, held them magnetized, fascinated, charmed, as men will be by the allure of a woman's lively calling essence, but left them entirely free below.

Jo Davidson first brought Hutchins Hapgood to see me. Everybody loved Hutch. He was the warmest, most sympathetic hound. God pursued him and he pursued God, looking into every dustbin for Him. He never thought he would find Him among the mighty, but always he was nuzzling among "the lowly, the lowliest, and the low." Neith let him think he was pursuing God, but she held the end of the leash in her enigmatic white hand and smiled a secret smile. For, like other women I have known, she didn't believe in this everlasting talk about his soul.

Whenever Hutch was touched enough by someone's pain, he got relief inside himself, and that made him feel God was there. He was a wonderful talker and his deep compassionate voice had a boom in it, and was like organ music. The book he wrote called *The Story of a Lover*, which told all about him and Neith, was just like organ music, too. It was suppressed (I mean by the censor!), because it was so essential it seemed strangely raw to the poor man. He had written other books when I met him: *An Anarchist Woman, The Autobiography of a Thief, The Spirit of the Ghetto, Paul Jones*, and several others. And some of these were about down-and-outs he'd met on park benches in his newspaper days, for he started as a reporter.

When Lincoln Steffens was the editor of the *Commercial Advertiser*, Hutch was one of his reporters and Neith sat in the window at a desk in the office where the sun came in on her red hair. Hutch never loved any woman but Neith. He tried to, but he couldn't. He felt he ought to. He believed that if he could become successfully the lover of a woman, enjoying her body and giving her pleasure, that it would be the gesture of purest comradeship. But it was a gesture he could not make completely. He called himself an intellectual anarchist, but while he was intellectual, he was not anarchic in his essence. He had not even an anarchistic influence it seemed to me, but maybe I was mistaken.

He was one of the most attractive and lovable human beings I ever knew, and I soon became deeply attached to him and wanted to be with him all the time. I told him all about myself—everything—and oh! how he sympathized. Tears stood in his eyes and he passed his hand tenderly over my hair. We spent hours and hours together in the white rooms, talking. And he brought all his friends to see me and took me to see them. It was through him I knew the anarchist group, the IWWs, the single taxers (of whom Lincoln Steffens was one, and also Fred Howe and Bolton Hall), and in fact, all the different kinds of radicals.

All that autumn Hutch and I were growing more and more attached to each other. Hutch, because I was such a perfect listener, so entirely understanding; I, because he was such a perfect listener and so entirely understanding. We told each other everything and we talked about our souls to our hearts' content. Each of us knew what the other meant. We sorrowed over each other and felt our mutual woe. We both felt like failures from the angle of worldly success, and we were proud of it, and we considered each other to be failures—and this drew us together into a luxurious, rich companionship. We thought we were the only ones in the world who longed for perfection; Hutch used to laugh and tell me [William] James said to him once: "I cannot understand this mad unbridled lust for the absolute!"—but it seemed to us we would long for it till we left this life.

When Hutch first took me to see Emma Goldman, I felt quite nervous as we climbed the flight of stairs to her apartment. I knew she stood for killing people if necessary. They called this Direct Action. And I knew, too, that she and her group had been close to the act. Alexander Berkman had tried to kill Henry Frick, and had been in jail for it for many years. Ben Reitman, Emma's present lover, was what was called a dangerous man. These people were not intellectual anarchists like dear Hutch living safely with Neith and the children. They lived under the constant espionage of the police. I dreaded going into the apartment.

But what a warm, jolly atmosphere, with a homely supper on the table, and Emma herself like a homely, motherly sort of person giving everyone generous platefuls of beefsteak (they were great meat eaters) and fried potatoes! She didn't look wild or frightening. She looked to me, from the very first, rather like a severe but warmhearted schoolteacher, with a very prognathous jaw. What willpower! Sheer strength in that jaw and no sensitiveness. Berkman, or Sasha, as they called him, was a heavy-jawed man, too, bald in front, with veiled eyes and thick lips. Hutch always said there was something very sweet in him, but I never could see it, though I tried. After I got to know him well, Sasha tried to kiss me in a taxi once and this scared me more than murder would have done. I don't know why.

I felt, though, that first time, that I wanted these people to think well of me. They were the kind that *counted*. They had authority. Their judgment was somehow true. One did not want their scorn. Emma and Sasha and the rest of them accepted me because Hutch vouched for me. They all loved him, though he did a great deal to make their cause weaker, in a way, because, by writing sympathetically of them, he helped remove the terror of them from people's minds. He was always bringing different kinds of people together and neutralizing their power.

I saw quite soon, in my New York life, it was only the separations between different kinds of people that enabled them to have power over each other. I remember Lincoln Steffens and Hutch both said, later, that Bill Haywood never made another really convincing and impassioned speech against capitalism after he knew me and came to the Evenings. He hated capitalists until he knew them. When he knew us, he couldn't hate us very much.

But though Emma and her bunch (as they were always called in the distinction from Bill Haywood and *his* bunch, or Carl and *his* bunch) had confidence in me and came easily to my house, still I always felt a reserve there that was never broken through. I felt they had Plans. I knew they had. I knew they continually plotted and planned and discussed times and places. Their obvious activity seemed to be publishing the anarchist magazine, *Mother Earth*, but beneath this there was a great busy humming complex of Planning, and many times they referred to the day when blood would flow in the streets of New York. That day was to be, truly, their blissful and perfect consummation, to be lived for, to be worked for, and sacrificed for. Any one of them would have died to bring it quicker, for they were all sturdy, robust people, unafraid of death. There was blood in the air that year—there truly was. One was constantly reminded of it.

Emma was the mainspring of her group. The one who had the initiative, the judgment, and the strength. The others were her hands, though they, too, were strong thinkers. Berkman had a good brain and his book about his years in prison is pretty strong material.

I remember we had a correspondence over the thing he wrote in his book for me:

Dear Berkman,

You have asked me to write you an article for *Mother Earth*. I wonder what you want me to write about? Perhaps you want me to define my attitude towards anarchism. You wrote in your volume of *Prison Memoirs*:

To Mabel Dodge, for a deeper social consciousness and a more perfect crystallization of a definite goal to make the world a better place to live in for men and women.

Now any crystallization seems to me only an opportunity for further disintegration. A new springboard from which to leap forward towards new truth. It seems to me that no sooner has an idea become crystallized into an institution, a habit, or even a party than it is ready for some spiritual dynamiting—the life that is in it [is] released, and put once more in movement, for only in movement is there any liberty, and life can only develop under freedom.

I do not believe or disbelieve in marriage, but I do believe in love, which may exist either within the institution or outside of it, providing that it is free. Free love seems to me that love which has been released from any limitation of personality or self-seeking, and which finds its fullest expression in service.

I cannot imagine myself ever crystallizing into an anarchist or a social-ist, any more than into a "society woman" or a Roman Catholic, because to become a member of a party signifies to me the exclusion of other par-ties. But I can conceive of being a woman of the world, taken in its broad-est meaning—or a humanitarian.

When I met Emma Goldman, my heart went out to her because she is a fine human being, not because she is an anarchist. Her genius lies, to my mind, in her rich capacious nature, and in the deep love of humanity that she has always given so abundantly to all who asked it, and to even those who have not asked it.

The party does not interest me; the individual does. His service is what counts. What difference does it make where he operates? The party and its "crystallized and definite goal"? Well, perhaps for some, but not for me. Some people are impelled to action by a definite goal, others, without any specific goal beyond love of progress in any of its aspects, are able day by day to illumine and enhance life for those with whom they come in con-tact, and this merely by the fact of their existence, and the love within them for all humanity, and in doing so they are making the world a better place for other men and women.

It seems to me that our friend Hutchins Hapgood is a good example of this. He is the true citizen of the universe, and he belongs to no party; rather he belongs to *all* individuals. I repeat what I said to you the other night: The true ideal with the largest reach would be to have *one* group of disorganized individuals if each carried in his heart just one essential—the love of *all*.

And so I am with you as one human being to another—and it is summed up better than I can say it in the words of Edward Carpenter—which you know.

Yours faithfully,
Mabel Dodge

One of Hutch's best friends was Steff. Lincoln Steffens had been the city editor of the *Commercial Advertiser* in past years when Hutch was a reporter and Neith worked in his office, and later he had become managing editor of

McClure's. McClure's Magazine was perhaps the finest magazine this country has ever had. Of course, old McClure, Steff says, knew how to pick winners. He knew genius when he saw it and gathered it up. First and last there were some wonderful people in that changing group: Ida Tarbell, Ray Stannard Baker, Witter Bynner, Willa Cather. McClure was enthusiastic about Willa Cather's quality before she wrote her first book, when she was there in the office. "Steff," he would say, "she's wonderful. She has genius. You'll see."

Lincoln Steffens had invented "muckraking" and had gone from city to city cleaning up politics, and these revelations appeared in *McClure's*. He was a delicately built little man, very flexible in his movements and with a rapier-keen mind. His brown hair came down on his forehead in a little bang, and he had sparkling steel blue eyes shining through gold-rimmed spectacles and a sudden, lovely smile. Steff had a way of flashing up the corners of his mouth in that almost rigid sudden smile. He called himself the only Christian on earth and he wore a plain gold cross hanging on his solar plexus attached to his watch chain.

He always believed in the young. Twenty-five years ago, when he was on *Everybody's Magazine,* he told his directors that they ought to be hunting out some new, young writers. They asked him where he thought he could find them and he replied: "I can find them. You wait and see," and he went to Harvard University and asked several of the professors there for lists of the likeliest boys they had in their senior classes.

One name that appeared on several of these lists was that of Walter Lippmann. So Steff sought him out and told him to report to him when he had graduated, and he returned to the magazine office and told the staff he had found a new writer. Of course they laughed at him—and they put the issue up to him in the form of a gamble. "You take him on, then, Steffens; call him your secretary, if you like. Give him a chance to write—to prove himself, and at the end of six months if he has done anything worthwhile we will pay for it." Of course Walter did!

It happened that Walter Lippmann's class had a number of other brilliant boys in it. Several "movers and shakers of the world" were graduated with him. For instance, there were John Reed, Robert Edmond Jones, Robert Rogers (he shook the world a few years ago by telling his class at the Boston School of Technology to be snobs!), Lee Simonson, and others.

Steffens had been a friend of Reed's father in Portland, Oregon, and they were both members of the old Bohemian Club in San Francisco. This father went to Steffens and said: "I have a boy graduating at Harvard this year and going to New York afterwards. I think he's a poet; I don't know, though. I wish you'd keep your eye on him." Steff did. He was amused at the antics of the young, and he liked watching them. He put Reed on the *American Magazine,* which he was editing at that time, but he told Reed he didn't want him to really *work.* Reed didn't. Steff even went down to live with a group of boys of which Reed was one, in that famous, ramshackley old house at 42 Washington Square South. It was kept by a couple of frowsy old landladies who cursed these young men when their rent was overdue and who nursed them when they were sick.

Margaret Sanger was one of the radical group I came to know in the first months I was in New York. She was the Madonna type of woman, with soft brown hair parted over a quiet brow, and crystal-clear light brown eyes. Eyes that were of a one-toned brown, not fusing and mixing with other shades as in the case of more complex natures. She had a husband, Bill Sanger, who tried to paint, and two children.

It was she who introduced to us all the idea of birth control, and it, along with other related ideas about sex, became her passion. It was as if she had been more or less arbitrarily chosen by the powers that be to voice a new gospel of not only sex knowledge in regard to conception, but sex knowledge about copulation and its intrinsic importance. She was the first person I ever knew who was openly an ardent propagandist for the joys of the flesh. This, in those days, was radical indeed when the sense of sin was still so indubitably mixed with the sense of pleasure.

Margaret Sanger was an advocate of the flesh. It was her belief that the attitude towards sex in the past of the race was infantile, archaic, and ignorant, and that mature manhood meant accepting the life in the cells, developing it, experiencing it, and enjoying it with a conscious attainment of its possibilities that would make previous relationships between men and women, with their associations of smirking shame and secretive lubricities, seem ignoble in their limitations and stupid beyond words in their awkward ignorance. For Margaret Sanger to attempt what she did at that time seems to me now like another attempt to release the energy in the atom, and who knows but perhaps that best describes what she tried to do.

It was in talking to her at home in my sitting room that I really got something from her, something new and releasing and basic. Nina [Wilcox] and I, I remember, had a wonderful talk with her one evening—just the three of us at dinner—when she told us all about the possibilities in the body for "sex expression," and as she sat there, serene and quiet, and unfolded the mysteries and mightinesses of physical love, it seemed to us we had never known it before as a sacred and at the same time a scientific reality.

Love I had known, and pleasures of the flesh, but usually there had been a certain hidden forbidden something in my feeling about it and experience of it that made it seem stolen from life, instead of a means to that great end, the development of life, and the growth of the soul. Margaret Sanger made it appear as the first duty of men and women. Not just anyhow, anywhere, not promiscuity, for that defeated its own end if pleasure were the goal; not any man and woman, but the conscious careful selection of a lover that is the mate, if only for an hour—for a lifetime, maybe.

Then she taught us the way to a heightening of pleasure and of prolonging it, and the delimiting of it to the sexual zones, the spreading out and sexualizing of the whole body until it should become sensitive and alive throughout, and complete. She made love into a serious undertaking—with the body so illumined and conscious that it would be able to interpret and express in all its parts the language of the spirit's pleasure.

Hutch had first taken me to "291." This was a tiny gallery on the top floor of a building on Fifth Avenue, and Stieglitz, who stood talking there day after day, was the spirit of the place. It was one of the few places where I went; it was always stimulating to go and listen to him analyzing life and pictures and people—telling of his strange experiences, greatly magnifying them with the strong lenses of his mental vision. His eyes, themselves, were like two powerful lenses surrounded by dark shades, and when he turned them upon one they burned through to the core.

He was always struck by the Wonder of Things, and after a visit to him one's faith in the Splendid Plan was revived. I owe him an enormous debt I can never repay. He was another who helped me to See—both in art and in life. His belief was that he never gave in to anything except what he believed to be the best; that he never did anything for money or prestige or power, that he cared only for what he called the spirit of life, and that when he found it, he fostered it. If, like the rest of us, he was in the dark regarding the masks of his colossal egotism, what of it? Only so could he get things done.

At "291" I met people who became the friends of a lifetime. There we gathered over and over again, drawn and held together by the apparent purity of Stieglitz's intention. He was afraid of nothing, and always trusted his eyes and his heart. Before the First International Exhibition he had already sponsored some of what were called the craziest painters in America—Marin and [Abraham] Walkowitz, Arthur Dove and Marsden Hartley, and he gave others like Andrew Dasburg the courage to paint things as they saw them. He provided an *ambiente* where the frightened artist dared to be himself.

I met Hartley there at "291"—that gnarled New England spinsterman who came to New York with his tragic paintings of New Hampshire and Maine landscapes where the trees were fateful, and Hartley told me how Stieglitz kept him from starving. He sent Hartley to Germany soon after I met him and supported him through the leanest years, as he supported Marin. He showed us some curious black-and-white drawings by a schoolteacher out west. Presently he hung them on the walls. One in particular was very intriguing: a pair of curtains, one partly drawn to one side but not enough to reveal what they hid behind them. This was the first work we saw of Georgia O'Keeffe.

Andrew Dasburg was one of the most touching people I met at "291." Lame, but slender as an archangel and with a Blake-like rush of fair hair flying upward from off his round head. There were always attractive people at Stieglitz's place. And strange, alluring paintings on the walls that one gazed into while he talked, until, gazing, one entered them and knew them. In those early years he launched nearly all those painters who count today in America and without a particle of apprehension he hung up the work of artists whom the physicians diagnosed as paranoiacs and *dementia praecox* [schizophrenic] cases.

The doctors couldn't see the difference between organization and disorganization. Because the patients in insane asylums made queer drawings and paintings, the doctors thought the artists who made pictures that looked queer to them were also insane. I asked Dr. Bernard Sachs for a card to Dr. Gregory at Bellevue so I could go and see for myself wherein they differed and wherein they resembled each other, but though he sent me the card, he disapproved completely of my wish to make such comparisons, and he said he thought it would be advisable for some of those artists themselves to apply for admission to the psychopathic ward: that the exhibition at the Armory was the best evidence of mental derangement flaunted in public he had ever seen and he advised me to keep out of it.

Stieglitz, however, never dashed, has lived long enough to see his psychopaths revered. What a dauntless spirit he had! Reviled by all the academic artists and critics, considered a freak, betrayed by some of the boys he had stood by and to whom he had given a chance to emerge from nowhere—Stieglitz was somehow tragic but never overcome.

CHAPTER FOUR ✤ THE EVENINGS

The first evening I can remember was engineered by Carl, who wanted to bring a pair of Negro entertainers he had seen somewhere who, he said, were marvelous. Carl's interest in Negroes began as far back as that, then. And it continued, taking him to Harlem, bringing Harlem to his apartment later on, so that others came to know that section of New York life, and it eventually grew to be very well known. How Carl loved the grotesque! He loved to twist and squirm with laughter at the oddity of strong contrasts. When he told me he was bringing two Negro entertainers, he said I had to invite some people for the evening, since entertainers required someone to be entertained. I didn't know it would be as outlandish as it was, not yet knowing how desirable all that was different from his own early surroundings appeared to him.

I sat, that night, among a number of disparate people while an appalling Negress danced before us in white stockings and black buttoned boots. The man strummed a banjo and sang an embarrassing song while she cavorted. They both leered and rolled their suggestive eyes and made me feel first hot and then cold, for I never had been so near this kind of thing before, but Carl rocked with laughter and little shrieks escaped him as he clapped his pretty hands. His big teeth became wickedly prominent and his eyes rolled in his darkening face, until he grew to somewhat resemble the clattering Negroes before him.

"One must just let life express itself in whatever form it will," I thought, to console myself. That was my only philosophy in those days. Let It happen. Let It decide. Let the great force behind the scenes direct the action. Have faith in life and do not hamper it or try to shape it. "I would rather be a leaf in the wind than the wind," I told Walter Lippmann in defiance of his own determination to decide everything himself, which I secretly admired a great deal since I knew he had extraordinarily good judgment for one so young. So as readily as I let Carl bring Negroes (once), I let Steff suggest another pattern.

"You have a certain faculty," Steff told me one autumn afternoon as we drank tea together by the fire that glowed in the white marble chimney place. "It's a centralizing, magnetic, social faculty. You attract, stimulate, and soothe people, and men like to sit with you and talk to themselves! You make them think more fluently, and they feel enhanced. If you had lived in Greece long ago, you would have been called a hetaira. Now why don't you see what you can do with this gift of yours? Why not organize all this accidental, unplanned activity around you? This coming and going of visitors, and see these people at certain hours? Have Evenings!"

"But I thought we don't believe in 'organization,'" I told him reproachfully, for had not he and Hutch said again and again that organizations and institutions are only the crystals of living ideas—and "as soon as an idea is crystallized, it is dead. As soon as one makes up one's mind, it is time to change it!"

"Oh, I don't mean that you would *organize* the *Evenings,*" he flashed at me with a white smile beneath his little brown bang. "I mean, get people here at certain times and let them feel absolutely free to be themselves and see what happens. Let everybody come! All these different kinds of people that you know, together here, without being managed or herded in any way! Why, something wonderful might come of it! You might even revive General Conversation!"

So, really, the Evenings were, in the first place, Steffens's idea. I never needed more than a hint of an idea, if it seemed a good one to me, to seize it and make it my own. Just a *little* push has always been enough for me if I liked the direction. Perhaps intuitive people like Steffens have sometimes seen the possibilities before I knew them myself—have noticed the bubbling before the artesian thrust and rise of energy—and by suggesting the activity already preparing to express itself have helped to bring it to the surface. Certainly this is what skillful psychologists try to do.

Anyway, ideas as congenial as this one Steff offered seemed to me already mine as soon as he uttered them, and months later, when the Evenings had become a feature of New York life, I was able to take the entire credit for them in an interview by a Mrs. Pearson:

"The Printed Page Will Soon Be Superseded by the Spoken Word," Declares Mrs. Mabel Dodge, Who Has Been Holding a New York Salon for Free Speech

All through the past winter at her apartment at 23 Fifth Avenue, Mrs. Mabel Dodge has been trying an experiment. A very puzzling experiment it was for those who were not in the know. For two or three evenings every week Mrs. Dodge kept open house, and in her drawing rooms foregathered interesting and interested people of all types and persuasions.

One was sure of an interesting evening at No. 23 Fifth Avenue, but one wondered sometimes what was being aimed at. You might find, for instance, one evening, a learned and eminent professor from Columbia University holding forth enthusiastically on Freud's theory of psychoanalysis to a roomful of absorbed highbrows. Or it might be that Mr. Haywood of the IWW would be expounding to the uninitiated what the IWW really stood for. Or Lincoln Steffens, or Walter Lippmann, would be talking about Good Government; a correspondent, just back from Mexico, would be telling about the war, or scientist from England would make eugenics a topic; or it might be feminism, or primitive life, or perhaps anarchism would bring a queer but harmless-looking crowd.

Every live topic, movement, and interest of the day has been discussed at her house, but Mrs. Dodge herself takes no part. Plainly she is not attached to any of these things, but her level brows and intelligent eyes make one know she has an interest. Pressed for an explanation of her evenings—this is her own account of them:

'They were a kind of propaganda for free speech, but with my own views about *free* and about *speech*. I never discussed it with the grave members of the Free Speech League, nor did they know I was in league with them! I wanted to try and free more than speech—I wanted to try and loosen up thought by means of speech, to get at the truth at the bottom of people and let it out, so that there would be more understanding. Understanding! That's the one thing that men go on trying for through all the changes of the world, quarrying it out of one material or another as time passes. . . .

'When I came back from Europe last winter, it seemed to me there were so many people with things to say, and so few places to say them in. There seemed to be no centralization in New York, no meeting place for free exchange of ideas and talk. So many interesting people only meeting each other in print! So I thought I would try to get people together a little and see if it wouldn't increase understanding, if they would talk among themselves and say what they thought.'

Imagine, then, a stream of human beings passing in and out of those rooms; one stream where many currents mingled together for a little while. Socialists, Trade Unionists, Anarchists, Suffragists, Poets, Relations, Lawyers, Murderers, "Old Friends," Psychoanalysts, IWWs, Single Taxers, Birth Controlists, Newspapermen, Artists, Modern Artists, Clubwomen, Woman's-place-is-in-the-home Women, Clergymen, and just plain men all met there and, stammering in an unaccustomed freedom a kind of speech called Free, exchanged a variousness in vocabulary called, in euphemistic optimism, Opinions!

I kept meeting more and more people, because in the first place I wanted to know everybody, and in the second place everybody wanted to know me. I wanted, in particular, to know the Heads of things. Heads of Movements, Heads of Newspapers, Heads of all kinds of groups of people. I became a Species of Headhunter, in fact. It was not dogs or glass I collected now; it was people, Important People. I vaguely believed that anyone who reached eminence in the community, raised themselves above the level of the others, must have attained excellence, and excellence I always revered, and also individuality, difference, originality, any tendency that showed above the old tribal pattern. Each of these "leaders" brought his or her group along, for they had heard about the Evenings (by this time called a Salon) and they all wanted to come.

Every Evening promised a problem. Did I long for other people's problems, or what? For instance, one Evening, when many artists were present, there had been a great deal of talk about the corrupting influence of money, of trying to please the public taste for money, of the sacred freedom of the artist, and all that, and among them all Carl Hovey was there, listening with a smile on his intelligent lean face. Following that talk I wrote him a letter. He was co-editor of the *Metropolitan Magazine*. This magazine was the most popular, and the most expensively printed and illustrated, ten-cent periodical of the day. Sonya Levien, a beautiful girl of Russian parentage, was Hovey's secretary and I always felt her judgment and her strength were a strong element in the office, as was the case with countless other anonymous women who were running things behind the scenes in New York. Sonya had that most enduring quality: worthy weight and substance, character in short. I adored it wherever I saw it.

So I asked Hovey to come for an Evening and to bring his art editor, Will Bradley, to meet the editors and artists of *The Masses,* a small radical affair that was the very antithesis of the plutocratic *Metropolitan*. In fact, the illustrators of *The Masses* often tried to get the *Metropolitan* to support them by buying illustrations so they could afford to contribute to *The Masses* for nothing, for Max Eastman and Floyd Dell couldn't pay them anything.

I had lunch with Carl Hovey at the Ritz a week or so later, and he told me that Will Bradley went to bed after the Evening and wasn't up yet! "It quite knocked him out," he told me, smiling. "He had no idea those young men felt like that. I think he means to try and have a more human relationship with them after this . . . if he ever gets up!" he added.

"Well, my idea is to get people together so they can tell each other what they Think," I answered. "These Evenings are making changes in a lot of different ways. Enmities fade away as soon as people talk. I have had people meet there who had been enemies for years in print, like Abe Cohen of the *Staatszeitung* and some of the editors of our New York papers, and when they met face-to-face and talked, they found their bad feelings melted right away. They couldn't feel the same anymore."

One night Bill Haywood, Emma Goldman, and English Walling, aided by their followers, arranged to tell each other what they thought. Now this meant that Emma and Bill and Alexander Berkman would try to convince the socialists that Direct Action was more effective than propaganda or legislation.

They believed in killing, they advocated it when it was possible, and they had done it, some of them openly. Of course, the IWWs led by Bill Haywood, Carlo Tresca, Elizabeth Gurley Flynn, and [Arturo] Giovannitti advised sabotage for industrial machinery no matter what the risk might be to human life.

I always decided more or less the *kind* of evening we would have, and usually they were on the same evening each week so that people saved that time and did not make other engagements. I would ask some specialist, some Head of something, to come and tell his views to start the ball rolling—the Head of the Poetry Movement, or the Head of the Free Speech League, and so on— and then all the other Heads of movements and leagues and ideas would come, and they would question each other and tell their views as freely as they liked.

One night the artists were there listening to "Big Bill" Haywood tell them that he thought artists thought themselves too special and separate, and that someday there would be a Proletarian Art, and the State would see to it that everybody was an artist and that everybody would have time to be an artist. Of course the Modernists who heard this—Andrew Dasburg, John Marin, [Francis] Picabia, and Marsden Hartley, among them—weren't so mad as Janet Scudder, who rose slowly to her feet, her eyes like pinpoints beneath drooping lids, her lips drawn down at the corners, as she glared at the big man who grinned back at her. She said in her drawling voice, with an accent of scorn:

"Do you realize that it takes twenty years to make an artist?"

In a flash, I saw Janet's memories running through her mind. Her struggle to get enough money to leave Terre Haute, years of working for a scholarship. Her long journey to Paris, her years of drudgery there, drudgery and joy too, and her great need for adjustment. Her hungers, her thirsts, her sacrifices for her work; her gradual, her so slow and so gradual success in her métier, the dull clay eternally resisting! Her years and years and years in a brown holland apron, in dusty studios; no money and poor light, no money and small amounts of food—years of it, until she saw her *Boy with Fish* or her *Boy with Flute* standing, cinquecento, in the Luxembourg, or in some American-Italian garden.

How could Bill Haywood know anything of all this? He couldn't, any more than Janet could see the pictures flashing in his brain at her indignant speech. Yet I saw his pictures as easily as I saw hers—and the impossibility. . . . Well, it wasn't for me to reconcile different points of view, I thought.

There was the beginning, in those days, then, of a new attitude towards the artist. His sacrosanct vocation was being slowly questioned, his divine right to all forgiveness by virtue of his calling was being disposed of, little by little. John Reed, coming under the influence of the more intellectual radical Labor leaders, heard it all discussed over and over again, and in "The Day in Bohemia" he reflected the healthy reaction of those hearty realists against the privileged beings who consider themselves more sensitive than others, an assumption imposed by themselves for so long upon Philistines and Pharisees.

CHAPTER EIGHT 🐚 TENDENCIES

That I was leading an existence without any real direction occurred to me over and over again. I had been caught in the whirlpool of contemporary agitation and I seemed to be going helplessly around in circles, although perhaps my reserved expression made onlookers believe I was a leading influence who knew what she was about. The fact is, I had rapidly become a mythological figure right in my own lifetime, which, I am sure, is a rather rare experience. But the faculty I had for not saying much and yet for being there gave people's imaginations a chance to fabricate their own Mabel Dodge, which they did, attributing to her all kinds of faculties and powers.

The publicity I had been able to gain overnight for Gertrude had apparently been the starting point for the belief that I had only to be in some way associated with a movement of any kind for it to be launched. This belief spread in all directions and grew like a snowball, so that the success I was considered to be able to confer upon undertakings came to have a certain actuality. People attributed power to me and by their bestowal I had it, so I was able to secure a singular attention for anything anytime and this made people eager to have my name on committees and prospectuses, or to have me associated with new movements.

I had the reputation for being radical, emancipated, wealthy, and daring but in reality I was none of these. My reputation had nothing to do with me. It never had had anything to do with me. At the same time I had a vague sense of responsibility about this automatic influence I seemed to have, and I wanted to do things with it. I had a sense of power but it didn't seem to have any savor in it, no real enjoyment. A feeling of power that translates itself merely into a sense of duty is no fun. I even missed the kind of sadness I had sometimes suffered at the Villa Curonia, for there was more real color in that than in my present life. There was no feeling of richness for me in this confusion of ideas and activities; it seemed like trying to live in one's own head, to the neglect of the heart and the senses. But nothing touched my heart and there was not much to stir one's sight and hearing unless I made an effort to go to theaters or outside places, whereas before in Florence everything about one had been nourishing to the eyes and ears and we had rarely gone to places of entertainment, so I had not the habit of going out in the evening. The most that happened to me, then, was an excitement somewhere in the region of the solar plexus and a growing restlessness.

Dr. Brill had begun his Freudian analysis before that time, and it was thought to be just as queer as all the other attempts people were making to achieve some kind of social adaptation. We had him come down and talk to us one of the Evenings and several guests got up and left. They were so incensed at his assertions about unconscious behavior and its giveaways. Although I had invited Dr. Sachs to come on the Psychoanalytic Evening, he repudiated my invitation with the tone of an admiral who has been invited to tea on an enemy submarine. He said he was not at all in sympathy with the subject or with the manner of presenting it to the public, and, he added, he considered the subject a dangerous one for me.

It was a very tentative period in many ways. For instance, we had the idea of starting a club for men and women where they could meet and talk together. The old Liberal Club down on MacDougal Street had been in existence for some time but there was nothing very attractive about it; no place to sit, no place to eat, and only useful, really, for meetings or lectures.

There was a club called Heterodoxy for unorthodox women, that is to say, women who did things and did them openly. Women who worked. New York was largely run by women; there was a woman behind every man in every publisher's office, in all the editorial circles, and in the Wall Street offices, and it was the judgment and intuition of these that determined many policies, but they were anonymous women. They didn't seem to mind being so, for the most part. They seemed to be content just to function without the credit. But the Heterodoxy was composed of women whose names were known: Charlotte Perkins Gilman, Mary Fels, Inez Haynes Irwin, Edna Kenton, Mary Shaw, Mary Heaton Vorse, Daisy Thompson, Fola La Folette, and others were already members when I was asked to join. Beloved Marie Jenny Howe was chairman of the club from the time it was created until the day of her death. She was a rare person who did a great deal for the liberation of women, and her loving wit helped her accept the sterility of her domestic life. She was married to a man [Frederick Howe] who was deeply engrossed in humanitarian problems, who, while he was Commissioner for Immigration, made Ellis Island bearable for thousands where before his time it had been purgatorial. He really tried to make it hospitable and a temporary home, while in his own home he was one of those husbands who seem to be perpetually engrossed in thought and never on the spot. When he wrote his autobiography and his wife read it, she exclaimed: "Why, Fred, were you never married?" He had neglected to mention this small fact.

There were a good many courageous people to know in those days, people who risked shattering themselves for the sake of their ideas. All kinds of people suffered and sacrificed and tried this and that. Life was ready to take a new form of some kind and many people felt a common urge to shape it. Everyone seemed to fumble and feel uncertain a good deal of the time, blind and unable to look ahead. The most that anyone knew was that the old ways were about over, and the new ways all to create. The city was teeming with potentialities.

My correspondence grew voluminous, and it had tentacles stretching in all directions and through many layers of the New York world. It is surprising what a curious resemblance the letters of that epoch have to letters of all other epochs! As I read them over I find they show the same eagerness, hope, despair, and envy that present themselves in some of the social patterns in decade after decade. The only changes seem to be in degrees of hours, and amounts, or in matters of title or neighborhood.

There were letters from unemployed and desperate people who did not know where to turn, letters from eager solutionists like Upton Sinclair:

Dear Comrade—Come to the *Call* office this afternoon or Rand School. Get others! In haste,

Sinclair

Letters from publishers introducing young writers, angry letters from people who did not sign their names:

DEAR MADAM,

Women that smoke are similar to the streetwalking class; they are vulgar immoral people.

No refined Lady would lower herself.

Those women that smoke regret that they were not born males.

They are trying to ruin their health, cause their breath and fingers to smell, and learn their children the same habits providing that they have children instead of dogs.

Yours very truly,
M.A.

Will you take over April or May number of *The Masses* magazine? Fill all space you can with plays, stories, editorials, verse, articles, suggest cartoons, anything you choose. Unconditioned freedom of expression. Will advertise

you as editor of the issue. Probable circulation 2 or 3 hundred thousand
from Atlantic to Pacific Coast. All profits yours.

Max Eastman, Editor

And invitations to join all kinds of organizations such as the World Order
of Socialism in England were interspersed in the morning mail with insult-
ing anonymous outcries and comments from people who had been at an
Evening and wanted to tell their afterthoughts. There were all kinds of communications from people who had something to say and no place to say it and
who sought for a chance in my house: ("I shall be delighted to receive notice
of an audience with you for any evening and the chance to tell you more about
Esperanto!") Then, often letters from old friends who still tried to guide my
opinions!

Demands for money for every sort of project, from birth control to new
kinds of engines to supplant steam, gas, and electrical ones! Ingenious plans
to bring all the labor class together, and pathetic notes from old servants in
need who knew my father and mother in the past; many offers of positions on
committees where periodicals were being instituted, like the *New Review,* etc.
Was it any wonder my head was spinning with the contrast between these
days and the Florentine dream life? I wondered what happened to these fabricated personae of society—such as I had become. What was to be the end
of them?

This legendary Mabel Dodge lived alongside me for many years while I went
alone, cut off from the ways of other people who all attributed to me far more
participation in rich living than they themselves enjoyed. To be sure, at times
I tried to identify myself with contemporary social changes, and to be guided
by what Naomi Mitchison called "praxis," to persuade myself as she does that
I lived purposefully with a predetermined social outlook. But truth to tell, this
persuasion, which never lasted long, was usually the undying longing to share
a group activity, the simple herding instinct. I had been brought up in an environment where altruistic attitudes were unknown, and afterwards the life in
Italy had been all too concerned with aesthetics to be troubled about reforms.
But I wanted a life in common with others.

CHAPTER TEN 🖎 REED

One night Hutch and Neith came in town to spend the night with me and go
to a party at B.'s and I, who so very seldom went anywhere, particularly in the

evening, went along too because I wanted to meet Bill Haywood. Hutch had told me so much about him and about the Paterson Silk Strike that he was leading that I was curious to see him for myself. So we walked down to the square and beyond it to one of the quiet streets, and there was a large bare room lighted with candles where a few men and women stood about chatting, or sat together the floor, for there weren't many chairs. Haywood sprawled in one of the few chairs, a great battered hulk of a man, with one eye gone and an eminent look to him.

Haywood's one eye had acquired a steady watchfulness. As Max Eastman had said, he looked like a sturdy old eagle. He was telling about the long, unremitting strike over in Paterson, New Jersey, at the silk mills; of the patience of the strikers over their fight for an *eight-hour day*.

"But there's no way to tell our comrades over here in New York about it," he growled. "The newspapers have determined to keep it from the workers in New York. Very few of them know what we've been through over there—the drama and the tragedy. The police have turned into organized gunmen. God! I wish I could show them a picture of the funeral of Modestino, who was shot by a cop. Every one of the silk mill hands followed his coffin to the grave and dropped a red flower on it. They cut their geraniums from the pot in the window—and those who hadn't any made a little red flower of red tissue paper. . . . The grave looked like a mound of blood. As they marched they sang the 'International.' By God, if our people over here could have seen it, we could have raised a trunkful of money to help us go on. Our food is getting mighty scarce over there."

"Can't you get any reports of it into the paper by hook or crook?" someone asked.

"Not a damned word," answered Haywood.

"Why don't you bring the strike to New York and *show* it to the workers?" I asked in a small, shy voice.

Haywood, who hadn't noticed me before, turned his eye on me with an arrested look. I went on, feeling engulfed in blushes and embarrassment, but unable to be still, for this idea was speaking through me. I hadn't *thought* it consciously.

"Why don't you hire a great hall and reenact the strike over here? Show the whole thing: the closed mills, the gunmen, the murder of the striker, the funeral. And have the strike leaders make their speeches at the grave as you did in Paterson—you and Elizabeth Gurley Flynn and Tresca!"

"Well, by God! There's an idea!" exclaimed Bill Haywood. "But how? What hall?"

"Madison Square Garden! Why not?" I was excited now by my own inspiration that, coming to me without any volition or expectation of mine, appeared simply wonderful to me. I sat there in an exalted, uplifted bubble of energy that had somehow arisen from some source within to delight me.

"I'll *do* it!" cried a voice—and a young man detached himself from the group and assumed a personality before my eyes.

"Well, if anyone can 'do' it, you can, Jack," someone laughed.

The young man came and sat by me. He was young, big, and full chested. His clothes wrinkled over his deep breast. He wasn't startling looking at all, but his olive green eyes glowed softly, and his high, round forehead was like a baby's with light brown curls rolling away from it and two spots of light shining on his temples, making him lovable. His chin was the best of his face, for it had a beautiful swinging curve forward—the real poet's jawbone, strong and delicate above his round throat. His eyebrows were always lifted and he was generally breathless!

"My name is Reed," he said. "That's a *great* idea. I'll go over to Paterson the first thing in the morning. . . . We'll make a pageant of the strike! The first in the world! Why, I see the whole thing!" he cried exultantly. "Why hasn't anyone ever thought of it before!" I thought in a flash of the cinquecento pageant in Florence when I had failed Gordon Craig, and it pricked with a small shame.

"Where do you live? I'll come and see you when I get back," he went on; his eyes were full of light now and he didn't see anyone around him. Already the strike pictures were forming in his mind and he saw them vivid and alive. I told him where I lived, and again he said: "The minute I get back I'll come to see you. I want to look over the ground in Paterson. Then we'll work this thing out." He didn't *ask* me if I would—he assumed from the very first that I would work with him and carry this thing through. Had I not suggested it? He never realized how little I had to do with suggesting it—that it had just popped out of me.

When Neith and Hutch and I were back in that other world that my apartment was to me, I was glowing and enhanced. Neith said: "You look like a big red rose tonight, Mabel, in that dress. Maybe you should always wear skirts of full crimson silk and sit on the floor and have Ideas! It's so becoming to you!" She was laughing at me with her gentle cynicism.

"You love ideas better than anything in the world, don't you, Mabel?" queried Hutch, smoothing my hair as his eyes filled with his usual tears. His other arm, a glass of whiskey in his hand, rested on his knee as I had seen it so many times that it is photographed forever on my memory.

"Yes," I answered him slowly, "alternately with emotions."
"Whatever that means," added Neith.

Meanwhile I had become interested in *The Masses,* a real, true radical magazine, fearless and young and laughing at everything solemn and conservative, with Max Eastman for editor. I liked him very much, and Ida Rauh, his wife— noble looking, like a lioness. I became one of their advisory committee because I had such good "ideas" always surging up out of nowhere. All sorts of people made use of me and of the free-flowing magnetic influence I seemed able to exert; also I seemed to them to have a lot of money. I was always getting letters like this:

Dear Mabel:

I am appealing to you as the ablest committeeman of your sex.

Will you please call together the Finance Committee of the International Workers' Defense Conference at your house Wednesday afternoon, or if that is not convenient for you, the next available afternoon? You have somehow the magic of making people come to committee meetings, which is a rare gift.

Faithfully,
Joseph O'Brien

Reed blew in one day, pale and excited, and ready to start immediately upon the pageant! From that moment I was engrossed by it. I gave up everything to work on it. Reed was the executive. I kept having ideas about what to do and he carried them out. We called a meeting at Margaret Sanger's house and got all the people interested who were good workers. He and I worked shoulder to shoulder and we were a perfect combination for work—untiring, full of fun, too, and perfectly thrilled by the handful we had taken up.

Everybody worked except me. But I was occupied, I thought, in inspiring Reed. Dolly Sloan accomplished prodigies of labor on this pageant, and I did a good deal of begging, for we begged, we borrowed, and we somehow raised the money to accomplish it. Girls went to all the flower shops and asked for their red carnations for the night of the pageant. The generosity of people— especially the poor people—was splendid. Reed worked night and day, half the time in Paterson, half the time in New York. When he went to Paterson, he coached the hundreds of people about the procedure of the pageant, and he rehearsed their songs. One of the gayest touches, I think, was teaching them to sing one of their lawless songs to the tune of "Harvard, Old Harvard!"

In New York he was here, there, and everywhere at once. Imagine suddenly teaching 2,000 people of various nationalities how to present their case in a huge, graphic orderly art form! Imagine planning an event to fill Madison Square Garden, a whole city block, where we were used to going to see Barnum and Bailey's Circus, with three rings and two bands going at once, and have it audible, visible, and composed enough to be convincing!

"Our Bobby Jones," as Reed began to call him, insisted on making it a Gordon Craig affair, and having a long street scene right through the audience and up to the stage, and this was a most dramatic idea because the actors entered at the far end of the hall, and the funeral procession marched right through it, so that for a few electric moments there was a terrible unity between all these people. They were one: the workers who had come to show their comrades what was happening across the river, and the workers who had come to see it. I have never felt such a high pulsing vibration in any gathering before or since.

But the time was short in which to prepare it all, and Reed was physically wearing out; we were caught into the magnetic, powerful force that people can contact at such levels of the impossible—and we were both exalted spiritually, though very, very tired. That we loved each other seemed so necessary a part of working together, we never spoke of it once. There wasn't time, and that it was no time for lovemaking was accepted without words between us. I knew I was enabling Reed to do what he was doing. I knew he couldn't have done it without me. I felt that I was behind him, pouring all the power in the universe through myself to him.

Here is a description of how it appeared to the newspapermen:

Fifteen thousand spectators applauded with shouts and tears the great Paterson Strike Pageant at Madison Square Garden. The big mill aglow with light in the dark hours of the early winter morning, the shrieking whistles, the din of machinery—dying away to give place to the "Marseillaise" sung by a surging crowd of 1,200 operatives, the fierce battle with the police, the somber funeral of the victim, the impassioned speech of the agitator, the sending away of the children, the great meeting of desperate hollow-eyed strikers—these scenes unrolled with a poignant realism that no man who saw them will ever forget.

Immediately after the night of the pageant—I believe the very next day—Miss Galvin, ever present help, John Reed, Bobby Jones, and I sailed for Europe.

Although scarcely a word of the personal kind had passed, we had taken for granted the inevitability of our love for each other, Reed and I. I had never experienced before such a passionate unity as there had been between us all through those days we worked together. He told me later that he had been constantly reminded of something George Meredith wrote about two lovers, of a perpetual flame that played back and forth between them. It had been like that with us. It had carried us on and on through those days, supporting us, and enabling us to do more than we could ordinarily perform. We were free and ready to turn to each other. But, strangely, something in me resisted him strongly. I wanted a lover and I wanted to be loved, and Reed was entirely lovable, and admirable, too, I thought. Yet something in me held back from taking that step into love.

We went to the dear old Hotel des Saints Pères, and I sent Miss Galvin and John down to Florence on the train, for we planned to stay a few days and then rent a motor and drive through the south of France and along the coast to Italy.

And then . . . then Reed's room and mine were close to each other the first night in Paris. . . . And now at last I learned what a honeymoon should be. As soon as I gave myself up to Reed, I was all for love and everything else well lost! Nothing else in the world had, any longer, any significance for me. I had built up an interest in life, a love for beautiful things, for noble ideas, and for interesting people; I had learned to be satisfied with flattery and adulation and influence. I had consoled myself with a belief that I was a maker of history, since people had told me I was doing that day by day, and because I remained silent and mysterious, while my life poured out of me and made itself felt without words, my own silence had finally convinced me, beyond the strength of any formulation, that I was indeed remarkable.

When we motored away, somehow Carl was with us—and we rolled through the June day—I in blankness—suspended—waiting for the night, the boys eager and interested in all they saw. Everything interested Reed. His imagination was on fire in the Old World. I hated to see him interested in Things. I wasn't, and didn't like to have him even *look* at churches and leave me out of his attention. When we reached Concarneau, I thought I had lost him to the stones of that place, and when we found the Italians giving *Aida* at night in the amphitheater in Verona, I was inclined to force him to go on, drive all night, anything rather than submit to the terror of seeing his eyes dilate with some other magic than my own. Everything seemed to take him away from me, and I had no single thing left in my life to rouse me save his touch.

But I could not hold him day and night. Only at night. Our journey, just the same, was happy and carefree and gay. Carl, glad to be away from his newspaper and his everlasting reports of music, was amusing in his florid, hilarious fashion. Every morning as we drove rapidly out through the quiet streets of some old town, Carl stood bowing right and left to the astonished citizens: *"Au revoir et merci"* ["good-bye and thank you"], he called to them, raising his hat, his face twisted in his crooked smile.

There stood the villa waiting! Was it possible only a year had passed since we left it for a new world? So much had happened! And now Reed came to me down the silken ladder from Edwin's dressing room upstairs and we were together in the low bed that had four gold lions at its corners, and for the first time that place was the cradle of happy love for which it had been created. But was it? What is the matter with life that nothing is ever right, I wondered. Now nothing came between me and my desire in the short summer night, but I was not happy [though] things were very gay at the villa.

It was in the fall of 1913 when Reed and I returned to the apartment at 23 Fifth Avenue to live there together quite openly; though I was still accompanied by Miss Galvin, I felt courageous and high-minded about it. I hated the thought of clandestine nocturnal life, and I believed that I was strong enough to do openly whatever I did. Reed gave me that strength. And because I persuaded myself to feel this, I persuaded others, too.

The Evenings, of course, had been in full swing before I met Reed and when we came back everyone expected them to continue, though I was fainthearted at the semipublic character my life in New York had taken on, and I would have been content to settle down now to a quiet and cozy fireside with him. But no! Hutch and Neith, Steff, who knew Reed well and loved him dearly, Carl, and all the others simply insisted upon owning me, my house, my life itself, and they all just came along as usual. Reed himself was ready for anything! Ready at any moment to pop off into some new enthusiasm. He always seemed to have his lungs too full, and he would draw in his round chin in an effort to quiet his excited heart. *Always* there seemed some pressure of excitement going on in him.

I didn't want only to sleep in his arms. I wanted to *live* with him. It seemed to me, now, that to live quietly with him would be just as good as to work at high pressure with him had been before we went away for the summer. It seemed to me that I could live happily with him simply and quietly and slowly. But it did not seem so to him. Life—just everyday life—little things and gentle hours were not enough. He was too young and too full of urgency and excitement. From the break of day he was eager to be off and *doing*.

I took my breakfast in bed, and he ate his at a little table by my bedside because I wanted him to. But he might as well have been gone from there for all he was with *me*. He drank his coffee with the morning newspaper propped up before him, his honey-colored round eyes just popping over *"the news!"* Any kind of news as long as it had possibilities for thrill, for action, for excitement.

I invited more and more people to the Evenings and I tried harder than ever to interest and attract them, making the ancient mistake of believing my victories would act upon Reed like an aphrodisiac and that when my value appeared greater to others, it would appear so to him and would make him want to be with me all the day. On the contrary! My triumphs served to stimulate him to greater achievement in that world where men *do* things in order to prove themselves powerful to themselves. So a spirit of competition sprang up between us! If I had power, he, then, must have more power. Desperate, I tried to hold him closer by laments. I grew pale and wept and I held him tighter and tighter.

When he came in one night and told me he had walked and talked with a strange, beautiful prostitute on the street, had felt her beauty and her mystery, and, through her, the beauty and the mystery of the world, I threw myself on the floor and tried to faint. Overcome by commiseration for an unhappiness he could not understand but that he knew he caused, he promised me he would be faithful to me forever—and that no one should ever separate us. Believing that since it was a *streetwalker* that had been the cause of my grief, if he cut out talking to them in order to learn their secrets and their mysteries, he would no longer hurt me, he had no hesitancy, one night, in telling me that the young wife of a friend of ours and he had stood talking at the front door while the early fall snowflakes came powdering down on their faces—and all the time they talked he felt her strange purity was whiter than the snow, and colder—and yet that she revealed without knowing it a peculiar impersonal attraction that was as hot as hell and spoke directly to him behind her shy, correct, Nordic demeanor.

I was perfectly stunned. He seemed to *have* to have these imaginary experiences with everything and everybody, and to *have* to come and tell me about them. I shut him up hard about his girl, whom I had only known for a short time.

Hutch had to hear all about the peculiar struggle going on between us and had things to say about Sex Antagonism. He was so eloquent that Steff suggested an Evening given to the discussion of this subject. Everybody thought Hutch and the others would probably be so brilliant that we'd better try to record the conversation, so Steff secured a stenographer and put her, unbeknownst to Hutch, behind a screen where she was instructed to take down the whole evening's talk in shorthand!

Reed brought F. [Fred Boyd, an English socialist] in one night and they talked all the evening while I sat forgotten. They talked wildly—over the possibles: the possible revolution, the possible New Art, the possible new relation between men and women. I felt defrauded and left out and also very mad to have such a common little thing spend an evening with me whether I wanted him or not. I went to bed long before he left—and heard him flattering Reed as I undressed with the door ajar. I kept Reed awake for hours arguing with him about this new friend. About his mediocrity, his superficiality, his unworthiness. "Why don't you pick out someone *worthwhile* for a friend? F. is craven."

When I came in from the swimming pool where I often went, at eleven o'clock the next morning, I found a note from Reed.

Goodbye, my darling. I cannot live with you. You smother me. You crush me. You want to kill my spirit. I love you better than life but I do not want to die in my spirit. I am going away to save myself. Forgive me. I love you— I love you.

Reed

I turned ice cold all over and rushed down to the motor, where Albert still waited for the afternoon orders. "To the Hapgoods'," I gasped. "Hurry—hurry!"

All night I lay awake floundering in a black empty place. There seemed no place to come to rest. Reed had gone away, taking the universe with him. And all next day I wept weakly and without hope. I had not cried like that since I had my heart broken in Buffalo. I felt my flesh dissolve in salt water—and my head grow lighter and more empty. Neith and [Hutch] left me alone for a good part of the day—and I wept silently, sometimes angry, and sometimes just lonesome. The third day I woke up in the morning and saw the sun was shining. I felt weak and cold as one does after a great illness—but I saw the sun was shining. I mean I saw this as a fact that lived in and of itself and because it was itself. It had nothing to do with me or any man. And I loved it and felt grateful to it.

I enjoyed feeling frail and sensitive that day at lunch! Every sound was clear and magnified many times. Everyone stood out sharply like objects in a garden after a heavy rain. The world looked particularly bright and sparkling and I felt as though I had been drenched and was drying in the sun. Everything looked new to me, every street and every house was terribly interesting and vital. The world had been given back to me once more.

Of course when I went back to 23 Fifth Avenue after lunch and found it so empty and cold, my exaltation fell a little. What was I supposed to do with myself? I scarcely knew what to do next. I groped like a baby learning to walk. But I made an effort and asked someone to dine with me—Walter Lippmann, it was—and I listened to him talk and although my mind was rusty because I hadn't used it much lately, I began to be interested again in impersonal things, and I moved through the hours as though I saw a new world, and I saw myself undress and go to bed alone in the still room as though I watched a stranger.

The next morning I woke alone and just a faint beginning of gladness for aloneness itself was lifting in me when Reed burst into the house. Pale, with black shadows under his eyes, his curls on end, he fell on his knees by me and buried his head against me. "Oh, I couldn't *bear* it," he cried. "I can't live without you. I missed your love, your selfish, selfish love," he cried. Composed myself, I saw my hand smoothing his rough, round head. "Your way, not mine," he murmured deeply into my side. So it began again.

Now I had, in a way, cried myself inside out when he left me. I could never weep like that for him again. Yet when, some weeks later, Carl Hovey asked him to go to Mexico and send back articles about Pancho Villa and the land, for the *Metropolitan Magazine,* I was devastated. I lost the sense of the world I had recovered as soon as Reed was sleeping with me once more, since, as usual, I had easily forgotten what had happened to me. I tried to make him give up the commission. I tried in every way but he would go.

"It won't be like leaving you the way I did last time," he said. "I will take you with me in my heart. But we must be *free* to live our lives—dearest!"

"But I don't want to go with you in your heart—I want you *here!*" I moaned. "I can't be free without you!"

Ordinarily, to be alone was to doubt my own being, so little did I live in the life about me. And to live with Reed stimulated something in me so I felt a flowing appreciation of little things. Not his things, not his ideas. I really didn't care much for his ideas and neither did he in any ultimate way. He had successive bonfires in him and I wasn't burning in the same kind of fire he was at that moment. I wasn't dying to alter everything. The outside of the world wasn't enough to hold me. No. What he did was to make me myself feel real and like other people. He was able to make me contented and reassured, and as I had had precious little of this I craved it; while he, the instrument of my reestablished equilibrium, had nothing but contempt for contentment and believed it was only good enough for slaves.

When Reed came back from Mexico, he was, once more, The Hero. He had gone through a great deal of dangerous adventure successfully. Everyone was enthusiastic about his articles in the *Metropolitan Magazine,* which had had the effect of winning a great deal of sympathy for the Mexican peons in their battle for the land. Reed published the articles in a book called *Insurgent Mexico,* and had two deluxe copies made bound in red morocco, for his mother and me. He dedicated the book, however, to his mother and this made me silently angry. I, myself, obscurely, wanted to be his mother.

Reed was not home for long. Carl Hovey sent him to Colorado to write an article about the coal strike. There had been a good deal of bloodshed at Ludlow at the hands of the militia, and Trinidad was the center of trouble when he got there. When Reed came back from Colorado it was evident to me that he was becoming more and more The Hero to everyone, especially to Women.

I am relating, in these volumes, my intimate memories, and in the life of any woman these are recollections of love or the devilish ingenious substitutes for love procured more or less deftly by her unconscious being. By love I do not mean only the ultimate sexual act, though this is perhaps the cornerstone of any life, and its chief reality, but I include that sweet, deep psychic relationship that enables one to live more fully than anything else, and for the sake of which all power, influence, success, achievement, discovery, ease, or wealth are thrown aside and known for what they are, the second choices of less fortunate people.

This is especially true of women. It is indeed the happy woman who has no history, for by happy we mean the loving and beloved, and by history we designate all those relatable occurrences on earth caused by the human energies seeking other outlets than the biological one. It seems we must include the mystic marriage of the essential spirit in human beings when we use the word *biological,* for unless the spirit is satisfied and fulfilled, the creature is not satisfied. Coition alone never released or satisfied anyone, lacking the needful intrinsic elements of what we call love.

That I have so many pages to write signifies, solely, that I was unlucky in love. Most of the pages are about what I did instead . . . many, many pages that I leave unwritten would be filled with accounts of how I passed the time—the innumerable activities of an energetic woman crossed in love. That I was crossed in love—"unlucky in men," as Mrs. Hopkins said—was due to my own selection, of course. But why I chose men too immature to satisfy me, or too lacking in essential qualities—ah! That question must be answered later on. Perhaps my unsatisfied maternity helped me choose the younger ones: since I had no maternal feeling for my own son, I must take it out on other women's sons. Certainly Reed was a child compared to myself. Well, since I wanted sons, certainly I got them. . . .

When Reed was away from me I seemed to be able gradually to accumulate an essence of myself that permeated me and made an atmosphere around me. Added to my own distillations were the opinions of people who had watched things happening, and as I have related had come to believe that I had a peculiar faculty very valuable to any undertaking. Besides, the Salon idea had hit the New York people very hard. They were never tired of talking about it, and the stories were fabulous.

So I experienced in between times again that phenomenon of power conferred upon one by opinion. And maybe that is where all power comes from, that of witches and saviors alike, and of all leaders. But the peculiar thing about it was that when I was living with Reed at home my power seemed to leave me, for he seemed fundamentally hollow in activity and could give no rest to one. At least it seemed so to me. And he never satisfied me. The substitute for love called power thrilled me more than he, though I always preferred to have him there and to feel uncertain and unsure of him and of myself rather than to triumph, with him away. Finally I believed the lack to be in myself when I found myself perpetually unassuaged—and, I thought, only religion will fill me; someday I will find God.

CHAPTER TWELVE &ebd; APPROACHING END

Everywhere hope—everywhere expectancy.

Reed was at his most expressive moment in the spring of 1914. The poet is destined to give words to life, and he, feeling the pressure of forces in and about him, tried to tell of it. He never completed these breathless, groping phrases. They are only snatches of happy and hopeful words that noted what so many were already calling the New Day, and they are the last happy and innocent words he ever wrote:

Only the mass . . . the multitude . . .
Only the majestic sweep of people:
The seeping stream blends everyone.
The brain that thinks, the body that is capable of action, the space animate
    with form unseen, the object tangible . . . all the expansive breath of life . . .
A stretch, unending, of expression . . .

The plain, smooth, merging crush of birth and death.
Nothing separate, nor lost, nor helpless, nor oppressed . . .
But greeted, welcomed, challenged . . .

When it grew warm in New York, Reed and I went to Provincetown. It was just a double line of small, white clapboarded cottages along a silent village street, between the bay and the open sea. A few people we knew took these cottages in the summer. The Hapgoods, the Jig Cooks, Mary Heaton Vorse, and others. People amused themselves with private theatricals. The Provincetown Players put on plays by Neith and George Cram Cook and Gene O'Neill—that wide-mouthed, anguished, sunburned boy—in an old barn on the shore, and Helen Westley found she could act. In fact they all found they could act as well as write plays!

Neith and I had planned to go to Florence for the summer, and I think I left Reed in the cottage in Provincetown when we went. Either that or he was off reporting something for Hovey. I can't remember. I only recall Neith; Miss Galvin; John; and Boyce, the oldest Hapgood boy and John's best friend; Beatrix [Hapgood], aged three; and I, all together on a dreadful Italian steamer bound for Naples. Reed was to join us later at the villa—and Carl, too, was to come down from Paris to stay with us.

There was a queer atmosphere on that boat. Neith and I wondered about it. It is hard to name what it was, but the days seemed dreamlike and unreal. The summer ocean was oily-smooth, there was a glare in the light that came off the water, and there was, too, a peculiar calmness over the aspect of things, so that we lost the sense of time. We just slid along silently suspended in a void, emotionless and unaccented.

I myself had sunk into the unrelated blankness from which I suffered when I found myself unattached to someone, and no longer borne up and supported by the male contiguity through which alone I seemed to become real to myself. When I was out of tangible connection with someone outside, everything seemed to run down in me and I did not respond to anyone or anything. I experienced nothing but the fatal inner immobility from which I had suffered as a child, feeling nothing but an emptiness that became a positive pain in its agonizing negativeness and I carried about with me the awful vacuity that was like hunger and thirst.

It seemed to me that the dreadful suspension of life that I was experiencing was a reflection of the outside world. Everything was abated within and without. But whereas Neith continued to function, agreeably enjoying herself, and observing, with detached interest, the changed look of sky and sea and the light upon them, and was about to comment with a smile: "The world looks queer. It's as though it were dying or dead, somehow," I partook of that death—dying with it.

We reached Florence, where the villa awaited us as usual—smoothly in order, servants assembled. And here I revived a little in the interest that Neith took in it all. How beautiful, after New York, the Villa Curonia appeared, serene upon its hill, with the roses and jasmine about it.

Then, suddenly, a crash came that threw us all into activity. War was declared. What a scramble! Into the bank and to the consular office for Carl and Neith, for all they thought of was to get home while they could. Everyone in confusion—difficulty in getting money—moratorium declared—voices raised—all the usual vibrations of life upset.

As for me, it didn't mean a thing. It didn't interest or excite me, or even reach me. I dwelt alone in a deep contempt for wars, for anxieties, for humanities. My isolation at that time was doubtless at its zenith. Then by some chance, at whose instigation I do not know, I sat in the small dark salon of a Christian Science healer in a narrow street in Florence, a woman whose name and face made no impression, but whose presence raised me. Presence? Being? Vibration? Whatever the alchemy, I left her after half an hour restored to life, to the world about me, happy, elated to come back, a trifle ashamed of my recent darkness, but adjusted once more to the pattern of which I was part and able to function in it naturally. I didn't need to force myself to smile, to think, to be. I was.

I sat alone in the yellow salon and closed my eyes and had a vision of the nations changing form like the bits of colored glass in a kaleidoscope. The world was undergoing a mighty shift, and the hard foundations of all things moved under them. It seemed that there was a total change to realize and accept without hindrance or demur. Of what avail to go against the evolutionary will? In New York we had sensed the approach of a vast overthrow and had worked for one. That it had occurred in a manner unexpected to us and in Europe, instead of locally, was none of one's business. We had had the intuition of an imminent revolution—and a revolution was upon us. The revolving of the wheels would perhaps crush our conveniently systematized lives—but possibly, I thought, a new world is being born today—a new cycle, a new beauty. Had I not written of Gertrude's work: "Life at birth is always painful and rarely lovely"?

Among the cables from Hutch, my family, and [Carl's wife] Fania [Marinoff], calling us all to come home, one came to me from Reed telling me to wait and meet him in Naples. He would sail at once and we would go up to Paris together. I caught his excitement and enthusiasm—his eagerness to be on hand to "report" this war. I was quite surprised at the extreme self-centeredness of my companions. No one was thinking of anyone but himself. I was a little appalled at the idea of being left all alone in Naples—I who had never been alone in my life anywhere—and though Miss Galvin wanted to stay with me and see things, I did not want her on my hands when Reed and I should be going to the war together, and I told her she would have to go home. There was some altercation about her ticket and I believe I could not get the money out of the bank for her, so that she had to use her salary. Anyway, whatever it was, I recall her for the first time in a towering rage that made her go into the street in Naples and smash a plate glass window where a portrait of the Kaiser gazed at the agitated passersby.

Reed burst in upon my even days like Miss Galvin crashing through the plate glass window. He was untidy, curls damply disordered, breathless, and evidently containing more excitement than he could conveniently hold. My calm seemed to amaze him. He had never seen me so self-contained—neither happy nor unhappy, he said. But I thought I was happy and I smiled a complacent small smile like the one I had seen on many people without understanding it. The smile of unknowing, the secure smile of obliviousness! He was eager to get away to Paris immediately, yet he had never been to Naples and he said he *had* to see Pompeii, and Vaia of Dante's time.

How recount the gradual fall from bliss? Did the return to earthly love bring it about? Did I forfeit my wholeness when I lay in Reed's arms again, tearing open the entrance to the nether world until I was like a wound that gaped between heaven and hell? The darkness and depression were down upon me again like a heavy world shutting me away from those who stayed outside in the sun. Reed stayed outside. Even though his had been the hand that thrust me below once more, he himself remained above in the light. The alternations of influence that people have upon each other are hard to understand. Once Reed had given me life and a feeling of reality—and losing it in his absence, an unknown woman in Florence had restored it to me. And now Reed was the one to take it away again. How can one ever call one's soul one's own while one is so at the mercy of others?

In Paris we established ourselves in a somewhat dreary apartment on the Rive Gauche. Or was it I who was dreary? I stayed in bed a good deal of the time. Lifeless. Reed was out all day. Panting with pleasurable activity, his eyes shining, the two highlights on his round forehead gleaming below his nodding curls, he rushed with his friends into the affair of the war. It was always activity he adored, almost any exciting activity. He was not essentially radical or revolutionary; he loved it when things happened and always wanted to be in the center of events. Any great events. All the other American journalists were already in Paris and everybody was excited, pleased, happy. Everybody but me, I thought. Afterwards I wrote an article for Max Eastman to publish in *The Masses* called "The Secret of War," describing the happiness of those men in Paris. The cafés surged with officers in brand-new uniforms and shining eyes. The male population in Paris was as lustful as the Roman mob.

One day before we left for London, where Reed wanted to go, he came in and told me he had seen R. T. [Arthur Lee, a sculptur] in the Luxembourg Gardens. N. [Freddie Lee] and he were living nearby in a studio. I begged him not to force me to see them. I had no energy to pretend either pleasure in them or that mutual interest that people feel for each other. I was jealous, too, or envious, of the easy give-and-take of flowing intercourse. I was a weak, unstrung creature—at war with myself and lost to life. At such a disadvantage that I felt like shunning everyone, yet dreadfully lonely when I was alone. I really wanted Reed to be with me every moment and he was never there.

In London it was worse—and I decided to go back to New York and be miserable at home, where at least I could be comfortable, for to sit solitary in a hotel room was growing to be more than I could endure. I think Reed was relieved when I told him, though in a way he liked to have me there waiting for him, longing for him to come back. Men do not really mind a woman's agony and loneliness; it gives them a sense of their own independence and security, and they like women's jealousy, too.

I had always tried to hold Reed to me so firmly that he couldn't pass the barrier of my will and take another woman, and though one part of him declared independence, and he always argued with me about "freedom" and the right to live one's own life, yet another part did not want to be free—that element of his soul that escaped both him and my own grasp did not want to be loosed. So for the most part he was firmly welded to me. In all these months he had never even touched any other—and no matter how weak I grew in my split, disintegrated substance, at least I held him close. Sometimes he felt rebellious and cheated of some part of life, but he was caught nevertheless and tightly held.

A new life began at home in New York. That fall I moved from the apartment on the third floor to the one that had been below me—and this change seemed to be the beginning of a different existence. The depression gradually wore off. Hutch and Neith were there, and Walter and Andrew, and others whom I liked. The sun came into my bedroom in the morning, and as I drank coffee and opened my letters and waited for the telephone to ring, life seemed lively.

I had had a letter from Reed from Paris. A brutal, reckless letter written in a café on blue-lined paper. It told me desperately, wildly, that the night I left London, he had got drunk in a sailor's dive and slept with a prostitute. It seemed written in a spirit of dismal levity. I did not feel badly. Somehow I understood it and felt sorry for him. I guessed the utter relief that he had felt to have me gone and his regret that he should feel relief—the reaction after restraint when the pressure was lifted. And anyway I did not love him anymore. How it passed or why, I did not know at all. There was no reason, no cause. It seemed that with the lifting of the black mood I had been under, the whole of the old life had lifted itself out of me with it. I was someone else. I scarcely knew Reed, my lover. But I knew well and affectionately Hutch and Neith and those whom I had not loved in that way. My sense of significance returned and I wanted something else again.

One morning a cable was brought in to me from the Brevoort Hotel. It said:

N. T. AND I HAVE FALLEN IN LOVE WITH EACH OTHER
MY HEART IS BROKEN

REED.

I laughed. I called Walter on the telephone to tell him about it and I sounded more rueful than I felt. After I read him the telegram, I cried: "Isn't it childish? I'm tired of being the mother of men!"

Well, I thought, as I faced forward into the year 1915, that is the end of *that*. I had said good-bye forever to Reed in my heart. To the gay, bombastic, and lovable boy with his shining brow; to the labor movement, to revolution, and to anarchy. To the hope of subtly undermining the community with Hutch, and to all the illusions of being a power in the environment. My young lover was gone, and, it seemed, gone with him were the younger hopes of change. With a world at war, one somehow ceased to war with systems and circumstances. Instinctively I turned once more to Nature and Art and tried to live in them.

Part Two

CHAPTER ONE 🖎 LITTLE ELIZABETH

Still like a bird within a glass-walled room, the spirit was desperately beating its wings against the impediments between it and freedom. This had been a time when many people frantically tried to find salvation outside themselves. They consulted psychics and they went to all kinds of healers and doctors and psychiatrists. Within myself I felt an ever increasing need for help of some kind and I looked for it where I could. At least I was not worried about money as were so many of my friends. But there is a peculiar sense of insecurity that finally comes to people who have money they have inherited. I had never done any work of any kind, for nothing had obliged me to and so there never seemed to be an incentive. Reed had tried to tell me about work: "Any job has something more important in it than the job itself," he said, but whatever he was trying to tell me was incommunicable. I had no idea what he meant.

I remember he had come in one day and found me idle and unhappy and terribly bored with everything. He had just been talking with an old professor of his—George Baker. When Reed had asked him how he was, he had answered, "Oh, busy and interested."

"Busy and interested," repeated Reed, looking at me meaningly. "It seemed to me so significant. I thought of you. Why *don't* you *get busy,* Mabel?"

"I'm not going to *fool* myself into anything," I had replied angrily. "Why should I *make up* a job? If there's a job for me, it will come after me. If there isn't, I'll live on my income the best way I can. Why should I make up work just for its own sake?" I felt too proud to work at anything less than an *inevitable* job, though I suffered from an emptiness of living that ate into me, except when I was caught up by some vital experience.

It is my impression that this empty feeling is really the most insecure sensation known to human beings. When one is not wholly occupied by some absorbing and congenial work, or all caught up and unified by a vivid love affair, there is a dreadful frightening burden of time and space and energy deep down in one that seems to threaten one's safety. Oh! The alarming danger of a regular income, that means for many people time to think and nothing to think about!

After Miss Galvin smashed the shop window in her attack upon the Kaiser in Naples, I never saw her again. Reed had disappeared somewhere into the war zone in Europe with his new love. I was alone in my apartment for a while, until Bobby [Jones] came back from Germany.

I began to wish for a baby very much. At last, it seemed, instinct needed a chance to express itself. When John was born, I had been too occupied with another kind of emotion to have any feeling left over to give to him, and all through his first years of babyhood, it was as though I had been away from him, though he was always right there. I never knew John as a baby. This thought comes back over and over and tightens upon my heart like a little hand. Now he was in Morristown School and I rarely saw him except for an occasional weekend he passed with me in New York.

I didn't feel in the mood for Evenings any more. I didn't feel like seeing anarchists or socialists or single taxers or members of the Free Speech League. Besides, they had all strangely disappeared from my life when the war broke out. No, the time had come to make a new pattern. The old form was broken.

I began to visit different orphan asylums and places of that kind to look for a baby to adopt, and I learned something that had not occurred to me before: there are very few healthy babies without parents. I had imagined there would be hundreds. No luck. I had almost given up. Over and over the matrons of places told me they had no good, healthy babies both of whose parents were dead. I had stipulated that because I did not want to be bothered or embarrassed later on.

Then one afternoon Albert drove me to the great dour building that housed all the different layers of Charity, and I went again to the children's floor.

"No, no babies. But there's a nice little girl. Why don't you take a look at her?" I looked to where she pointed to a blond child seated on the floor and playing with a doll.

"I don't want a grown-up child of eight or nine years!" I exclaimed indignantly.

"Take her home for over Sunday and see if you don't like her," the woman urged.

She was a jolly little thing with fine curly fair hair, like feathers; round, pink cheeks; very pretty blue eyes; and a turned-up nose that suggested the Irish very strongly. Something in the low forehead and the way her brows hung over her eyes was a warning perhaps, but the vitality of the child, the gaiety and the sweet pink and blue and blond colors of her covered it up. It was fun to take her to Wanamaker's and buy her some pretty clothes.

I did not adopt Elizabeth legally. I told them at the charity organization that I would take care of her and educate her. As I look back upon it now, I think all I wanted was to make a picture of her. The raw human blood instinct for a baby had been defeated, for I still had nothing in my arms. Elizabeth was too big. But it was fun to dress her in white muslins and her pink and blue ribbons.

I was not happy in those days. The heaviness and darkness were never far away. I read a great many mystical books, those by Evelyn Fitzgerald, the writings of the Saints, and Plotinus, Rudolf Steiner, Troward, and works on Rosicrucianism. Anything to help me through "the dark night" that always fell upon me when I was not either happy or unhappy over a man; for at these times I contained a vacuum and I had to struggle up through it by any means I could find. My life alternated between extremes, and I never knew which was the more real. Certainly love made me responsive and more like the other human beings about me, yet the dissatisfactions of love, or perhaps my way of loving, always plunged me down sooner or later into the dark abyss.

CHAPTER TWO 🦋 ISADORA DUNCAN

After some weeks of suffering I had reached a balance of some kind and apparently to belong to myself was good for me. It seemed to me now I could feel my roots reaching down to the center of the earth, where they fed richly. When Ducie Haweis wrote me from Florence after she went to live with the tempestuous [Emilio] Marinetti: "I feel uprooted and as though I were lost," I answered her: "You cannot be uprooted for your roots are in the universe," and this was something I had lately learned.

This was a very fine moment in life. I was not aware that, loosed from Reed, my powers ebbed back into my own reservoir and fed me where before they had been feeding him, and perhaps, too strong for him, had been poisoning him so he had needed to save himself from me. Anyway, I was agreeing with myself! I felt wonderful—adequate. . . .

I went to see Isadora dance with her young girls and the mass of little children she had brought from Russia. It seemed to me I recognized what she did in the dance, and that it was like my own daily, nightly return to the source. Power rose in her from her center and flowed vividly along her limbs before our eyes in living beauty and delight. We saw a miracle happen before us when Isadora stood there, passive, and Pure Being incarnated itself in her.

This was not something special to her and a solitary flowering. It was based upon a principle, not upon a personality. It was a way of life that she said could be learned. She said that, from the stage. She said she wanted to teach all the children of America how to be, how to move, how to walk and run. She said she called it dancing, but it was *being* that she wanted to teach. She asked for a place to teach in, a large place—and then for the children. She seemed to be hungry for children—many children—since her own two had drowned in the Seine. I saw her arms reach out with an expression of hunger in them when she talked to the great audience in Carnegie Hall, and asked for a thousand little poor children to teach, and I wondered what fatal mistake she had made in her life that had swept that automobile out of control, to go plunging into the dark waters.

Several of us conferred together. John Collier was the one who knew how to "organize" things, how to get things done in cities, and it was decided that the mayor, young Mitchel, must be brought to see Isadora in the "Ark," and she must ask him for an armory to teach in. She had taken, in a business building, a sort of loft that she hung with her vast blue curtains the color of robins' eggs, and there, with her young girls, and all the little Russian children she had brought with her from Europe, she made a life for herself. I had never been there, but many of my friends had, and told me about it. She called this refuge of hers the Ark!

Isadora came to my apartment to talk over the matter of an armory. I do not remember that much was said that day about [her] need for an armory, but we had promised her she should have one and we went about the business of securing it for her, or rather of giving her the opportunity of getting it for herself. How carefully we planned it! I got Walter interested in it because I knew he would give "cachet" to the event and we invited several "eminent" men to come to make to make it appear more significant to the mayor. Collier was to bring him at four o'clock, and Isadora was to do the rest.

John Collier still worked at the People's Institute, a little way above me on Fifth Avenue and 13th Street. Have I told how he looked then? He was a small, blond southerner, intense, preoccupied, and always looking windblown on the quietest day. Because he couldn't seem to love his own kind of people, and as he was full of a reformer's enthusiasm for humanity, he turned to other races and worked for them. He still had that job of trying to preserve the flavors of other nationalities when they came to New York. Singly, he tried to stem the ponderous tide of Americanization. He worked indefatigably; with committees and subcommittees he strove by means of pageants, parades, and prizes to persuade Italians, Russians, Germans, and all the others to keep their national dress, their customs, their diets, their religions, and all their folkways.

Walter and I, and Walter's inseparable companion, Alfred Kuttner, arrived at the Ark a little before four o'clock. The place was large and dim and romantic looking, with a few shaded lamps burning. It was a contrast to the hard, bright city streets we had left, and Isadora in a flowing Greek dress, ample and at ease, made us look and feel dingy and utilitarian. Particularly the men, as they stood beside her, appeared stupid, inexpressive, and as though cut out of wood, there was such a radiance about her compared with other mortals.

There were several extremely large, low couches with great piles of pale cushions, grouped about a couch larger than the others, and there was a great black piano with candles burning on it. The plan that had been arranged was that Isadora's young girls and some of the little children, whom we presently saw in groups in distant corners all in pale blue melting into the folds of curtains, should dance for Mayor Mitchel and show him what she had taught the little Russian proletariat, and then ask him for an armory in which to teach our own young proletarians from the East Side. She had promised to teach them for nothing in exchange for having the armory to do her other work in.

[Mayor Mitchel] stood for an instant, hat in hand, near the door, quite a large space between him and Isadora's group and us. Isadora started. She gazed. . . . All of her, with almost terrible expressiveness, revealed her classic disdain for everything physically meager or insufficient. She was disappointed. The beautiful girls behind her reflected her aloof and arrogant rejections; secure in beauty themselves, they gazed coldly at the spindling young man. He looked plain and miserable.

However, Isadora, recovering in a flash, made a noble gesture of resignation, large, magnanimous, and charitable. She swept forward, her dress fluttering out behind her, with shining, candid brown and outstretched hands. "Why," she exclaimed, "I thought you would be an old, old man with a long, white beard!"

We got ourselves seated somehow on those divans. Collier was the least self-conscious of us all and leaned back almost reclining, feet crossed, shoes muddy, ashes dropping from his cigarette onto the silken covers. "I have told the mayor something of your methods of teaching. He would be interested, I think, if you could show him some of them."

"Oh, my methods of teaching are probably very different from anything *he* has ever known!" Isadora exclaimed rather truculently, throwing a disparaging look at the mayor's spare form. She gave a sweep of her hand towards the girls who lay like nymphs on either side of her and towards the children who sat on the floor at her feet, their flower faces turned up towards her as to the sun.

"These children have always had a *beautiful* life," she cried. "Look at them! *They* don't have to get up in the morning and go down to breakfast with their cross fathers and mothers! *They* don't have to go to school with horrid dirty schoolbooks in satchels! *They* don't have to go to church on Sunday and listen to stuffy old men in ugly buildings!"

A wave of consternation swept right through our party, uniting us, and Isadora's protégées glowed all together in their accord with her. On Gus Duncan's face I caught a glimpse of distress from his mingled thoughts. He agreed with this sister's ideas, yet he could see and understand how these men felt at her words. Marguerite Duncan was looking quite worried and came and sat beside Isadora, who was off on her great theme. Nothing on earth could have stopped her now.

"The greatest musicians come and play for these children, and the children dance for them and inspire them. Painters, sculptors, come and get life from them and teach them in return what they know. *That* is education. Living education." She was certainly living herself as she flung these words at our young Catholic mayor. She glowed and burned, her dark hair flowing off in crisp waves from her righteous white brow. Her dress slipped from her shoulder and showed her breast.

The poor young man was all at a loss. Anything to bring this terrible thing to an end so he could get away and never come back—get away to join his wife, as he had promised, at five o'clock to dance at the Plaza Hotel.

Isadora had either forgotten what the mayor was there for, had forgotten the armory and the thousand little poor children she wanted to teach in it and that she must ask him for it, or else she had revolted too far away from him and all he represented. Perhaps he did not seem real at all to her. Anyway, she threw away her chance.

CHAPTER THREE ✺ ELIZABETH DUNCAN

Elizabeth Duncan marched into my sitting room one early spring day, sent to me by the ubiquitous Collier. She was a vivid spark of life with her little body erect and prim in a long, burnt-orange velvet cloak trimmed with red fox fur, and a bristling red fox turban on her head. Behind Elizabeth was the eager face of Max Merz! He was the manager of The Elizabeth Duncan School, lately escaped from Darmstadt. Elizabeth was a great teacher. She had taught Isadora from the time she was a child. Hour after hour she sat and coached her in the long past days, while their ma played accompaniments on the piano.

I wish I could remember in Elizabeth's own words the long saga about the struggle between her and Isadora to show the world the Beauty. How they tried to work together and could not. How Elizabeth secured a "patron" in the Grand Duke and a beautiful school building in Darmstadt. How Max Merz, seeing Isadora dance for the first time, was infected by the magical vision and forthwith was sucked into the Duncan constellation first by Isadora, then by Elizabeth, who seized him when her sister ignored him, and made him manager of the school.

Elizabeth took a handful of German children and worked over them for years in the school; years of disciplined living, of exercise, of careful diet. She made a perfect small world for children—she made it lyrical and lovely with the music of Schumann and Schubert, and with the great poetry of all the ages. Their bodies unfolded gradually in the rhythm of the years and no fashions in dress preoccupied them with anguished queries about becomingness, for they always wore the same little blue tunics and they were always becoming. They were lovely, clear-skinned, wide-eyed little girls from eight to eleven or twelve years, with beautifully tended bodies and well-brushed, shining hair. What had happened to their parents, no one seemed to know. Least of all, I think, Elizabeth. She gave an entertainment and everyone who saw them dance their little compositions to the music of Schumann, Chopin, and Schubert fell in love with it all, and straightway believed that life was not so awful as it had seemed before that hour.

CHAPTER FOUR 🐚 THE ELIZABETH DUNCAN SCHOOL

Here was something to work for, I thought. If people can be developed like these children, then we must have a school in America where Elizabeth can make American children beautiful like these little nymphs. It was Collier's idea and he began to plan. In the meanwhile money must be found to rent a suitable house for them and to furnish it somehow.

Now I had saved a thousand dollars that I had meant to spend buying an abandoned lifesaving station on the dangerous coast across the dunes from the village of Provincetown on the bay. It was a lovely weathered building half covered over with sand with an old boathouse near it. There it was, lonely and aloof on the high sandbank above the beach where the fierce waves pounded in all day—a wild enough spot to suit anyone. I had meant to dig it out and do it over, painting it inside like a ship and furnishing it like one. But when Elizabeth came along with those children, I knew it would be more fun to do something with them than with paint and sand and sea, so I told Collier I would give that money to start them off and we would try to get some other people interested in them, too.

The perfect house was found for them on a high hill over the Hudson River at Croton. It was a large, airy, brown house with a view of the country for miles and miles on all sides; that lovely rolling New York State country, crossed by the stone walls that separated the rich fields, country where the deer wandered and rabbits flickered in and out, and where the wild pheasants passed to and from with mincing steps, dragging their long tails.

Meanwhile, Collier told Sam Lewisohn about my decision to interest myself in a school instead of in an abandoned lifesaving station. Sam, the son of the copper king, liked this. He told Collier to tell me he would buy the station himself, and if I would do it up for him exactly as I had intended doing, and for the same money I would myself have spent on it, we would share the place, turn and turn about. For all Sam's delight in the place, he used it very little, and I only used it once, which was the following summer of 1915, with Maurice. Sam finally sold it to Eugene O'Neill, who loved the sea, and for whom it seemed, really, to have been designed.

Of course, one of the first things I did was to turn Little Elizabeth over to the school. Elizabeth Duncan was rather dubious about the child. She judged illy of her from the shape of her fingers and fingernails and by her brow. Sweepingly, she declared that no "fine energy" could flow out of such unintelligently shaped bones. However, the exquisite, delicately spun hair was a good sign. We would see.

Elizabeth sized up intelligence and character by the qualities and shapes of the body. In the body she believed she could read the destiny of any mortal. Of course, there was a margin of hope even for clumsy and dull children if taken young enough. The human spirit could be drawn up through the coarsest materials, the most intractable forms. The little girl loved the school, as indeed all children did, though oftentimes there was not very much beyond porridge and milk on the table. But in that bright entourage there was a full reassurance of quick and golden life, the golden age we all so wistfully search for among the gray shades that surround us.

I myself could scarcely heed anymore now the continuous flood of letters that kept coming as usual about birth control, industrial relations, free speech, and all the other forms of social maladjustment. Little by little I ceased to attend meetings that required my presence as an influence for change. I just lost interest in that fabricated puppet, Mabel Dodge, as a Creature of Importance in Her Time, and I longed only for peace and more peace, for innocent fun with Elizabeth and to share the Irish glee that flooded her.

When they moved into the house on Mount Airy, high above Croton village, at Elizabeth's suggestion I rented the Sharkey Cottage, just below them on the winding country road. It was a little, old, white house of four rooms, with a tiny attic. In the front, there were a dining room and a sitting room, and behind these, a kitchen and a bedroom. It was small, old, simple, and supposed to be haunted. Bobby, who had a shack on the place for a bedroom studio, saw the ghost once or twice: a nice old lady.

My life was thus divided for a while between New York and the country. In New York the hastening, frantic stream of traffic flowed through the streets, sometimes overflowed them into the apartment fighting, struggling, grasping at shadows that seemed essential could they once be caught; it was all flowing away from me and I was glad to let it go. The lovely, quaint countryside seemed to have the truer living in its deep pulse.

My life was gathering and accumulating in me. Now I felt full of abundant life. I learned a way to sink back far into myself and there I found more and more strength—as though I contained a deep pool of refreshment and delight. This I called upon often, always naming it Nature. I felt the rich stream of life that rose out of the earth and I loved to lie upon it, under some strong tree. I had attained a perfect and unfailing contact with the country where I lived. Max, who was sensitive to women, felt, I suppose, the mediumistic part I had come to play and seemed to feel the earth life that was using me to pass through to whomever could take it.

I was not interested anymore in a personal relation because I was satisfied. Little happenings were beautiful in this new life. It was life without colored glass, or French furniture, or hanging white silk. To see the evening sun come in the door from the porch and fall on the supper table, shining through a tumbler of red wine, falling on the orange-colored cheese and the fresh brown loaf while we sat idly, at rest, after the purposeless day. How good it was! While in New York the women hurried to check the population, or to raise wages, or to "swing" some urgent affair, we sat in Sharkey Cottage and sipped our wine and watched the beautiful plumes of the asparagus bed move as though a hand had passed over them. Of course, the asparagus bed shouldn't have had plumes at all. But I didn't know that. I didn't know anything practical about the country. I only knew how good it felt to be there.

Now I drew John from the atmosphere of the stuffy boarding school and I gave him, too, to Elizabeth Duncan. Of course, Elizabeth put short, blue drawers and a short blue-belted tunic on John. Barefooted, with the bow and arrow raised in the archery class, he was beautiful. There he was, transported to Mount Olympus on Mount Airy. The earth has no age. The children lived in its early Greek expression, that's all.

CHAPTER FIVE 🐚 MAURICE STERNE

It was sometime in the spring and Elizabeth and Merz thought it wise to give another entertainment in New York to show the children's work. I sat with some friends in the ballroom of one of the big hotels and in front of me I was happy to see dear little Alice Sprague and Mr. Sprague. Alice Sprague was one of my earliest memories, dating back to twilights in Buffalo when, as a little

girl, I had seen her pass down Delaware Avenue in the dusk, more like a creature from one of my favorite books than a flesh-and-blood-go-to-market-and-
dance-at-the-Charity-Ball woman, like all the others there.

Between her and her husband sat a black-haired man with red cheekbones
and a white brow. One noticed him at once in a crowd, for there was something vivid and colorful about him that marked him out among the other more
neutral personalities. He seemed sensitive to attention, for he moved as I sat
examining him and turned, with a slow, almost secretive caution, his large brown
eyes in my direction.

"Well," I thought, "who might *that* be? He really has a face!" His straight,
fine, black hair, fine, almost, as feathers, fell back in long locks in the manner
of Liszt, and his broad forehead had a pale, innocent look, especially at the
temples, where people show for good or bad. His long-lashed brown eyes were
nothing more or less than *orbs*, there was such a splendor in their liquid regard. The nose, of a biblical dignity, had a good bone ridge, but below it, oh,
dear! his mouth, when he forgot to arrange it, was not so good—more or less
a thin, straight line, without curve or meaning. When he did arrange it (for it
was his instinctive preoccupation to do so) he could at best only shape it into
a self-conscious kind of smirk or tighten it into a stingy, pursy bunch of lines.

As our eyes met and we regarded each other, he let the unbecoming grimace fade, and quickly drew his lips into the line that expressed self-control,
determination, and poise. He held my glance with the most practiced and impelling stare, not quite rude, very stealthy and exceedingly magnetic. He managed to keep it under cover and unseen by others.

"Well, *really,*" I thought, "such technique!" I was becoming very curious
about him, for he had a certain force, a conquering air despite his lips. I always loved the slightest appearance of masterfulness in a man, because it hinted
at an opportunity for me to exercise my strength. In the intermission, Alice
Sprague turned and introduced us: "Mr. Maurice Sterne," she said.

I had heard of *him,* of course: the Russian painter who was having an exhibition at Birnbaum's Gallery. He had spent a year on the island of Bali—
practically the first white man other than traders ever to go there—and he had
brought back a big collection of drawings and paintings of native life.

As we talked together for those few minutes, several well-defined phases of
his makeup showed themselves; the man had form and everything he expressed
was clear-cut and had a certain massive quality to it. When he changed from
the studied and cautious hunter of dames to an aspect of naivete and bubbling
delight, then he had something juvenile about him. His lines grew younger.
He looked like a little boy. His body looked square and as though he would

be taller when he grew up. What an anomaly he was! He was a mixture of old and complex racial turmoil, a darkness shot through with lightning; something dangerous in him threw out the warning to beware of him, yet how easily he was moved by goodness, how appreciative of little Alice Sprague, of the Duncan children, of Elizabeth herself. He loved goodness. I thought him very romantic. He represented the unknown, the undisclosed soul of Russia.

The next day I went to see his work. The first thing I told Birnbaum was that he was a sculptor, not a painter, for that impressed me immediately. His forms were so plastic, so tactile. He was a magnificent draughtsman but his color seemed unrevealing and uncertain. His vision of things was strange. The Bali people seemed to be a distinguished, reptilian race, elegant and haughty in their frenzied dances and in their dark magical rites; a dark and livid race made somewhat gruesome by the artist's predilection for yellow-greens.

Birnbaum, professionally enthusiastic at all times, seemed quite overcome by the genius of Sterne, and exclaimed that no one for years and years had arrived in New York with work of such magnitude and individuality. "What an original!"

"He would be more original if he had not seen Gauguin," I answered, rather pertly, I fear. I bought one of the smaller drawings, a pyramidal priest in brown chalk, and took it home with me. It was the effect of Sterne's magnetic *look*. Like his paintings, he interested and repelled one. I thought it would be amusing to see him again sometime.

CHAPTER SIX ✍ REED AGAIN

Yes, he came back as he had done before. Always, as soon as I had regained my independence and the physical and emotional life that he aroused in me had subsided in his absence, he returned. But this time I was determined to go on possessing myself and not to lose my balance. I had my deep exchange with Nature now, and this satisfied me more than any man had ever done. I would not be fool enough to lose all I had gained, for I had arrived at this security after a great deal of searching and unhappiness.

Reed had left N. After going through the drama of reaving her away from R. and taking her to her family in Germany, announcing to them his intention to marry her, all the usual conventional difficulties a man will undertake for a passionate indulgence that is masking all the world for him, he had come out of it and remembered me. Well! Well! Well! Yes, there was no one like me. Once a man loved me, he said, he could never get over it. . . . He could not live without me. So he had come back to me.

Another new idea had him in its grip. As soon as he had finished this thing in Russia for Hovey, he would rush back and we would be married! See—he had already bought a ring, two gold circles that were linked into one: that could be divided but not separated. But I was worse than cold or hard with pride. I was indifferent.

"No, Reed, I can't. It's all finished for us," I repeated over and over. He just couldn't believe it.

"But *why?* What's *happened?* What has come between us?" he kept hammering at me, and when I answered, "Nature," he was completely baffled.

Reed tried to clinch us together in every possible way. He told everyone we were to be married upon his return and he told Hovey to regard me as his wife, to refer all questions to me that needed decision and to communicate to me every cable or message he sent the magazine from Europe. When he left, after a long, passionate, more loving farewell than he had ever expressed when I had really cared for him, I forgot him before the day was over; nothing had happened so far as I was concerned. From the tender, he sent me the first verses of a poem ["Pygmalion"] that he had begun about us.

I returned to Croton and the mild, sweet country enveloped me. I participated in the moods of the day and the nights and grew more serene and more secure than ever. Whether it rained or the sun shone did not matter. There was strength in either way.

CHAPTER SEVEN   STERNE

Sterne, more than any artist I ever knew, craved reassurance. He had a large-boned frame, he was broad and strong; in a flannel shirt, given an ax, he would have had the appearance of a Russian woodsman. I do not know how soon it was that I felt impelled to turn Sterne into a sculptor, but very soon, I think. I simply longed to have him work in clay and execute in the round his insistent need to express bodily life and the action of muscles and bone. I do not mean that I realized about him then what I do as I write this in later years. I did not think it out. I simply saw that his painting was sculpturesque, plastic, three-dimensional, and ugly in color. I thought: "The man is meant for a sculptor—what fun it would be to make him into one."

But he was alien, standing there in the Duncan School smoking his black cigar and fixing that heavy, concentrated look upon me across the room over the glossy heads of the Duncan children. Trying to catch one's eyes and hold them, to pour the stream of magnetism from him into one's being through these small loopholes, to get and hold one so.

I saw Maurice frequently after that. He came to the apartment in town and talked by the hour and told me all his problems. He was a good talker and though he was not an intellectual man, he had a lot of fanciful ideas and intuitions about everything. He was quite clogged with art theories, with theories about "significant form" and all that. He was what is called a self-made man and he had had practically no schooling, no training in the customary human behavior, and had had to pick it up as best he could; in Europe he had amassed a great deal of the kind of culture that comes from loving nice women and talking with their more or less cultivated husbands, sitting in cafés or strolling through art galleries.

He had swallowed the culture of the ages too rapidly and perhaps it poisoned him a little. The slow growth that should have taken three or four generations to produce him had been crowded into twenty years. When a man or a race has to make a new adaptation it is sometimes unsuccessfully hurried, like an apple that is rotted before it is ripe, as are many of the Negroes in Harlem.

It was not long before Maurice began to make tentative efforts towards me. He would assume his rigid look of concentration and with lips firm in a straight line, he timidly advanced his large, white hand to lay it on my knee or on my hair. He acted a good deal like a man unaccustomed to horses who attempts to ingratiate himself by a cautious caress while remaining well on the lookout for a kick. But I did not kick him. I realized that he had a small range of behavior with women, that his experience of them hadn't given him a very good opinion of them, and that while he felt no real impulse to make love to me, was in reality quite indifferent to me in that way, he really believed that all any woman could want of a man was caresses. He was grateful to me for buying his drawing; perhaps I expected him to repay me with love, he thought. Very well, he would carry on the same old game he had always played. Perhaps I would buy another!

I drew away from him and laughed at him. "No, Maurice, it's your work I'm interested in, not you!" I was immune, I thought, what need had I for men, I who had so far outrun them, and their limited understanding, and capacity for life? I was inflated and I felt very superior. This inflation is self-sustaining. I had no one to tell me or show me I was selfish and antisocial or that I was headed for a fall, as are all who try to preserve a separated pleasure.

One night I motored him out to Croton for supper in the Sharkey Cottage. We took a lunch basket with us and a lovely bottle of Graves. Maurice loved to drive in automobiles. He lay back on the leather seat luxuriating in the ease of it. He was always very conscious of his surroundings, observing and estimating them. "At least he is a *man,*" I thought. He had a acquired a poise in the course of his years. He was dignified and massive—villainous, perhaps, in spots, but something to grapple with. There was nothing flighty about him as about the lovable, immature Reed. He was a "Serious Artist."

The supper and the wine were good and it was a pleasure to eat and drink with him because he had a grave, pleasurable way of appreciating such things, and he gave a proper value to them, so that they were enhanced for one, and made more important by his consciousness of them. He had a sense of food, as many Europeans have, and it too was a part of his seriousness. After the meal was over and the sweet evening air was filling the room from the hillside beyond the open door, both of us eased by the wine of the apprehension of life, we talked together of many things. He seemed to want to come closer and be confidential, tell me his secrets, and he told me about the love of his life.

He was the victim of one of those so-called fatal attachments, whose intensity and apparent inevitability make them appear admirable in a world of easy love. Hutch had taught me too to admire the inevitable wherever I found it—so now I read more significance and weight into Maurice than I had before and by the end of the evening I was about to respect him and look up to him.

When I went to my room to get my hat, for the motor would soon be there, he followed me. He came up behind me and flattened his body against me until I felt all of him. I tried to get away—and only dragged him along with me. I fought and wrestled in that ludicrous backward embrace and took to kicking him. Well, he had expected that. I got free of him for a moment and stood panting, with my back against the foot of the bed. I held on to the footboard with both hands and tried to get my breath—and in an instant he had lunged again and clamped himself onto me!

"Darling!" he breathed hotly into my ear. "Darling! I *love* you!" How many times had he practiced *that* in his life? *Darling.* How I hated the word!

Heat burned into me now. I got really angry. Maybe he had meant it so: meant to somehow arouse some feeling in me, something to work upon. The man had method. He leaned over against me and I was bent back upon the hard metal until it hurt me, but I kept my face beyond his reach. He himself enjoyed the struggle, for his body had a chance at last to wrestle and constrain its material, and his muscles, pent up for too long in paint, expanded and contracted in a great burst of rude delight. But muscle for muscle, my own were adequate! I managed finally to throw him off.

The drive home was far more pleasant than on the way out to the country. We were more intimate, more cognizant of each other's flesh, more realistically aware of each other's hair, skin, limbs, and lips and all their odors than we had been before. We were as cold, as strange, as distant in heart as ever, but we existed, each for the blood cells of the other. Besides, Sterne was solaced by his struggle and I was pleased by my success in overcoming him. We were as lonely as ever, but more comfortable. Exercise, no matter what kind, will overcome horror.

When he reached his home that night, he sat down and wrote me a note that he dispatched to me in the morning. The sentimentality of it only made me realize more strongly that he was playing some game. I could not feel he was sincere, and I felt a weariness at the thought that actually I had undertaken a task with that man that would be horribly difficult if I had to put up with boring flights of fancy all through it. I would certainly stop any more pseudo-classic love letters, however! I would harry and taunt and enrage and injure him. I would light a real fire in him before I was through: when I had him malleable I would make him throw away his yellow-green paint and take to clay.

I knew that something had got started that no matter how weary I grew, no matter how bored or disgusted, I would see through to the end. I was grappling now with the essence of the man hidden deep below his insincerities, and his incongruities. His essence was strong and pure, though overlaid with so much of the world's harm. I turned to it and went forward.

CHAPTER EIGHT 🖎 FINNEY FARM

One day Elizabeth asked me to walk over and see Finney Farm. This was an old place she had already visited herself because one of her American pupils lived there. She said it was beautiful—a picture of real life. How peaceful it looked! A complete human habitation. The large farmhouse had the somewhat dingy color of old white paint and the windows were shuttered with turquoise blue blinds.

"I am going to come and live here," I announced suddenly. Life was shaping itself for me. I saw, dimly, the form of the future crystallizing in a new pattern. The luxuriance of it all, the country opulence and wholesomeness were full of reassurance to me. How had I put up with my New York apartment for so long? I contrasted it with this shining, cleanly spaciousness and remembered with distaste the flakes of black soot that lay each morning on the tarnished ivory windowsills left open overnight, and then out here the little Sharkey Cottage was only a tiny playhouse.

I don't know how, but in another week I had leased it for two years—Charley [an old horse] and the cows and Jerry the hired man and all—and the Finneys were able to go to Florida or California or somewhere as, they said, they had longed to do for ages.

My long struggle with Maurice was already under way. I unhesitatingly did all I could to strengthen my influence over him, and to bind him to me. I invited him to Provincetown for the summer and told him he could have the lifesaving station to work in. The name appealed to him, with his undercurrent of apprehension! He said he would come if I would let him do a portrait of me and I shuddered inwardly at the thought of the color it would be, but I agreed. I realized that part of his reason for doing the portrait was for the advertisement it would give him, for artists often think in these values, but I was not averse myself to the advertisement a portrait by him in the New York gallery would give me. I determined, however, to help along as much as I could with this production so it would do justice to us both!

Maurice really did like and need something I had in me. My certainty and assurance about life at that time gave him a great feeling of security. He liked to feel I was taking the responsibility of him, he who had fended for himself for so long. He was curious about my apparent strength, and questioned me.

"What is it, Mabel? What makes you so fearless about life?"

"Nature," I answered him as I had answered Reed. But he could not understand that. Whatever it was, he loved it. He told me he had always loved the most gentle, feminine women until now—helpless and delicate ones. But now, he thought, he was beginning to love other qualities. Decision and courage and that honesty he felt in me.

I felt very weary and emancipated. When he argued that it would interfere with his Work if I didn't let him make love to me, that old persuasion convinced me that I might as well be hospitable to him without stint and not be narrow-minded. Since I had told him it was his Work that counted with me, and this was true, and I had taken on myself to mold and change it, then I had no right to withhold anything that prevented him from being free to function as I intended he should. I was as cool and logical as possible about this. He was not—yet—physically attractive to me, though his Scotch tweed coat had begun to have an endearing influence with its whiffs of wholesome scent. I stifled all tendencies to soften and melt and be at rest, though I was already tired of the attitude I had assumed. I put my attention onto Work.

Is it surprising that I should have really seized upon this man, determined to change his whole scheme of work? To pull him about and alter his makeup? No, countless women have done that to men, are doing it, and will go on trying to do it. The surprising thing is that one tells about it and gives the show away! But that is the way I was thinking and planning then and that is the way many women do, and will go on doing until they learn better. (Forgive me, all you women!)

CHAPTER NINE 🐙 PROVINCETOWN

Motoring to Provincetown with Maurice, we had to spend a night somewhere on the way. After riding for miles in the long, summer twilight, I remember standing, dazzled by the light at the hotel desk, in a large mahogany lobby, hearing Maurice ask for a double room and bath, and feeling perfectly limp and miserable. I had accepted what I called to myself the minor inconvenience of a physical relationship with him to further my scheme, thinking that by so doing I would remove our two bodies from the foreground, since they had become obstacles to the work I planned, and stood in the way of a complete influence over him. So it only meant (at least that is what I thought at the time) that I must be extremely vigilant and, separating my body from my soul, offer the one to him and withhold the other, reserving the spirit, keeping it intact and uninvolved.

Really, I never felt less emancipated in my life than I did that night! I knew the man considered me an experienced woman of the world and that actually he was rather nervous, in spite of his feeling of increased importance at being alone with so sophisticated, so dangerous, a person as myself, and I knew that, to preserve and add to my power over him, I must never let him know my childish and bourgeois Buffalonian trepidations. In his white pajamas with large bedroom slippers on his feet, he recovered a hint of the innocent patriarchal atmosphere I had noticed about him, and the potential Hebrew prophet reappeared once he shed his tweed overcoat and his soft brown felt hat, and drew from his tie the sinister black opal pin that gleamed intermittently with a dark and baleful blue light. He laughed with the gasp that sent the air in a rush from his lungs as he climbed into bed and I obediently received him. And this for ART!

We labored in the dark, he with his eyes closed, trying to imagine he had B., his early love, there with him. He had unfortunately told me that this was his habit when making love to other women; I, with a certain commonsense thrift, endeavored to get as much enjoyment out of the exigent situation as I could. His strong, rather bland hands traveled over me, sizing up shapes, as sculptors' hands are made to. His fingertips were more interested in form than in sense. They were always studying. No sooner was the spasmodic embrace completed than it was forgotten in the thoughts about Art that surged up in his mind. He began to talk about his work.

"I have a great gift of visualizing," he said. "If I can first visualize a thing, I can draw it. To me, it seems, I grasp Essential Form more completely if I visualize it to myself than if I *look* at it. Now these curves, darling, these volumes and masses, I can see them in my mind; I could get up now and draw them without *looking at* them; I have taken them into my psyche by touch, that is really 'knowing' a woman as it speaks of it in the Bible. . . ."

"I think you were meant to be a sculptor," I murmured drowsily into his shoulder. I fell asleep, worn out by the dreary vicissitudes of evolution, while his voice went on and on in the night, delivering a little lecture upon Form.

We arrived conspicuously in Provincetown. I had engaged one of the beautiful little white clapboarded Portuguese fishermen's houses that lined two sides of the long main street and the salty smell of the bay permeated its small, tidy rooms. It was a curious setting for the dark, ornate stranger I had in tow. But I soon had him settled in the building adjacent to the lifesaving station across the dunes, busily preparing his materials for his work.

I organized my life. It had different parts to it that must be brought somehow into a whole. I had two houses to live in. Across the sand dunes the Peaked Bar lifesaving station on the coast, and a fisherman's cottage on the bay! I had John coming soon from school for his holidays, Bobby Jones coming from New York, and I had asked several friends to visit me. I wished to consider Sterne simply as one of a number of elements of the summer. I did not intend for him to fill up my foreground, for he had not that importance for me. In the first place, I wanted always to feel the lovely, new, free, unattached ownership of myself that enabled me to retire alone to my depths, forgetting the whole world, and I didn't want people to begin to assume that we were having a love affair, because I didn't want them talking about it all around us, for that kind of attention vitiates the air, sucks the life from it, steals one's freedom and spontaneity and energy. Besides that, I was afraid of criticism.

The Hapgoods were already there and I made an arrangement with Neith to form a joint household for meals—thus taking care of John and the others.

"I never saw you more self-possessed than you are this summer, Mabel," [Hutch] told me. "You seem to belong to yourself at last. Do you hear from Jack?"

"Hutch, I do. And I wish he'd leave me alone. I don't care for him anymore. It's *over*. Steff made me pretend it wasn't, but it is! Hutch, won't you write and tell him this for me and send him this ring? *I* don't know what to tell him. You'll know what to say."

I had been receiving many letters and postcards from Reed ever since he left, and the end of "Pygmalion," where he tried to voice my vague feelings for what I had called "nature."

Pygmalion, Pygmalion, Pygmalion—
He wrenched the shining rock from the meadow's breast,

And out of it shaped the lovely, almost-breathing
Form of his dream of his life of the world's women.
Slim and white was she, whimsical, full of caprice;
Bright sharp in sunlight, languid in shadow of cloud,
Pale in the dawn, and flushed at the end of the day.
Staring, he felt of a sudden the quick, fierce urge
Of the will of the grass, and the rock, and the flowering tree;
Knew himself weak and unfulfilled without her—
Knew that he bore his own doom in his breast—
Slave of a stone, unmoving, cold to this touch,
Loving in a stone's way, loving but thrilling ever.

Reed wrote joyously, his thoughts centered on his new house across the Hudson River in the Ramapo Hills. He was overflowing with happiness; even when he got sick in Bucharest, it did not seem to affect him. I have his Russian passport; out of sheer exuberance, he wrote on the outside of it for all to read who could read English:

I am a German and Austrian spy. I do it for money.

Reed.

He felt, he told me afterwards, immune from sin, sickness and death, as though nothing could ever hurt him again.

CHAPTER ELEVEN 🍂 OH, MAURICE!

The imperceptible shift I made, from the source of power in myself to the power in Maurice, took place so unconsciously that I did not realize what was happening. All my attention was on him and so all my satisfaction or discontent had to come from him. In the last analysis, what one wants in oneself or another is their energy, their power. This makes virtues and vices lose their values, and Maurice's value for me, his irresistible and all but priceless possession, was the power in him. Neither of us defined this to each other, but he was aware of something in himself.

I continued to pose for Maurice every morning, and to limit him to the single tubes of blue, or to the sanguine. He made a large number of drawings, some of them very fine, all of them of Mabel Dodge, that now are scattered about the world so widely that while one of them hangs in Mrs. Gusdorf's dining room [in Taos], there is one in Peiping [Beijing] and another in Nova Scotia!

Maurice and I continued to play with the idea of marriage in much the same way that one pokes at a snake with a stick. The idea was dangerous and revolting; yet we couldn't leave it alone.

Every morning I traipsed over the sand to the studio with a basket of lunch for us. One morning as I plodded along, and my mind was as usual seething with the problem of Maurice, and the conflict between my revolt about him and the fixation I had upon him, I rehearsed as one does what I should say to him when I reached him. I saw him before me in my mind's eye, earnest and serious and convincing, at his best, suffering from his own conflicts, dignified by agony.

("We must separate, Maurice. We are too dissimilar. I want to be alone again. . . ."

"But Mabel, you help me so much. You are helping me to smoothen out my life. You are showing me something so much finer than I knew before. If you send me away, I will only drift as before. . . . I need someone to hold me up as you do. . . . You are so strong, darling.")

I knew how it would go. It had become a routine for us, and I would be unable to withdraw my essence from the sticky blend it made with his. We had pooled our energies—how could we ever separate them again?

CHAPTER TWELVE 🐚 LEO STEIN

Leo Stein had left his villa, his Cézannes and Renoirs, and come to America. He was in Provincetown, probably staying with us. Leo meant a great deal more to me in America than he had in Europe. More and more nowadays I needed people of solid worth, people with ideas and character instead of those who were "intriguing." Oddities of nature had ceased to appeal; reality drew closer.

Reed's letters continued to come to me all the while Hutch's letter was on its way, following him from place to place. They were wistful letters, full of a humility that I had never known in him. Reed seemed so familiar to me, his American essence was so plain and unequivocal, natural as bread and butter compared to the rich, exotic, dubious unfamiliarity of Maurice, who was darkness shot through with golden gleams. Maurice's large, dark, secretive eyes, gleaming with pain and struggle or tender with pleasure at some aspect of beauty, then suddenly glazed and fixed with sensuality when his perfervid imagination took hold of form and converted it into a vehicle of sex—all his aestheticism so sexed, his sex so mixed up with sight and mind—those eyes of his, constantly conveying to one how his centers shifted and borrowed each other's function so that in his own being there remained no form and no integrity, gave me no peace or security.

I needed something certain and familiar and real near me, and I wondered whether I couldn't persuade Reed to come and join us at Finney Farm, where we could be real friends. When I thought of him he seemed like a young green tree, strong and immature, with potential fruit concealed in promise, while Maurice was indeed like the uprooted pine tree the Independent Society of Artists had chosen for their symbol!

CHAPTER THIRTEEN ✍ THE END OF REED

Reed came and I gave him the third floor of the farmhouse. I liked to think of him up there with his typewriter in the window, working and occasionally looking out over the still orchard. I went into town every day to fix a studio for Maurice on Tenth Street, for he was incapable of doing it for himself. Reed tried to live in the attic room for three days. Then one morning he came to me and said, "I can't do it, Mabel. It's not natural. You and Sterne here and everything. . . ."

"Why can't you people *live* your theories anyway?" I cried. "You always said one should be emancipated and true to oneself."

He looked at me. "I love you," he said.

I rolled my eyes. "Well, what difference does one house make from another? Here it's convenient for you, you have your work to do, I like to have you here. If you go somewhere else, how does that alter things?"

"I don't have to see and hear," he said.

"Where are you going, then?"

"I'm going to see if I can buy the Sharkey Cottage."

"And you'll come over often and everything?"

"Perhaps," he said, and left that day.

But the change was effected only by breaking something. He had to stiffen inside himself and feel coldly toward me so as not to mind too much. Soon I heard that he had bought the little Sharkey house, where I had hurt him so badly, but he had [also] taken a room in Washington Square and he had met a girl down there and taken her to live with him. I was curious about her, and one late afternoon I knocked at his door. It was opened by a very pretty, tall, young woman with soft, black hair and very blue eyes, who held a lighted candle in her hand.

"Is Jack Reed here?" I asked.

He appeared suddenly behind her with rumpled hair and hurt eyes, and his temples shining as of old.

"This is Louise Bryant," he told me gravely.

Shall I tell here how the story ended? Louise had been married to a dentist in a small town in the West, but the girl was clever with a certain Irish quickness, and very eager to get on. I think Reed was a stepping-stone, and through him she met a lot of people she never would have known otherwise. It had not seemed to me that she cared very much for him. When he was away on one of the writing commissions he always had for the *Metropolitan Magazine* and others, she had a brief passage of passion with a friend of Reed's and mine. The following summer Reed took a cottage in Provincetown with her and we used to pass each other on the street but never stopped and spoke.

Reed had never been quite well, I think, since his illness in Galicia, and finally it was decided that he must have a kidney removed. He married Louise, before he went to the hospital, for convenience's sake. Rumors of their quarrels came to me from friends of both of us. "Oh, *you're* not so much," Louise cried to him bitterly. There was the old competition in importance again!

Finally they went to Russia, like so many others looking for an escape. For Louise it was an opportunity to be on her way, and she wrote quite a good book; for Reed it was an adventure again and perhaps a chance to lose himself in a great upheaval. He threw himself into action close to Trotsky and Lenin and when he died of typhus the Russians gave him a splendid public funeral and set a stone with a tablet to his memory over his grave, and Louise, draped in crêpe, the wife of a hero, threw herself on his bier long enough to be photographed for the New York papers.

Andrew saw her when she came back to New York, married then to William Bullitt, and she told him that as Reed died, he whispered: "Listen . . . I am singing a little song for you. . . . The whole world came between us. . . ."

CHAPTER FOURTEEN ✦ LIFE AT FINNEY FARM

Finney Farm was bright with sunlight and wood fires, and ruffled white muslin curtains so sheer that the movements of the leaves and branches on the trees outside made a lively dancing pattern at all the windows. In the big, homely kitchen, there was always a smell of baking and roasting, of cinnamon and apples and hot coffee. I loved the beautiful sense of home in the country. Maurice, when he was not in New York, wore high boots and his Scotch tweed clothes, and carved a turkey as we all sat at the wide, long, dining-room table.

It was a perfect setting for an American country gentleman and his wife, but though the environment was perfect and I myself, I thought, could have settled down into a bounteous peace, Maurice was so Russian here that he seemed to complicate the dream. Somehow the very innocence and sweetness of the place showed up his difference from us and made him stand out instead of blending innocuously like a piece in a picture puzzle!

I imagine that what I really wanted was someone more like what Dr. Harding has called "the phantom lover," one who would exist mainly in my imagination, a projection instead of a reality, or perhaps, after all, I was conditioned to prefer the kind of American husband who is unobtrusive when he is at home, and that rarely. But Maurice was no phantom. He was more definite and real than anyone I had ever lived with. He had a strong presence, and the qualities that had made me capitulate to him were more emphatic than ever here at Finney Farm. He was darker and more ruddy against the white muslin curtains; his cigar permeated the house and blotted out the mild conservatory perfumes. Sitting in the room beside the fire he diminished my other friends, Bayard, Bobby, or Leo Stein, or whoever was there. He diminished me, too, and made me seem more of a brown wren than ever!

My poor Maurice! I had dragged him into this New York country life and wanted him to be no more than a table or a chair or a canary in the conservatory, just a part of the setting, but the man was a man after all! He was very much of one, in fact! He walked around with heavy steps upon the hardwood floors and without even trying he became master of the house. It was natural to him to overlook and forget women and often he forgot I was there. Sometimes if I saw him concentrating on some visitor, looking right past me, I would go up to him and murmur gently but with all the force I could inject: "Stop that, Maurice!" and he would flash a bright black-and-white smile up at me and exclaim, loud and disingenuous, "Stop what, darling?" Really, I couldn't do a thing with him!

Sometimes he tried to leave me. He would say he couldn't stand it and he would dress himself in a silk shirt and leave the house with a long cigar between his teeth. At the split between us my whole nature would stretch out after him; the unseen antennae in every cell that reach out all around us would strain, moving to find him in the empty space he had left, every nerve on end and crying for him. Why? Why? Why did I have to want him there? At any rate, I had to have him back no matter how he hurt or repelled me.

"Darling, sometimes I feel that I *must* get away. The other day I just ran from Finney Farm and I thought I would go and see some of those simple people having a good time. Then that old *hunting* instinct awoke in me! I began to look at the girls. They are beautiful, those girls of the common people. But as soon as I looked at them and began to desire them, my feeling for them changed into the *artist's!* I began to see in planes and masses and my sexual desire turned into a terrific wish to draw—to reproduce those forms. That is always the way, darling! I wish my Art would let me enjoy myself!"

"Oh, Maurice! Surely there is another way still! If you really loved me you would be faithful in spite of yourself. You wouldn't have that hunting thing always leading you astray. You wouldn't have all those sexual cravings and you would be free to work."

"Oh, darling, I do love you! Perhaps I have lost the capacity for that young thrill I had over B. but I know I love you, and need you, seriously."

"Maurice. Let me order some clay for you. Try modeling. It seems to me your hands just long to handle some solid substance."

"Later on, dear. I want to work out some problems first. I know I can make form as plastic with paint as a sculptor does with clay. . . . I think I'll get one of those young shop girls for a model," he mused.

"I don't want you to have models down there in that studio! I know just what *that* means. When you can't paint, you'll make love instead. . . ."

"Really, Mabel, you are impossible. I must be free. I don't see how we can go on like this."

CHAPTER FIFTEEN   Dr. Jelliffe

I decided I must have help from outside and I thought of Dr. Jelliffe. I launched into a description of my situation with Maurice. It was a great relief to talk, to tell it all . . . to tell how I hated things about him even while I loved him and was unable to live without him.

I enjoyed my visits three times a week to Jelliffe's office. He had a speculative mind with an amusing intuition. As he turned my attention more and more upon the inner working of my own nature, curious spiritual events began to occur, and my starved perception, which had been centered for months upon Maurice, reveled in the new direction of interest. It became an absorbing game to play with oneself, reading one's motives, and trying to understand the symbols by which the soul expressed itself.

Psychoanalysis was apparently a kind of tattletaling. I was able to tell, not only everything about myself, but all about Maurice. I grew calm and self-sufficient, and felt superior to him in the evening when, returning from New York, I found him still in the grip of his nervous fears and worries.

It was customary during an analysis, Dr. Jelliffe told me, for the patient to be separated temporarily from the family, or from those nearest one, who were in some way involved with the compulsions and complexes of the case. I did not doubt now but that Maurice was the complete picture of whatever was the matter with me; that, could I but read it aright, would explain to me the difficult, incomprehensible makeup that hid the real self somewhere deep down in me. But I found I just couldn't define my impulses, no matter how strong or how real they were. Why, why did I have to wrestle with this man, compel him to an exact fidelity, determine him to be a sculptor, lift him up and chasten him? Really, was it only myself I was working on?

At Jelliffe's request, then, I got him off to Pottsville to paint landscapes of snow, and the strain immediately lessened, and I resumed a way of life less concentrated and bent upon changing him. I found everything much pleasanter. For me it was exactly like a holiday, as though Maurice had been a tremendous job from which I was granted a vacation—and what was left of the strange grind that constituted our love affair was the love without the strangeness or the strain. It seems to me I never loved him with any ease except when we were separated, and then tenderness and a kind of compassion entered into me. Alas, poor Maurice! How sorry I am when I remember it all! With the same pity I used to think of him alone in Pottsville in his boarding house, so earnestly trying to be good and to love me as I insisted he should, in the particular, dignified, worthwhile fashion I required. I was always so afraid he was not *noble* enough for me! Heavens!

Maurice had not been away long enough for me to resume much of my real poise; only long enough to allow my great craving for love to grow stronger—fastening more securely upon him for its satisfaction. While he was away, I had felt love in me and supposed it was for him, love that had only occasionally reached the surface of my perceptions when we were together, and this love that I wrote to him about in exalted letters attracted and drew him back to Croton where, alas, his presence caused it to sink down in me again, leaving only the strain and the agony of wishing for a different and more adequate object for its fulfillment. When I looked within, I saw myself floundering, yet would not—yet—save myself. I continued to believe that somehow, someway, *I* could be fixed, or Maurice could be fixed, so that we would fit together like the covers of a book.

We struggled on and on through the winter, through the spring.

CHAPTER SIXTEEN 🕮 STRUGGLING ON

The exhibition of "Portrait Drawings of Mabel Dodge" came on at the Bourgeois Gallery with success. Maurice was there most of the time, talking to women who also aspired to be drawn by him. He had a good time while that was going on, for the critics were flattering and many people attended the show. The sculpturesque quality of the work was commented upon, and I tried to draw Maurice nearer to my unfailing wish for him to model in clay, but he continued to put me off, although he was accomplishing nothing in paint.

I built a studio for him in the orchard, and got him to give up the New York room, and I used to go into New York and buy him fresh flowers to work on, hoping that if he must paint, that the contemplation of their color would help to lift him out of the greens and browns of his palette. He worked assiduously, but without delight, upon flowers and fruit, and they came out looking more like him than like themselves!

I ordered several hundred pounds of clay, which I had mixed in a big box in Maurice's studio, and I set to work myself to build an armature for a heroic figure! There was no limit to what I was ready to do or try to do to make that man start to model! It seemed to me that the sight of wet clay would prove irresistible to him. I slyly persuaded him to help me hammer the big armature together, believing there was magic in getting actually involved in an undertaking, that it drew one imperceptibly into itself. But it was a miscalculation. While I hung handfuls of the damp clay onto the skeleton, Maurice, his face distorted in an exasperated frown, continued to paint hyacinths and tulips and felt affronted at my interference.

My friends were surprised to find the large, sad figure of a clay woman in the studio after a short time. I kept her covered with a wet sheet at first, but when I realized that Maurice was indifferent to the chance to model and go me one better (as he could have done with his eyes shut), I could not continue with it. I was not at all interested in modeling for its own sake. So the moisture slowly dried into the clay and folds of the sheet stiffened upon the figure beneath it until there was left only the unmalleable effigy of an unfinished female thing, gradually turning into stone. Oh, Galatea!

CHAPTER SEVENTEEN 🦋 EMMA CURTIS HOPKINS

Jelliffe couldn't really help me to understanding, and when the amusing speculations had gone on for a few months, they finally ceased to amuse, and the old fatigue and depression came back. Then someone introduced me to Emma Curtis Hopkins, and she, for a while, soothed me into "the effortless way." "Be still and know that I am God"—that sort of advice. Her teaching was based upon intuition and there was a great deal of truth in it. Her counsels were full of quaint turns of phrase and native spice, for Emma Curtis was an old-fashioned

New Englander from Boston. She had made her debut with Mary Baker Eddy, who called her her star—but then had come one of the periodic upheavals when one star displaced another in the Eddy constellation, and Mrs. Hopkins had started to teach her own doctrine. She had formulated Twelve Lessons in Mysticism, and each lesson consumed one hour to tell.

She stimulated and renewed one—causing the love and faith that life congealed to flow again. And she was so flattering! She loved us all, or seemed to, and she appreciated us. She called me her "child from Atlantis," and to the others she explained me away by telling them that I was Atlantean and could only be understood by other Atlanteans. This explained me nicely to myself and lessened my feeling of doubt and conflict. I gradually impelled all my entourage to her quiet asylum. Bobby, Maurice, Nina, Elizabeth, Andrew, and others—they all followed me there.

Maurice, she told me, was "a great soul, a giant among men." I liked to hear this, for it endorsed my suppositions about him and dignified our relation. So for a while things went better for us all, since we did not *try* so hard. We all endeavored to live more like the lilies of the field, and sure enough all things came easier to us when we ceased to go after them, and even Maurice's work was, for a time, more free and flowing.

CHAPTER EIGHTEEN 🙞 CHANGE

Sometimes we went down to the Hapgoods' in Dobbs Ferry, and quite often John and Boyce went back and forth visiting each other. The two boys had a real passion for everything "Western." They pored over Sears Roebuck catalogues and when they could they ordered Stetson hats, chaps, quirts, and all kinds of cowboy paraphernalia from Chicago. They cultivated hard, ruthless expressions and thrust out their lower jaws. "The West" had become for them both the land beyond pain, beyond fathers and mothers and their appendages. John and Boyce spent long hours lying in the grass in the upper field comparing notes, voicing their miseries. For John, Maurice—that "guilty stranger" as he once called him—was the constant, galling presence that poisoned his home, and for Boyce, it was Hutch, who criticized and kept after him the way fathers do until he was sealed up like a rocky cave. Perhaps Hutch was a little jealous of Boyce, as so many fathers have to be of their sons, for Neith undoubtedly loved him so much that she drew her out more than others did.

Finally, resolutions formulated themselves within me and began to come to the surface. I decided to go and stay with the Hapgoods, who had gone to their little fisherman's house in Provincetown. I asked Maurice to go, hoping he would refuse, and he did. I really wanted to get away from him and be with John, so he and I started in our car, and the good Albert, who had been with me so long, drove us. Away alone with John, we both had a good time. It was too bad it so seldom happened. Since I had made plans to undo the Croton Cosmos before we reached Provincetown, once there all my taut nerves relaxed in the soft sea air. Nothing ever pleased me so much as that lovely salt breeze that bathed the little town night and day. "Untied are the knots of the heart!"

I fell into the Hapgoods' embrace. We had always liked each other and we always would. I loved to be once again in that entourage with Neith's quiet, aloof smile to arm me, and Hutch's booming voice rumbling through the board partitions!

CHAPTER NINETEEN 🕸 DEEPER CHANGE

Of course I wrote to Maurice and tried to inject a little love into the pages. Also I summoned up the physical strength to write directions for those I had left behind me. By letter I dismissed Domenico, the Italian who had been with me in the New York apartment and who was caretaker there, and I ordered it closed up. I ordered old Charley shot to save him from some hard, unknown master, and then Maurice was left on my hands! I told him to come and live nearby in Wellfleet, where I would take some rooms for him and he could do that portrait that always hung in our minds' eye, waiting to be painted to justify to ourselves and to the world our painful liaison. This magnificent *Mona Lisa,* we both hoped, would make up for it all.

While I paused in Provincetown during these first days, trying to collect myself, trying to fill the emptiness with God, I wrote rather cold letters to Maurice, for when feelings left me I could not remember how it had been when they filled me. So I could never deceive him. I know I encouraged him impersonally to get away from the enervating air of Croton and to come to live at a distance from me. But these signs of my independence of him aroused the instinct of self-preservation and he who always appeared lacking in initiative when there was anyone to act for him suddenly packed up and went to Ogunquit on the Maine coast, where his friend and great admirer, Hamilton Field, operated a little art colony.

Maurice had decided he wanted to paint rocks. My energy ran out like quicksilver to find what he wanted, only it should be of the most superior quality, of the highest distinction available. If he had to have rocks, then they must be the rockiest rocks in Maine in the most distinguished setting I could find—

rocks really aloof and undomesticated, something different indeed from the intimate and overused coast of Ogunquit that I visualized from his letters, with the boardinghouse and the art school all mixed up together and easels stuck up all over the place. He wrote me that a girl's hat peeped out from behind every rock! Also that one of the first evenings he got there, a girl got at him almost in spite of himself, and he had her out on the beach in the dark.

This peculiarly abundant incontinence in Maurice made me absolutely furious. I could not understand it or condone it. All I knew was that I would not permit it. The only way to stem the uncontrolled flow was to be on hand and superintend it myself. Was this to be my lifework? I regained a sense of significance from Maurice's lapse on the beach, for again he reappeared in my imagination as a *job*. I must personally direct and canalize this rich stream and see that it was metamorphosed into Art. That portrait of me should take care of this.

CHAPTER TWENTY 🐠 MONHEGAN ISLAND

Monhegan! A black rock in the Atlantic Ocean with cruel cliffs against which the water, always of a nondescript color, angrily lurched and broke night and day. A small boat motored one out to that gaunt and repellent island, then turned around and hastily left. Near the boat landing a few dwellings clung together, also the post office, the store, a small hotel. But away across a kind of moor, covered with coarse grass, there were several wooden houses facing out to the open sea, built low to resist the wind, and weathered to a dark brown. I was able to rent the largest of these seaside homes. It had character. It reminded me of Charlotte Brontë, George Sand, and Brittany, only it was more austere, more tragic, than any of these. It was a suitable background for the turbulent artist and there were rocks piled all along the edge of the water below the cliffs—black rocks, terribly indented and carved by the intransigent sea.

The only neighbors were a couple called Lee, [who] rented it to me. They were very cordial to John and me, hoping for company, I suppose. They instructed me about meals for since I could not cook, we had to carry them over from the hotel. I had sent for little Elizabeth from the Duncan School: she and John would be able to bring our food to us in baskets. We would live as simply as possible—the rocks were the principal consideration!

Everything about Monhegan was ascetic and screwed up to the endurance of life, rather than to an enjoyment of it. Every outline was hard. There were no amenities. One had to get one's pleasure out of the qualities of salubriousness, briskness, and rugged strength.

I had undertaken something that was really too much for me, for this was the first time I had ventured out into the world alone with Maurice. Every morning after our silent breakfast, he departed for the rocky shore, his portfolio under his arm. The two children disappeared—and what did I do? I haven't the faintest idea, for not the vestige of a recollection of my days there is registered anywhere in my memory—so I suppose I did nothing.

Maurice ignored it all. He was deep in his subterranean world and my own darkness deepened day by day. I tried to comfort myself with the thought that I was a pioneer in living openly and honestly with Maurice instead of clandestinely, as so many other people conducted their unmarried affairs. But it was no good. I was not interested in being a pioneer. It was no comfort at all. The nights were worse than the days, for my awareness of what I believed public opinion to be regarding our sensual relation froze my blood and prevented me from enjoying the sin for which I endured it. I had never suffered this way with Reed! Why did I imagine such things off here with Maurice? Was it because there was really something sinful in our conjunction that had been absent when Reed and I were together, or was it because this was the first time I was out alone in the cold, cold world, unprotected by the walls of my own environment, away from my friends and admirers? I had no admirers here— no legendary glamour to reinforce me. I had not even Maurice, for he absented himself more and more every day. I felt I ceased to exist and this negative sensation deepened as the weeks passed.

One of these sudden decisions that always arose to save me at the ultimate hour came to me now. I decided to leave Monhegan Island with the children— to leave him there with the rocks and the storms and to rush out of these depths back to Finney Farm. Maurice was mildly surprised, but he did not try to stop me. He wanted those rocks more than anything else and he let us go.

I was alone: I had to have help and I thought of Dr. Brill. When I went to see Brill, he told me he could not take me until later in the fall, but I told him I was badly in need of something, I didn't know what. I was frightened, for I felt I could not endure my terrible burden of melancholy. He said, oh, yes, I could, and he turned me away. I found out he was right.

CHAPTER TWENTY-ONE ✆ DR. BRILL

The "analysis" with Dr. Brill was very different from what I was accustomed to! When I sat down before him with his flat, mahogany desk table between us, I started right off to initiate him about myself.

"I have a very bad Oedipus complex . . .," I began, but he interrupted me.

"Never mind about that," he said. "I want your dreams. I want you to organize your life so that you have plenty of occupation and I want you to bring me in at least one dream every time you come."

"But I hardly ever dream," I protested.

"Well, you will."

"How can you mean 'organize' my life?" I went on, somewhat impatiently.

"Make a program for yourself and stick to it. How do you occupy yourself at home?"

How *did* I?

"Do you attend to your household? Do you like to paint or write? My impression is you are out of place in the country. I think you should be working with a number of people. I may be wrong, but I believe *people* constitute your best medium."

"That's because you saw me first at one of my Evenings here in New York. Oh! I got tired of all that! I hate the city!"

"That doesn't make any difference. Perhaps you belong in it just the same. Why do you hate it?"

"Oh, the noise and the smells—the hurrying around after nothing! I can't stand it. . . ."

"It is the *norm*—the usual environment of the period you are living in. If you can't stand it, you are maladjusted. That's why you are here this morning. We're going to see about that." He smiled a kind of owlish grin.

"Do you mean to say you're going to adjust me to the wild, crude noises of city streets, barbarous horns and yells, and the stinking smells of gasoline, hot asphalt, and all the others that most people are too insensitive to notice?"

"They may be insensitive—but they are able to *stand* them."

"Why *should* they? Why *should* one accept a perfectly uncivilized environment? I don't *want* to. I can imagine *altering* an environment, but I can't imagine meekly accepting it if I don't like it. That's subnormal. I'm interested in the supernormal, myself."

"Oh, but you should at least *be able* to accept it. And you say you are not able. Well, my job is with the norm. I'm not interested in the supernormal. *The normal* average life—that is quite an achievement, you know. Do not call it subnormal until you can live it."

Thus began our unending argument. . . . Brill was all for action, whereas Jelliffe was speculative and considered the play of the psyche and the mind a good outlet in itself. Brill believed in externalizing things. Apparently nothing counted unless it was painted, written down, or formulated into some life pattern composed of persons and their movements. Of course, my previous existence at 23 Fifth Avenue, with its Movements, Leagues, Unions, its Evenings and all, evidently had, to his mind, constituted the perfect adjustment for me. Something in me had risen to spoil it. We must find out the destructive agent within and analyze it away. He did not seem to attach much importance to Maurice, but looked upon him more or less as a mere element in a composite arrangement that I had carefully but mistakenly built up to defeat my own best interests.

I liked Brill immensely from the very first. One could have confidence in him, for his integrity was apparent at once, but it took me quite a while to learn that I could not continue my interesting speculations with him. I would begin hopefully:

"Do you believe a manic-depressive can cure herself? Jelliffe—"

"That's enough," he would interrupt. "You are not here for conversation."

Then he refused to accept my belief that one could drive one's energy from the lower to the higher centers and so increase power. But I thought, later, he did have much the same idea when he talked of repression and sublimation, only he apparently considered that repressions were involuntary and that only sublimations could be directed. He seemed to consider that neurotics were the only people who accomplished anything in this world. I asked him if, from his standpoint, sublimations of sex in painting, writing, inventing, and so on were not to be considered merely by-products and their chief function not to create beauty and a more abundant life, but to keep people out of insane asylums. What would happen, I asked when sublimations were exhausted, used up and no longer sublime? Perhaps the world was already overfull of these productions, of pictures, books, music, inventions!

"Is civilization just an effort not to go crazy?"

He told me not to try to be clever but to tell him a dream!

Brill was certain from the first that I had no use for the country, that I was wasting my life in Croton. He had an idea, I think, that I would be more at home in some skyscraper with telephone, push buttons, and alert secretaries to carry out my plans than among the sweet williams and the pheasants of Finney Farm!

I fought this notion with all my heart, for I did not want to go back to New York. I remember more vividly than anything else sitting in my bed and writing short articles for the *New York Journal*. For more than any other reason, I began to write to appease Brill, and get him off that idea of my return to town! So I had asked Arthur Brisbane for work on the *Journal,* and since he had been insisting for fifteen years that I was a *writer* he could not very well refuse me a chance to be one.

These little feuilletons of mine took me an hour or so to write and they amused me very much. I held my public in my mind, the shop girls and young clerks who, Arthur said, read the *New York Journal,* and I wrote down for them all I learned about psychoanalysis and about myself, and anything else that came along. The editors immediately boomed them and advertised them in black letters two inches high: "Mabel Dodge Writes About Mother Love!" "Mabel Dodge Asks Do You *Work* for a *Living?*" The city editor's captions were always embarrassing! They were syndicated in every Hearst paper in the United States and "Mabel Dodge" entered the circle of Dorothy Dix and suchlike.

But this was not *work* at all. It was just to enable me to live at Finney Farm where, in spite of Brill, I thought I wanted to live, and indeed it seemed to pacify him. He seemed contented if my name appeared in large black type and if I brought him my dreams. Once I confessed to him that I had made up a dream when I hadn't really had any real one to bring, and he had nodded and said, "Just as good. Any one you make up will be as revealing as any you could dream!"

I continued to see Mrs. Hopkins now about once a week but I had to keep this dark as best I could, for Brill called all my mysticism a fantasy life and frowned upon it severely. He became arbitrary and dogmatic. Anything "religious" was anathema to him. He consistently tried to remove every vestige of my belief in an inner power, and when I haltingly endeavored to convince him of something that counseled me and impelled me from my depths, he said scathing things about a Jehovah complex! It was only later that I realized I should have referred to God and Nature as "the Unconscious"—and then they would have gotten by!

CHAPTER TWENTY-THREE 🕮 SISTER BEATRIX'S ADVICE

Sister [Beatrix, a lay nun who ran a girls' school nearby] came across the river for lunch one day and I noticed she had a purposeful look. When we were alone in the living room by the window where the afternoon sun came through the ruffled white muslin curtains, she suddenly leaned forward impulsively and seized both my hands. Her soft draperies fell into biblical folds. She might have been Martha on a visit to Mary. "I want to say something very frank to you, dear. May I?"

"Surely, Sister. What?"

"It is about you and Mr. Sterne. You are in such a false position here! People who *know* you admire and respect you, of course. But those who *don't* know you are bound to misunderstand."

"Well, I have to accept that, don't I? I can't live to suit everybody. If my friends don't mind, that is all I can hope for."

"They may not tell *you* they mind—but I'm sure *every*body would rather see you living differently. Mr. Sterne is such a fine person—just as you are yourself. Surely you have a responsibility toward the public, as an example, I mean. You are neither of you insignificant or obscure people; everything you do is observed. Come! Think it over. I know you will decide to take a step. . . ."

One night in August, on the seventeenth, to be exact, Alice Thursby brought Agnes Pelton to stay for a couple of days. Agnes, whom I did not know very well, awakened some of the old, strained feeling about "my situation." The need to pretend, to say good night in a somewhat obvious and conscious way to Maurice when he and Andrew withdrew to the Green House. Then something flared up in me. The need to be done with all that once and for all—to demonstrate its lack of importance by being casual about it! When Maurice came over to breakfast, I called him up to my room.

"Let's go and get married!" I said, raising one eyebrow.

"But dearest! Why this morning? Are you sure you want to?" A flush broke over his face and a look of pleasure.

"Yes, I want to. We'll have Alice and Agnes for witnesses! We can go up to Peekskill and get a notary public or something!"

"Oh, darling! I hope we are doing the right thing!"

"Well, we're doing it, anyway," I replied succinctly, getting out of bed.

We motored along the river in the sunny morning hours and Maurice bought a ring (a hideous, heavy gold band) and we found the right person to perform the ceremony—if that was what it was. I made the responses in a cold, tight voice, wishing it were over, but Maurice's voice shook and sounded solemn. When it was finished, I was surprised to see tears in his eyes! We went and had luncheon in a dismal hotel, and when Alice got me alone, she said:

"You didn't care at all, but Mr. Sterne really felt what he was saying."

Mr. Sterne! This man I had married would always be that to my friends!

"I'd like to go away on a little trip," said Maurice that evening. "Shouldn't we have a little honeymoon, darling?" he continued. He gave a gusty, involuntary laugh, half nervous, half tender.

"Oh, Maurice! *You* go. I'd rather stay here and go on with what I'm doing. Where do you want to go?"

"Bourgeois wants me to go out west with him on his vacation. Somewhere near John's camp, I think. I might look in on John while I am out there and see what kind of place the Rumseys have. I am very fond of John, you know, Mabel," Maurice went on seriously. "I want to have him like me, and come to me if he needs anything. I have wondered sometimes if he was not a little jealous. But now everything will be smoothened out—won't it?"

"Well, Maurice dear, you go on a little honeymoon with Bourgeois and I will stay here. You know my lease on the apartment at 23 is up the first of September. They are going to tear down the Sickles house. Too bad . . . Maybe I'll look around for another place. I have to put the furniture *somewhere*. Shall we stay in town this winter for a change?"

"Well, darling, you know *I* always like the city. It is you who get so nervous about me. . . ."

The next morning the *New York Herald*'s caption was:

Mrs. Mabel Dodge secretly married to Russian artist. . . .
   "No romance," says Maurice Sterne, "we just decided to wed."

I was still alone upstairs that morning when Marie Howe, that great suffragist, came up to see me from her house below on the Highway. She was waiting for me down in the living room. When I came in, she came up to me and took my hands in hers and gave me a long, grave look.

"I suppose I should congratulate you," she said. "Probably everyone else will. But I cannot help feeling a little sad."

"Why?" I asked politely, seeing her pause for it.

"You have *counted* so much for women!" she exclaimed. "Your example has stood for courage and strength! I wonder if you realize that hundreds of women and girls have been heartened and fortified by the position you took?"

"Which one?" I asked.

"Why! By your life here! The fact that you had the nerve to live your own life openly and frankly—to take a lover if you wished, without hiding under the law. You have shown women they had the *right* to live as they chose to live and that they do not lose respect by assuming that right. But *now!* When I think of the *disappointment* in the whole woman's world today!" Her beautiful dark eyes were filled with tears. I sighed. Everything seemed very tiresome and difficult. She kissed me and moved to the door. "I had to come and tell you," she murmured, and went away.

CHAPTER TWENTY-FOUR ❧ THE END OF THAT

While Maurice was away, I went all over town looking for a new apartment, and the most likely one was the top floor of a beautiful house on North Washington Square that Ralph Adams Cram had done over. It, too, was number twenty-three. If not a lucky number, at least a familiar one, I thought, and wondered if destiny had designed it, for I still thought in terms of fate, in spite of Brill!

When he returned, I was settled in the apartment. I had been absent from him long enough to create images in my mind of a domestic existence, with evenings of ease before the big fireplace, with embroidery and books and flowers and friends. A pattern that had always returned at intervals to allure me, but one I had never achieved. Something was always missing—generally the ease.

Well, he returned. The first night we went out to dinner at an Italian restaurant below the square, and before we had finished our spaghetti Maurice was fixing his eyes over my shoulder upon someone behind me. The unmistakable magnetism of his dark gaze flowed past me like a stream of lava. He had relapsed! I rose, instantly. Standing there and looking down on him, I announced from a great distance: "I didn't marry you for this, Maurice. It's not good enough." And I walked out of the place. On the way, I saw the amused and interested smile of the woman who had caught his attention. Quite an ordinary, nice-looking girl, with the casual manners of Greenwich Village.

He finished his meal and followed me home, where I sat smoking endless cigarettes before the fireless chimney place.

"Really, darling, you embarrass me," he began as he hurried in and laid his hat and stick on a chair. I interrupted him.

"It's no use, Maurice. We can't make a go of it here. One of us must leave. And *I* want to stay here. I'm going to send you out to the Southwest. I've heard there are wonderful things to paint. Indians. Maybe you can do something of the same kind as your Bali pictures. . . ."

It was as clear to me as that. I just gave it all up and began to plan something different and Maurice took to the idea at once. He always liked to go to new places. I procured letters for him to people in Santa Fe and to the Hubbells in New Mexico, and before long he was gone.

Then I fell ill. The weeks passed without incident in the kind of hinterland one goes to when one is not physically well. Maurice wrote enthusiastic letters about New Mexico and he seemed to like Santa Fe very much. He had a little house and friends across the street from him. He even encouraged me to come out and join him, but oh, no! I had no heart for that. In his absence, though, I gradually grew better and felt like myself once more, but I did not resume my analysis; I was off that. It seemed to me I had gone as far as I could with Brill, and away from him I began to resent his interference with my fancies about the unseen powers and influences that appear to guide us and that are not all, as he would have me believe, the promptings of our own unconscious wishes. No, I reverted back to my earlier beliefs.

Elizabeth sometimes came to spend a night and slept beside me in the other bed in my room. Once I awakened in the middle of the night. I passed from unconsciousness into a state of superconsciousness without transition. I lay staring into the darkness, when before my eyes I saw a large image of Maurice's head. Just his face, there before me, with its handsome features and its alien oriental expression. It frightened me and I shuddered. Then, as I gazed, his began to fade and another face replaced it, with green leaves twinkling and glistening all around it—a dark face with wide-apart eyes that stared at me with a strong look, intense and calm. This was an Indian face and it affected me like a medicine after the one that had been before it. I sighed and let it take me and cleanse me. . . . A movement in Elizabeth's bed and she sat up. So did I, and when I turned on the bedside light and looked at her, she giggled nervously:

"Oh! I thought you were dead! I woke up and looked over, and right along the whole length of your body there was another form, like a light. I thought it was your spirit outside you! Oh, dear! You *are* a queer one!"

"I've had a queer dream or something," I said, rubbing my forehead. "I saw an Indian face in some green leaves."

Then Maurice wrote me from Santa Fe:

SANTA FE, NOV. 30TH

Dearest Girl—

Do you want an object in life? Save the Indians, their art-culture—reveal it to the world! I hear astonishing things here about the insensitiveness of our Indian office—through ignorance, solely, for they mean well—the stupidity and the pathetic crimes committed by its agents through a sense of superiority of the white color and white civilization (including, I suppose, the "Great White Way"—Broadway at night, over anything that has *color*).

That which Emilie Hapgood and other are doing for the Negroes, you could, if you wanted to, do for the Indians, for you have energy and are the most sensitive little girl in the world—and, above all, there is somehow a strange relationship between yourself and the Indians. You'll say it is different with the Negroes—they are scattered all over the U.S.A.—so that it is easier to bring them before the public. This isn't at all an advantage, for we have become too familiar with them, and our antagonism towards them was deep-rooted, whereas, as far as the public is concerned, no prejudice exists against the Indians, only a patronizing attitude, which to my mind is worse as far as the Indian is concerned.

And it would be the easiest thing in the world to get a number of Indians from different parts of the country to perform at N.Y. and above all at Washington, to make the American people realize that there are such things as other forms of civilization besides ours.

I spoke to some people about it here, and they told me that they were doubtful—for several years ago a number of very fine dancers were taken to Coney Island by an enterprising Yankee, but hardly anyone went to see them: the people preferred to shoot the chutes. This signifies nothing—so would an exhibition of Sung paintings fare at Coney Island. . . .

It is to be done on a *great* scale—beautifully.

I saw a wonderful dance yesterday. . . .

With all my love,
Maurice

VOLUME FOUR

❧

Edge of Taos Desert
An Escape to Reality

[1917–1918]

CHAPTER ONE ✑

The last evening I spent at 23 [North Washington Square] is still vivid in my memory. The large living room was softly lighted at each end, and dinner was served before the oakwood fire. We left that room, with the fire glowing and the lights burning upon the patient household gods that had moved around with me, as though I were just going to pay a visit next door.

I went out of there intending to return. I was going to the Southwest, a little known neighborhood, for perhaps a fortnight, because I wanted to see what Maurice was doing, for his letters had intrigued me. I had always heard of people going to Florida or California, and more occasionally to the West, but no one ever went to the Southwest. Hardly anyone had ever heard of Santa Fe.

"Well, I want a vacation," I said to myself. "I've had a horrid time lately. I feel like a change." I got it. My life broke in two right then, and I entered into the second half, a new world, that replaced all the ways I had known with others, more strange and terrible and sweet than any I had ever been able to imagine. Whether it was to Atlantis I went or not I do not know, nor have I ever been interested in conjecturing about it. I suppose when one gets to heaven one does not speculate about it anymore. And the same must be true of hell. Anyway, I was through with reading books about Atlantis, Rosicrucianism, the Seven Worlds of Theosophy, or about any other mythical things. I entered into a new life that they were concerned with and I was done with reading any books for a long time.

CHAPTER TWO ✑

Not accustomed to traveling by myself, I got on all the wrong trains, and the final one was the kind that is full of children eating bananas and apples, and that stops at every station, and as the last afternoon dragged on, I could hardly endure it. My heart was pounding with impatience, for in spirit I had already arrived and only my body was left behind on the smelly train. Every time we stopped I went to the door and sniffed the clean air that was so good after New York.

Finally about five o'clock, we stopped at a little place for quite a while. From the window I saw two girls in big hats and riding clothes waiting on their horses 189 beside the station platform. There were two or three old cars standing there too. The station house was of ancient gray wood, and the open space behind it was worn and dusty, but there was the loveliest light all over everything and an empty road leading away, and beyond, just beyond, the bluest mountains I had ever seen. In an instant I rejected that train and ran out to where the automobiles stood. No drivers were about, so I blew a blast on one of the horns and this summoned a long, slow boy from somewhere.

"Listen! This train is supposed to reach Lamy by eleven o'clock. Can't you motor me to Santa Fe quicker than that? Isn't there a road?"

"Guess I can," answered the boy, without much interest.

"Well, wait until I get my bag." I was breathless and excited. Out in the still air everything sounded so strange. My own voice sounded out of key in my ears. "Why does it feel like church?" I wondered.

I rushed into the train and secured my bag and my fur coat, and left behind on the seat *The New Republic,* the *Atlantic Monthly,* and the *Mercure de France.* And I left behind the staleness and the dull, enduring humans all dressed in browns and blacks, with their grimy handkerchiefs in pockets gritty with the deposit of their dull lives! And then I hurled myself at the big boy who stood dazed beside the waiting automobiles.

"Now we must hurry!" I cried. "I want to beat that train."

"This hyah is my car, lady," said the boy, leading me to the end one. It was the most dilapidated vehicle I had ever seen. It had no top and its black, shiny leather seats were ripped and gray. Horsehair bulged through the rents. I didn't care. I hastened into the backseat, my bag in front with the driver, and ['Lisha] started to crank the engine.

In that bright winter evening light we started off down the alluring road towards the mountains. I heaved a sigh of relief. How good it felt! How *good* this fresh air, this clear simplicity.

But all too soon I began to notice a painful jarring under me.

"Wait a moment. What *is* this bumping, anyway?" I tapped him on the shoulder.

"Oh—them back springs is busted. I guess we'll make it, though. If these two cylinders hold out . . ."

"How much is this trip going to cost?" I asked angrily.

"Oh, 'bout sixteen dollars if we make it," he returned. He was leaning forward now, in the crouching attitude of a racer. He had a cigarette hanging from the corner of his mouth and his ashes blew back into my eyes every time he turned towards me, so I stopped talking to him. Holding myself as firmly as I could in the hopping motion of the back end, I began to watch the country we were careening through. I thought I had n.ever seen a landscape reduced to such simple elements. The desert on either side of the road changed to black velvet, unfathomably soft and wide, and suddenly it was night.

"Gee! We got no lights," suddenly said 'Lisha.

"No lights? Well, how do you think we can travel until ten o'clock or eleven without lights?" I cried. I was beginning to get mad.

"Dunno. P'rhaps we can make Wagon Mound."

We bumped into it. There was a station beside a railway track, dimly lighted by oil lamps, and I suddenly longed for a train! "When does a train go through here for Santa Fe?" I asked the old man in the ticket office.

"Tonight's train goes through in 'bout twenty-five minutes," he told me. "You kin get on her then."

I hastily sent another telegram to Maurice, saying:

COMING BY TRAIN AFTER ALL LOVE

I got out [of the train] and he seized me timidly by the arm, his face a conflict of ruefulness and pleasure, for he never was unmitigatedly glad to see me. But then, I wasn't glad to see him.

"Dar-r-rling! What *have* you been doing, jumping on and off that train?"

"Oh, I got tired of it and got off. And got on again," I answered, uncommunicatively. "Where's John?"

"Well, he met this Sara Parsons. *I* introduced them. She's a ve-r-r-y attractive girl. And they invited him to stay there."

"Oh, Maurice!" My heart was sinking. "What about this girl?"

"John seems quite smitten! I am myself. A little. She has a pair of fast horses she drives around. Very jolly!"

The stage rolled from side to side and bowled us into town through the silent streets that were lined with leafless trees. There were very few streetlamps. It seemed a sleepy little place. We drove into a large, empty plaza that looked European. Then we drove up a hilly, narrow street. I saw a great many little low cottages of mud along this street and I began to wonder where Maurice's house was. Presently he stopped the stage at one of these mud huts. "This is it," he said, and helped me out.

My thoughts were all in a turmoil at the unexpectedness of everything. To reach this distant city finally, and to find both John and Sterne more or less *in love* (yes, they are—they're *in love*) with the same girl—and to be left standing on a dark street in front of a mud hovel that I had to enter and *sleep* in. I could hardly believe it was true. So *this* was the Southwest! *"Well!"*

CHAPTER THREE 🖎

The following morning Maurice's house shone in the deep yellow sunshine that flooded the three little rooms and made one ashamed of ill humor. From the very first day I found out that the sunshine in New Mexico could do almost anything with one: make one well if one felt ill, or change a dark mood and lighten it. It entered into one's deepest places and melted the thick, slow densities. It made one feel *good*. That is, alive.

Maurice looked changed. He had on a gray flannel shirt, open at the throat, riding trousers, and high, black riding boots. He looked really Russian now. This life and this place suited him. When we had eaten, he said: "Go outside and sit in the sunshine. I'll wash up."

Behind the house, the land sloped upwards. It was hard and stony and dotted all over with small evergreen trees. He told me they were cedars. I broke off a twig and smelled it—and then tasted it. Bitter, pungent, strong taste of cedar! It entered and took possession right then forever. I climbed the hill until I could look down over the town and saw that it lay in a large hollow with the snow-topped mountains all around it except where the long stretches of desert country sloped away southwards in vast, shimmering, gray-green masses that pulsated in the clear light. Everything was in such a high key that one couldn't tell whether it was light or dark, and the town, though it looked very still as it lay pale and flat on the ground, seemed to vibrate and to breathe. It was a living thing.

Out of the crouching buildings a pale yellow church lifted two square towers from which deep bells were ringing with a full, gay sound. It was curious how round and complete all sounds came to one's ears. Sitting there on that stern hillside, that had nothing soft and comfortable about it like other hills in milder places, I had a complete realization of the fullness of Nature here and how everything was intensified for one—sight, sound, and taste—and I felt that perhaps I was more awake and more aware than I had ever been before. It was a new enchantment and I gave myself up to it without resistance.

"Then John came, calling, 'Mother!'" and I went down to meet him. He looked excited and happy. His hair was untidy and his fingernails, I noticed, were terrible. But he had a yellow silk handkerchief knotted around his neck and spurs on his boots. "This is a *swell* place, Mother!" he told me at once. "You'll love it!"

Going across to tea at the Burlins', later, was the first really tiresome thing that happened. There was a good deal of bright paint about—yellow and blue—and Paul Burlin's Modernist paintings here and there on the walls. Natalie

Curtis, his wife, was a little old doll that had been left out in the sun and the rain. She had faded yellow hair, cut in a Buster Brown bob, and faded blue eyes. Paul was much younger and looked fresher. He had curly red hair about a round forehead, and the absent, speculative, thoughtful look of an intelligent Jew.

A small woman sat on one of the daybeds, knitting a khaki-colored sweater. She was presented: Mrs. [Alice Corbin] Henderson. She smiled; they all smiled. Maurice smiled. I tried to and couldn't. I felt dead. We had tea and Mrs. Henderson began to talk about Harriet Monroe. Did I know her? I did. She framed words that showed me she and Harriet were coeditors of the *Poetry Magazine*. I didn't care. She told me how many sweaters she had knitted for their Red Cross. I didn't care about that, either. I generally forgot about the war when Maurice let me.

The others were talking about an Indian dance on Christmas Day at Santo Domingo—making plans to go the night before and see the mass at the church at midnight. Quite soon I got up to go and Mrs. Henderson asked me to come to tea at her house the next day. To get out of this—I certainly didn't want to begin going to tea parties out here!—I said, "Well, I think we'll motor up to a place called Taos tomorrow."

"*Taos?* Why?"

"Oh, a friend in New York told me to be sure and see it," I said airily. Someone had—I couldn't remember who, though.

"But *darling*, it's quite hard to go up there, I've heard," began Maurice, plaintively.

"Well, I'm going up to see it anyway," I replied, getting up. They all got up. Maurice looked around at them apologetically behind my back, and then followed me out and across the street.

"Now, look here, Maurice. I don't like it here. All these people! I want to get *away* somewhere. I don't like living on this *street* and going to *tea parties!* You know you'll never work, living like this. I'm going to see what that Taos is like and rent a house there if it's nice. I'm going to find a car and motor up. You needn't go along if you don't want to, but I'm going. Tomorrow."

CHAPTER FOUR

We left the house soon after breakfast the next morning in Mr. Craft's Ford car. The road was narrow and full of frozen ruts and we shook and joggled from one side of the car to the other. The sky was a burning, deep blue over us and my heart rose higher and higher until I was thrilling all over. It seemed to me I had never been happy before just from being in good air and sunshine. Really, it seemed to me, I had never been happy before at all. I felt myself gathered altogether right there with nothing left behind in New York or anywhere else in the world.

"I am Here," I thought, with exultant surprise, and I looked at my hands and rubbed them together, feeling them both cold and warm from winter air and a hurrying heartbeat.

I cannot describe every step of the journey—it would take too long. But by noon, after passing several hamlets and crossing another desert, we reached the opening of a canyon where the Rio Grande ran narrowly between the walls of mountains. Soon after twelve, we crossed the river on an insecure and casual bridge, and drew up at a small, bleak, repellent-looking building. This was Embudo, where the little train of the Denver and Rio Grande Railroad stopped between Taos Junction and Santa Fe, and where the conductor and passengers got out for lunch. A woman brought us something to eat. She had a discontented, put-upon expression, and her dinner was ignoble.

I got outside again as quickly as I could and sat in the car, waiting for the others. It was intensely silent out there without a stirring of anything, and yet I seemed to hear, inside the silence, a high, continuous humming, like a song, and it made me happy. For the first time in my life I heard the world singing in the same key in which my own life inside me had sometimes lifted and poured itself out. But that had always been a solitary thrill before this. Now the world and I were met together in the happiest conjunction. Never had I felt so befriended.

I looked up at the hills that rose on either side of me. They were dotted with dark, deep, green cedars and the pinkish earth showed between. Along the canyon the branches of cottonwood trees were a film of gray lace, tinged with lavender: the most wintry trees I had ever seen. The river moved slowly here, profound and silent. Clumps of red willows melted into the shoreline, and some way up ahead, yellow spires of sandstone suddenly thrust their peaks into the Ionian blue of the sky.

"Holy! Holy! Holy!" I exclaimed to myself. "Lord God Almighty!" I felt a sudden recognition of the reality of natural life that was so strong and so unfamiliar that it made me feel unreal. I caught a fleeting glimpse of my own spoiled and distorted nature, seen against the purity and freshness of these undomesticated surroundings.

We moved along beside the twisting river as best we could over the rutted road. The shadows grew long before we reached the foot of the mountainside where we must turn from the river and climb to reach the tableland of Taos

Valley, whose long, level rim was so far above. As we climbed out of the shadowy depths, and descended again, and climbed again and wended our blind way through the dark trees, the light grew more golden and more fair, until suddenly we reached the top and swung around a curve onto level land: and there we were in a great blaze of sunlight, so mellow and so enveloping that we could see nothing for a moment.

The sun, with a great smile radiating from it, was just at the rim of the faraway horizon, level with our eyes where we paused to look about us. Its rays came to our faces straight and unobstructed across the gulf of the black Rio Grande Canyon over westward. The interminable desert beyond stretched between it and us like a soft, darkened carpet. Over towards the north, a crescent-shaped mountain range curved like an arm around the smooth valley. At its loftiest portion, a mountain shaped along the snowy heights like an Indian bow rested with a vast and eternal composure. The rays of the sinking sun threw its forms into relief and deep indentations and the shapes of the pyramids were shadowed forth in a rosy glow. The mountain sat there beaming—spread out in the bliss of effortless being. The lesser peaks linked themselves to join it; shoulder to shoulder they supported the central, massive curves. There they all waited, snowcapped, glowing like unearthly flowers, a garland of mystery beyond the known world. Not a house in sight! Not a human being! The wide, soft desert sweeping away to the half circle of mountains whose central curve was twenty miles away, its right hand reaching the canyon rim.

Quite soon it was bitterly cold, but fortunately it did not take us too long to reach the village. We wound in and out and reached a dark plaza. It was almost without any lights: quiet, empty, deserted; yet it could not have been more than half-past six or seven o'clock. A long, low building at our right had some lamps shining through the windows.

"The Columbian Hotel," Mr. Craft announced.

We went on inside, while Mr. Craft untied the bags on the rear of the car. "Can we get some rooms here?" I asked.

A stout Mexican woman took us into a huge room that led off from the lobby, a room whose windows were low and opened upon the plaza. Great double beds sprang into view as she lighted the oil lamp; huge, dark cupboards and washstands. "Nice room, no?" inquired the smiling landlady. "Where you come from?"

"Santa Fe!" I answered in an ingratiating voice. "How much is this room?"

"Oh, dollar and half. And meals, too," she replied.

"Are there any houses to rent here?" I asked her.

She looked at me in surprise. "People don't go away from Taos."

I wrinkled my forehead and began to worry.

"Well, I tell you, after supper you go see Doctor. Maybe he know some-body."

"Where does he live? Near?" I perked up.

"Oh, up the street a ways. I show you."

"Now, really, Mabel," began Maurice.

But I swept his words back into his mouth. "I have *decided,* Maurice. You must just trust me. This place has a feeling to it that is just *right*. I know my hunch was a good one—wait and see. There is something *wonderful* here."

[After supper] the landlady went out into the plaza with us and pointed out the way to Doctor's. We could not see much on either side of us: nondescript adobe walls, a dark store on the corner before we turned, then just house walls along the dirt sidewalk, with an occasional light inside behind the drawn curtains.

How to tell of the influence of places upon one, the spellbinding that does not have to come from sight or sound, though maybe smell plays a part in it? Anyway, Taos took me that dark winter night and has held me ever since. I am glad I capitulated in the dark, blindly but full of faith. It was a real conversion, and something accepted on trust—recognized as home.

Now we reached the door with the sign swinging over it: DR. MARTIN. It was a house of total darkness. The flashlight showed a bell on the office door that one twisted round and round. We twisted and twisted before anyone came. We sat down in the ice-cold waiting room. The doctor came in.

"We want to rent a house for the winter," I began firmly.

"What do you want to *do* here?" he asked me curiously.

"My husband is an artist and he wants to paint Indians," I replied, glancing at poor Maurice with a forbidding look. This was understandable, apparently. A look of partial comprehension swept over the doctor's expressive face.

"Well, I'll tell you. There's an old fellow lives next to me here. He has a big house; he might rent you part of it. He's cranky as the devil, but you might persuade him—savvy? Tell him I sent you, get me? Maybe he'll take you and maybe he won't. He don't have to. He's got plenty of money. You go and seem him in the morning. Name's Manby."

CHAPTER FIVE 🖎

We were awakened the next morning by the sound of wagons passing outside in the plaza, and by people going by the windows, talking in Spanish. It didn't seem possible that we were in the United States. Even the room looked foreign to me, with its low ceiling and whitewashed walls. The air was so cold that the water had frozen in the pitcher, and I wondered how we would ever be able to get up and dress. Soon, however, a black-haired child of sixteen knocked and came in, a bundle of firewood in her arms. *"Buenos días, Señora* [good morning, Madam]," she cried, smilingly. In no time she had a roaring fire going in the thin, round stove. A lovely perfume filled the air and warmth crept over us.

Maurice dressed hurriedly and went out to find some coffee for me. Soon the child brought breakfast, in thick, white dishes on a small tray and afterwards I dressed, with my heart beating fast inside me. Everything seemed so thrilling.

When we stepped out into the plaza and looked around, I did feel slightly disappointed. It was not particularly beautiful. Long, low buildings with shops faced with columned portals lined it on three sides, and the bare trees in the center were pinched and shrinking. Only the full, yellow sunlight over all gave it a certain look of richness. Long, wooden bars marked off the square of dusty yellowed grass where the trees grew, and to these were hitched wagons and saddle horses. If the people in Santa Fe had seen only the plaza, they were certainly right in saying there was nothing to Taos. But there was more to it than that, I felt sure. I could feel it coming to me through the air—the gay, compelling charm.

We hurried up to Mr. Manby's house. We hadn't much time, for we had to get an early start for our long day's journey back to Santa Fe. We rang the bell and waited, then rang again. Quick footsteps approached the door; it was opened a crack, and a heavy old, unshaven face appeared. His eyes were rimmed with red and were bloodshot—a most unprepossessing person. He was glowering at me, and I said timidly: "Are you Mr. Manby? Dr. Martin sent us to you. We are looking for a house to rent. Will you rent yours?"

He opened the door and said, "Come inside." And led us into a beautiful little patio. He was dressed in the dirtiest clothes I had ever seen on anyone. Filthy riding trousers and an old gray flannel shirt with a frayed waistcoat under it. His thick neck joined his heavy shoulders like a bull's, and he held his head lowered, looking up slantwise at us like an angry bull. He leaned upon a stout cane, and his whole personality breathed out a dark and bloody anger to the world.

He unlocked each of the long row of rooms that connected with this end of the house. Their doors opened upon the sunny corridor whose glass sides showed the central patio of the house with its trees and shrubs all withered now, and dry. Their large embrasured windows were on the garden side of the house, and they had heavy iron bars upon them like many houses in Italy. These bedrooms were huge and dark. They were furnished with heavy walnut and mahogany beds, ponderous bureaus, and washstands bearing heavy china sets.

He led us out to the garden. It was a great wide place, well laid out in broad paths lined with lilac bushes and bordered with irises. The paths led away in long vistas and at the end of them the mountain loomed blue.

"You see that mountain up there?" He pointed to the big one. "The Indians call that the *sacred* mountain. I could tell you some things about it if I wanted to. It is full of *gold* and *silver,* but those devils won't let anyone prospect up there. . . ."

"But listen—won't you rent this to us?" I interrupted him. I began to turn towards the outside road, slowly leaving. He followed, hitting out at dried garden things viciously with his cane.

"Hum! I'd have to have a very good rent, you know. It means a lot of trouble for me, getting it ready and all. And losing my privacy," he added, looking hatefully at Maurice.

"What do you *call* a good rent?" Maurice asked in a particularly cautious tone.

"Well, I would have to have seventy-five dollars a month, and for not less than six months."

"Six *months!* Who knows where we'll be in six months!" exclaimed Maurice. Little, indeed, did *he* know! I must have known more than he did, for it seemed perfectly certain to me that I wanted it for that length of time, and I cried: "All right! We'll take it. We'll go back to Santa Fe and we'll come back here on the first of January, and we'll live *right here* until the end of August!"

"Dar-r-r-ling!" exclaimed Maurice with a desperate look.

Mr. Manby tried to wither him with a glare of distaste. "Are you *German,* may I ask?" he inquired coldly.

"Russian," I offered hastily.

Taos village ended at Mr. Manby's place. There was only one other house beyond his, an ugly square wooden one painted gray. Beyond it there was a crossroad, with a graveyard at the corner, and in it the graves were marked with white and pale blue crosses—a very pretty cemetery! After this, empty fields bordered the road and we were in open country. Not desert, however: the land was cultivated and the brown, plowed earth looked opulent. The pale stalks of corn yellowed some places, but in others the land lay bare and dark and warm. Clumps of soft, rose-colored willows showed here and there like the glow of a gentle fire marking the creek that flowed down from the mountain.

Now there seemed to be a mild happiness pervading this land. The sun made everything luminous, and bathed the earth and the trees in a high light that brought out all the subtle winter tones. I had never seen so much color anywhere before this in December—not even in Italy. There were pale yellows and pinks and mauves, and dark shades of wine and bistre. Everything glowed and pulsated; the usual immobility of the dormant months was prefaced here by a gentle vibrating life, and the blue sky overhead, showing between the bare branches of the lacy trees, was of the most ineffable transparence instead of being hard and opaque.

We finally came along close to the mountain. It swept away above us, and there at the foot of it was the Pueblo, guarded by its heavy, green magnificence. On either side of a sparkling brown stream that rushed down from a canyon on the right were two piles of brown cubes, like children's building blocks, that rose in pyramidal-shaped masses, like the things I used to build when I was a child, or like a design by Gordon Craig.

The two big community houses were standing there in a smooth, clear space of earth, absolutely stark and undecorated, as economical as beehives, with little square holes for windows, but no window frames, plain doorways, and with many ladders, hand-hewn out of trees, leaning against the walls at all levels from one roof to another, so that the people who lived away up at the top must climb half a dozen of them to reach their houses. Now, strange to say, although the village seemed austere and certainly anything but domestic, yet one got a feeling of home from it. The very essence of it was of the home. Why? I do not know. That was the feeling it gave out richly. A stab of longing and of nostalgia went through me like lightning.

"Earthworks, aren't they?" I turned to Maurice and saw that he was quite excited.

"Why, it is *wonderful*—those pyramids composed of cubes! How mystical! And that mountain back of it—entirely made up of triangles! It will be wonderful to paint."

As we reached the little adobe church at the entrance to the village, I looked back and saw two Indians wrapped in white sheets standing upon one of the higher roofs. They had their heads together and they were looking after our little car. All of a sudden I had a realization of the illimitable distance between us and them—and of something powerful but quite undefined that shut us off from each other. It was as though the Pueblo had an invisible wall around it, separating the Indians from the world we knew—a wall that kept their life safe within it, like a fire that cannot spread. "How self-contained it seems," I thought, "and how contented it feels!" I mused to myself. "I wish I belonged in there!"

CHAPTER SIX 🐚

The next day was the day before Christmas and we were on our way over to Santo Domingo Pueblo in the little Ford car that we engaged with the Burlins to take us there and leave us, and then to return for us. It seemed a long, tiring trip, for the road south was rough and sandy, and a cold wind blew the fine grains into our eyes so that we had to keep our heads down against it. But between whiles I stole glances at the beautiful, mysterious landscape we were passing through. Out of the level desert over to the left rose a group of little hills, flat and blue and suave like those in da Vinci backgrounds, and farther beyond them stretched the distant desert with a high range of purple mountains against the sky. Like peaceful islands they seemed to float, these small hills with a quavering outline, upon a great green sea, and the same earthly sea surged up gradually behind them to the mountainous horizon. There was no disturbance in the scene, nothing to complicate the forms, no trees or houses, or any detail to confuse one. It was like a simple phrase in music or a single line of poetry, essential and reduced to the barest meaning.

I had a sudden intuition right then that here in this country life could come to one more concretely than in other places, and that meanings that were shut up in words and phrases out in the world could incorporate themselves in living forms and move before one. Ideas here might clothe themselves in form and flesh, and word-symbols change into pictured, living realities.

I heard the singing and drumming as soon as we reached the Pueblo, and it drew me strongly and I left the others and ran hurriedly towards it with my heart beating. Eighty or ninety elderly men stood close together around a great drum, singing, with eyes that seemed to look, but to be looking inward. They produced a volume of sound that was the glad solemn voice of the tribe, and at the same time it was like the wind that rose and fell above us. This secure and sumptuous music was not, as with our orchestras and chorals, the expression of one man, drawn from one heart and rendered by the obedient many to tell his experience: it was the expression of many, told altogether.

For the first time in my life, then, I heard the voice of the One coming from the Many—I who until then had been taught to look for the wonders of infinite divisibility and variety, for the many in the one, the elaboration and detail of a broken infinity. My world, all through my life, had been made of parts ever increasingly divided into more intricate and complex fractions. By our contemplation of pieces of things we had grown to believe that the part is greater than the whole, and so division had motivated all the activities of people I had known, of books I had read, of music I had heard, and of pictures I had seen.

The singular raging lust for individuality and separateness had been impelling me all my years as it did everyone else on earth—when all of a sudden I was brought up against the Tribe, where a different instinct ruled, where a different knowledge gave a different power from any I had known, and where virtue lay in wholeness instead of in dismemberment. So when I heard that great Indian chorus singing for the first time, I felt a strong new life was present there enfolding me.

Oh, fellow mortals out there in the world! Until you learn how to join together once more, to fuse your sorrowful and lonely hearts in some new communion, you can never make true music. The sounds you produce will continue to be but the agonized expression, called "modern," of separate and unshared life, the wistful, sorrowing complaint of individualism before it has reached the new communal level for which it has been creating itself. Until then, science, science, science—but less and less life. But afterwards—magic again: magical power instead of scientific power. When will the time for it arrive? When will we get together again and make a happy sound?

We form dancing classes, we try to do things in groups, we strive for a group consciousness, trying to raise our vibrations to greater heat by some means or other, desperate, like cold flies at the end of the solar year, crawling separately up the frigid, unfriendly walls of our cooling spiritual universe. But it is all no good. We have reached the last outpost of the warm and loving world of our kind of relationships. Our solar year is ending. We will give out and fall to the floor of the world and be swept away. Some such thoughts as these ran through my head as I watched the Indians dance through the hours.

But though my thoughts were rather dismal and envious, I was surprised to find how I felt after it was over, after it had ended in a sumptuous accelerated outpouring of forces, the dancers beating out the dance in two joined groups, to the drums and voices of two choruses who were singing contrapuntally. I felt made over. Renewed, refreshed, filled with life. Sometimes, after a deep sleep in fresh air, one awakes restored and full of unjustifiable hope—ready for inexpressible undertakings. The day in the Pueblo had given me a sense of new life, like sleep can give.

I looked at Maurice and I saw he felt it, too.

"It's wonderful, isn't it?" he said. "How it smoothens one out!"

The characteristic I liked best in Maurice was his ability to feel things, and to benefit by them, and even to know he was doing so. No, he was not so dead or so ruined as others I knew.

"Yes," I answered him. "It's marvelous. And it's hidden here where no one knows it! Why, if people knew about what is here, they'd rush upon it and simply eat it up. And there's no one here except just us! Why, that's extraordinary. I hope no one discovers it!"

"Why?" asked Paul Burlin, who overheard me.

"Why?" I repeated, staring at him in amazement. "Why? Do you want to see it eaten up?"

"Oh, I don't know what you mean by that. I think an art form like this should be known to the world, so people could enjoy it. There's no question of this being eaten up, as you say—"

"Yes, there is, too. This isn't an art form. It's much more than that. It's a living religion—it's alive like the Greek religion was alive before it became an art form and died out! Heavens! If people come in here—don't you see?—they'd grab all this and commercialize it somehow. As soon as religion is commercialized it has turned into an art form! Commercial value is the standardized, accepted foundation of acknowledged art. It is recognition! I'd *hate* to have these Indians get recognition! Why, it would be the end of them!"

"Well, I'm going over to Geronimo's to see if I can get some songs," broke in Natalie Curtis, who was bent upon her book of Indian music, and we followed along.

CHAPTER SEVEN ✑

John and I went up to Taos alone, for Maurice took so long to pack all his paints and paraphernalia I couldn't wait. Leaving orders at stores in Santa Fe, I expected boxes of provisions to come up to us every week, for I felt one wouldn't be able to buy *any*thing up in that village, far away from the railroad. I even ordered dry things, like coffee and sugar and cereals! It seemed to me that I was going into the wilderness and leaving the world behind me, and I loved that, for it was a new thing to feel.

Manby let us in, helped us with our bags and bundles, helped us light lamps and fires, for the house was cold as death as we came into our end of it through the thick side entrance door of the garden. In a short time, though, it came all alive. When I had the kitchen stove burning and potatoes and eggs and bacon frizzling upon it, we were Home!

While we sat there together alone, Manby having at last taken himself away into his own quarter with a baleful smile over his shoulder, I suddenly said to John: "I want to cut my hair off! I've always wanted to! Let's do it now! Can you do it for me?"

"Sure, I can," he exclaimed joyfully. He had always like to brush and comb it, to twist it into different shapes. I fetched scissors, and a mirror that I propped up on the table in front of me.

"Just straight around—just below the ears. . . ."

He clipped and clipped excitedly, and laid the long brown tresses in a pile. "I love doing this!" he murmured.

Soon it was all off. Straight across my eyebrows, then down a few inches and hanging heavily over my ears in an angular bob. I had no precedent for this kind of haircut. No one I knew or ever saw wore short hair like this, but I remembered Maxfield Parrish illustrations and medieval pages. That was the way I wanted it to feel, and that was the way it looked when it was finished. I tossed it back and forth and felt the satisfactory swing and freedom of it.

Like everything in my life since early days, this new phase was all a story-book to me, but these few months I am about to tell of are the last ones that had that fictitious feeling, as though things were happening around me but not to me. This book must first tell a little about the people who were there in Taos, who lived on the fringe of that other life that was esoteric and un-knowable to them. But this Taos village was not then more real for me, did not belong to me any more than the Buffalo world, or the Florentine world, or the New York and Croton worlds had. It was fantastic and funny and parts of it were delicious. The light and the air in those high regions were solemnly beautiful, but the people who lived in that beneficence were like the money changers in the temple.

Few were there except to make something out of the Indians, and the village had grown up on the outskirts of the Pueblo upon land stolen from them and settled by priests, traders, merchants, and finally artists. Even the pretty blue-and-white courthouse held no title for the land it stood upon, and no one had a title that had any real validity. There was no foundation to anything, no rights, no roots, and no security in Taos village. There was no law, no reverence, and very little beauty of living. But the small population thought it was real. They were spending their lives gathering enough money to remain on land that was not theirs, in a country that lacked everything they considered most desirable.

CHAPTER EIGHT

The Mexicans in Taos Valley seemed a sad lot to me when I first came. Apparently they hadn't much gaiety. They looked pinched, discouraged, and baffled. Their forefathers had come here ages ago and nothing much had happened to them since except conquests, so it seemed as though the most they had accomplished had been to keep alive. They are almost all of mixed Indian and Spanish blood, except for a few families.

It was so short a time ago that this whole country in the Southwest was a part of Mexico, and these Mexicans the slaves and soldiers of Spanish over-lords, that the resignation of defeat may linger yet in their blood along with the hatred and fear of the white American conqueror, who came eighty years ago. These feelings, and, added to them, a half-contemptuous, half-envious regard for the Indians, who have kept themselves to themselves through every-thing from the Spanish conquest and on through the American conquest, these dreary feelings seemed to me to rule them and sap their vitality and their hope.

But it was not long before I became attached to these people and enjoyed being with them, for they had a wistful pleasure in small things like the plant in the window and the handwork upon bright woven serapes or crocheted rugs. Whenever one entered their houses there was a welcome there. They were simple and brave and capable of enjoyment, possessing a quick humor and a warmth that was lacking in the more dispirited "Anglos," as they called the white people. They were capable of passionate loyalties once they became one's friends, and there was a thin, rugged tenacity about them that humanized and dignified their lives.

There seemed to be a happiness in the Mexican life, due to the Penitente exorcisms, wherein they flayed themselves, unconsciously perhaps, to dimin-ish the accumulated bitterness and despair that they could not pour out upon us. They came out of these ceremonies apparently refreshed. Turned inwards upon themselves, they drew their own blood, identifying themselves with Jesus Christ, who died for them, and who is still dying for them, in their flesh.

Their social and political life is still entangled with religion. Their Catholi-cism is violent and their violence is catholicized, and since the preponderance of the population in this part of the state is Mexican, the vote is a Penitente vote. Their *bailes* [dances] on Saturday nights frequently end in bloodshed, and the ensuing trials are decided by Mexican juries who rarely convict one of their own race. Even penitentiary sentences are usually remitted after a few years by the pressure Mexicans can bring to bear in this state upon those in office. Though they have a kind of power, they don't know yet what to do with it, how to pass laws that will lift their standards, or how to secure schools that will ultimately improve their conditions when their children are grown. The education handed out to them in the local public schools is unenlight-ened and it seems more calculated to keep them in ignorance than to raise them out of the darkness they exist in.

The churches were originally built like the Indians built their houses, with ceilings supported on huge pine beams, from which the bark was peeled when it was green. The Ranchos church has always belong to the community where it stands. There it squats, its massive rear heavily buttressed, painted a hundred times by the artists who have lived here and by visiting ones, its roof still leaking after cloudbursts, but as handsome as the day it was built. Only inside it, the Mexicans tore out a hand-carved balcony, and one day Bobby Jones found the pieces lying on the floor and brought some of them home in a wagon— and we built them into the big gates of our house.

When Bobby came he was spellbound by the leaning and irregular lines of adobe architecture, and the crooked crosses, all askew. He was, for a time, impressed by the curious powerful influences that linger around the Mexican Penitente *moradas,* those private chapels standing in remote spots, windowless and windswept, where unimaginable effluences escape into freedom. After his first visit here, he returned to New York and produced *Macbeth,* a semiabstract construction that made audiences feel faint and ill, that made Dr. Jelliffe himself stagger out of the theater, exclaiming: "But this is murder!" *Till Eulenspiegel,* at the Metropolitan Opera House with its fantastic towers and houses leaning and bowing towards each other, came out of Taos, too, after that visit.

CHAPTER NINE ✍

The day after we were settled in the dark, warm interior of Manby's house, John drove Maurice and me out to the Pueblo. I wanted to see the Indians, to know them, for, as they passed up and down the road outside the house all day long on their hard-bitten, gaunt ponies, I searched their faces and tried to penetrate their infinitely unfamiliar souls. But I could not. They seemed to have a barrier raised between themselves and the world—my world, anyway. Their eyes were not empty, but they were distant in expression. Sometimes cold, and sometimes smiling, but though they were alive and glowing, they seemed to keep a distance between us.

I took a bag of oranges out with me, for I had heard somewhere that one could ingratiate oneself with small presents like that. Just inside the Pueblo, across from the little Catholic church, there was a group of houses that looked less blank than some of the others. The doors were open, and when we stopped to decide what to do and where to go, a couple of small children ran up to us in a friendly way. Then a beautiful woman stepped to one of the open doors. She was full-breasted and her black cotton dress, sprigged with white, was brought in at the waist by a broad, red, woven belt that was wound twice around her and tucked in, so that it supported her deep bosom like a corset, and below it, the full skirt hung stiffly away from her, trim and rotund, while an inch or two of white embroidery showed underneath the ample folds.

She had a warm smile on her small, perfect face, and her eyes were dark and warm and amused. I got out of the car and just naturally went towards her and the others followed. Determined to make a good impression, I reached out to her from inside myself, and smiled a hesitant appeal as I approached her: but no hunter was ever more calculating, or ready to sprinkle salt on a tail approached unawares.

Near the door, I stopped, for I heard a low singing and the soft beat of a drum, and I became deprecating. But she made a smooth, round gesture with her small hand and murmured, *"Entre!"* in a voice that was low and rich and deep-toned.

Over the threshold and we were in a large, bare room with whitewashed walls that had along their base rows of rolled mattresses covered with white sheets and colored blankets. The room went far in and was shadowy at the end, but near the entrance, a bright fire burned and perfumed the air with wood incense, and sunshine came in at the door. There was a tiny little window in the left-hand wall, without glass and only thin bars of wood between it and the outer air. This little window, set high up in the thick adobe, let a beam of light come streaming in across the room, and suddenly reminded me of the window in the bedroom at Pierrefonds Castle, where Violet and I slept together.

A man sat beside the fireplace on a low wooden hassock. A thin, gray blanket came over his shoulders and fell in folds around his moccasined feet, and he tapped lightly on a little water drum that rested on the floor between his knees. He was singing in a low, faraway murmur, and his eyes were on the drum, his head bent so I could not see his face at first, and he didn't look up, even when we came crowding in, the three of us.

The woman motioned to the low, white bedrolls with a gesture that was grave and quiet and respectful to the song, and we tiptoed in and sat, in an atmosphere that was new to me. The room was impregnated with a fullness of life. It had a rich, slow peacefulness without being in any way solemn. Maybe the drumming and the song gave a measure in which one could relax and spread one's breathing fuller and deeper, maybe the deep being of these people enriched their surrounding air. Anyway, whatever it was, I had never felt more satisfied and at ease, although my attention was set upon trying to fit in and be a part of it without seeming to try.

I knew I could arrive at this unconscious, full equilibrium, but that I could only do so by adapting myself. I longed to simply *be* so, as they were, but I knew I must make it for myself as I went along. Not for me, alas, the simple, unthinking harmonies of life, but for me—yes! I thought fiercely—this sumptuous peace and content, this sunny gravity and fiery perfume in whitewashed walls at any cost, at any sacrifice.

And as I was thinking so, the man stopped singing and raised his head and looked at me for the first time, with a quick glance that penetrated to the depths with an instantaneous recognition, and I saw his was the face that had blotted out Maurice's in my dream—the same face, the same eyes, involuntarily intense, with the living fire in their depths. He bowed slightly, faintly patronizing.

"I sang you a little song," he said gently.

"Thank you ever so much!" I answered, feeling really deprecating now, and not having to pretend. "Would you like an orange?" I asked him timidly, and offered him one. He bowed again and took it graciously.

Maurice, trying to be sociable, said, "What are the words in that song?"

"Got no words. Just song," he replied coldly, becoming aloof and keeping his eyes on the orange as though he would not injure them with the sight of us.

The woman got up and altered the stiff moment by placing a stick of wood on the diminishing fire, so I got up, too, and said we must be going, and the others followed my example. I walked up to the man and held out my hand and said: "Thank you! I wish you'd come and see us down in Taos."

He said, "I seen you before, already," and he gave me another glance, swift and passing, but deep in the eyes, so that something vivid was etched into both of us.

I hated to go out the door and leave that good and lively feeling behind me in the room, for not in any room I have ever made and lived in had I achieved such a plentiful and active sense of living. Not with Genoese velvets and Renaissance chairs, nor with the repercussion of dangerous ideas fearlessly told, nor by any manner of means had I ever come so near before to the possibilities of abundant life, as in that empty place where firelight played upon bare walls and the air was sweet with woodsmoke, while some man unfathomably unknown to me, yet immediately recognizable, beat upon a small drum and sang a little song.

A few days later we stood in the gray air of the Pueblo darkened by thickly falling snowflakes. Several hundred Indians clad only in deerskins padded up and down in two long lines, bent forward on the deer sticks they carried in their hands. They uttered harsh animal groans and yelps as they followed the two implacable women who led them. The two women danced backwards with masklike faces and eyes downcast. They were majestic in their ancient Indian dress, and utterly compelling in their irresistible female way. They carried small pine branches upheld in each hand, and they shook them slightly to the rhythm of the chorus of singers. The snow fell quietly and unnoticed upon the deer people, who were naked save for the hides that were belted around them. They bore the heads of newly killed deer upon their own, their identities blotted out beneath the branching antlers. Among them, little boys were hidden beneath the skins of fox and wolf and mountain lion. All the beasts that came from the forest seemed spellbound by the magical women.

The power of the tribe was invested in the two women who gently danced before the helpless creatures, leading them to their doom. An old—perhaps the oldest—allegory was confronting us there. The feminine principle is the strongest one in nature—and the wild animal must follow where it leads, must be sacrificed, assimilated, and converted into a new energy.

"Marvelous!" exclaimed Maurice as he stamped into the house. "These Indians have a real art of their own."

But it was their life that seemed so real to me every time I got near enough to it to feel it. Real, real, and deep as fate, and full of wisdom and experience.

CHAPTER TEN 🕊

Soon a couple of women friends came to stay with us. They drove up from Embudo on Oscar Davis's stage and arrived late in the evening, because the car had broken down somewhere along the rough canyon road. Julia [Alice Thursby] was gibbering with delight. She was the nervous kind of woman who welcomed trouble because it was an outlet.

The next day I took them out to the Pueblo and as I saw the Indian woman I knew in the doorway of her house, I drew them over there. We went in and it was all as it was before. The man was singing beside the fire. When we left, Agnes [Pelton] said: "Your friend has beautiful eyelids!" I knew what she meant. His downcast eyes were nobly shaped under the three-cornered, veiling lids. The face was like a noble bronze—rather full and ample, with a large nose and a generous mouth. When we were going out the door, he gave us each a handshake and said he would come and see us someday. Like the first time, I carried away a sense of deeper being and more easy breathing. I began to be happy, then, in January.

The sun moved across the valley all day long, circling the house that was the new center of my life, and fell early, with blinding rays of purple and red as it sank below the faraway horizon. After five o'clock, when it would be gone, the sky showed a long, narrow bank of rose and yellow, just above the dimmed blue-white distance. The winter evening came quickly all about us in the village street, even while the west held its color for a long time. Then there was a magical, hushed feeling in the air and people's voices, out-of-doors, dropped to a lower key in unconscious reverence for nightfall.

Once, at this twilight hour, I came in the adobe archway that held the garden gate, after I had been to the post office for the evening mail, for I had the lifelong habit of letters and I still believed that sometime the letter would come that would make all the difference. I had three letters in my hand, but none of them was it.

I passed along the path beside the long house on my way to our entrance door, and as I moved in the cold, creaking snow, my heart began to beat tumultuously for no reason. I looked behind me, and then I saw a figure standing motionless at one side of the path down by the gate, under a tall, round lilac bush. Like a still column, he stood there swathed from head to foot in a dim gray blanket that covered all but the dark eyes that stared through the dusk. He faded into the surrounding gray evening and he seemed as immovable as the earth, and only came alive in the glance he bent upon me as I returned to where he was.

"You not see me if I don't want you to," he said gently. "I can come and go and if I don't want you to, you can't know it." It was half in joke, but half serious, too.

"Come inside," I said, "and get warm."

He sat down in a large chair beside the fire and never said another word. I took off my coat and hat and fidgeted around the way one does, making a lot of motions. I turned the lamp up higher, opened the door into the kitchen because I knew Anita [Mabel's servant] was there, shut it again, and finally came back to the fire. He had pushed the gray blanket off his head and it coiled around his throat like a wrapped toga.

"Will you stay for supper with us?" I asked him timidly. And he replied briefly: "All right."

We all sat down and conversation was started. "I think Taos is beautiful!" Julia broached. "Is the winter very long here?"

"Long enough to make summer. Got to have winter. And snow. Then everything come right."

Then Agnes said, "You have a fine mountain. Do you hunt up there?"

"Boys hunt when we want meat. Fishing pretty good, too, in summer. Do you like that mountain?" he asked, turning to me.

"Oh, yes!"

"I take you up there when summer comes."

Maurice came in, stamping his new black boots.

"Maurice, this is Tony." I saw his thoughts as they ran through his brain. "This is my chance," he was thinking.

"How do you do?" he said, and smiled.

"All right," Tony replied.

"I am almost ready to work! And now I need a good model. Can you recommend one of your friends to come and pose for me?"

"Some will and some not like to. I ask Pete. She used to work at some artists."*

"She?" queried Maurice, obtusely, I thought.

"Yes. She very nice-lookin' boy and artists like him."

"Oh!" answered Maurice.

"Well, let's eat supper." I hastened to the table and they all gathered round.

CHAPTER ELEVEN

The weeks passed. Maurice was working on a bust of Pete, a Buddhistic-looking young Indian who slept on the model stand, much to the artist's irritation, but the head and shoulders, modeled in black wax, grew daily more solid and suave. Two long braids came down on either side of the strong neck, the eyelids drooped, [and] there was a slight smile on the voluminous countenance.

Occasionally large wooden boxes were delivered to us, containing groceries from Santa Fe. These were unpacked in the stable yard at the far end of our part of the house, and stored in an empty pantry. But we were growing tired of Anita's unvaried cooking and I was unable to teach her anything, for I had not learned to cook anything more complicated than beefsteaks and eggs. Then we heard that Dasburg and Bobby Jones were coming to visit us in answer to my enthusiastic letters about the simple, beautiful, remote valley, and I wired them: "Bring a cook with you."

Julia and Agnes had gone, now, Julia promising to return later in the spring. Andrew and Bobby drove up from Embudo on Oscar Davis's touring-car stage, and they had a pale, gentlemanly stranger with them whom they introduced as William von Seebach [who claimed to be the nephew of General von Seebach]. He was the cook.

Maurice and Andrew had a map of Europe pinned to the wall of the living room, and every evening they discussed the progress of the armies and stuck little pins into it to mark the advances. They were quite pro-German, and wholly free to admit it in their talk in this outpost of the world. As for myself, I maintained the broad-minded attitude I had tried to keep since the war started, and to remain impartial and uninvolved in the wartime manias. The Germans were just another people to me, I thought, and the war a stupid misery.

Gradually I began to know people in the village. There was Mr. [Bert] Phillips, across the road, who was one of the first artists to come to Taos. He was a small, worried- looking man with a long, straight nose and kind brown eyes.

*Many Indian languages have an all-purpose third-person pronominal (he-she-it-they) that sometimes resulted in reversed gender designations when translated into English.

He and Manby had not spoken for years, though they were constantly meeting each other. They had developed a feud because when Mr. Manby planted the long avenue of cottonwood trees along the road, Mr. Phillips had also planted some along the stretch that passed his house. But *he* had planted the female cottonwoods and in the autumn all the air in the neighborhood was full of the white fuzz. Mr. Phillips was married to Dr. Martin's sister, and he had a boy and a girl about John's age. Around the corner from his house on the side street lived the Bateses. He had been one of the mounted police somewhere in Canada, a young tough with a baby face, married to a woman older than he, short, plump, with pale, protruding eyes and the look of reformed dissipation.

The village seemed to live on feuds. Almost everyone had some kind of cherished hate for someone else. There were the two stage drivers, Oscar Davis and John Dunn. One drove to Embudo station, and the other to Taos Junction, but they did not speak. Oscar was handsome in an Irish way, with black hair and merry blue eyes, large bony features, and an attractive look to him, but John was immeasurably tall and lean, with a drooping tobacco-stained mustache and melancholy eyes. He had a Yankee drawl that came out through his nose and he emphasized it because it made people laugh. He was a character— but so was everybody here.

CHAPTER THIRTEEN

Never had I known a spring to awaken with such a sweet violence as it did in Taos Valley—after weeks of sunny rigidity while the earth was either hard and white, or hard and brown, then suddenly something happened. From one hour to another a sort of heaving and the change came. There was breathing in the valley, all over the valley, in fields, in flesh, in people, in cattle, in birds, and probably in the gay fish flickering in the rivers. Now all the larks were singing on the fence posts, and in the pastures the shaggy, ungainly bulls struggled to mount the passive cows.

It was not really so long before the plows were cutting open the wet steaming furrows and there was a smell of flowers in every breath and breeze. Hastily the spring dug and delved among the tissues of earth and the men and beasts upon it. It made the hearts in all of these species to swoon and bound again, and the blood was renewed and freshened on its course. All over the valley the coupling went on to an accompaniment of singing birds, and a delirium of bleating, mooing, whinnying, and barking. The perfume of spring caused a madness in the nerves that was stronger than all caution and restraint. A girl was raped in a nearby village . . . a boy was knifed in Peñasco; all through Lent the Penitentes gathered in the *moradas* and sang on the roads to Calvary Friday nights.

Each of us in that house was happy in our own way. Maurice was a sculptor at last. He saw the Indians in the round, plastic fullness of another medium than paint. Wax, clay, plasticine occupied him all day long, while Pete dozed on the stand before him.

"Really, da-a-rling—you were right, I believe. . . ."

Andrew had started hunting, an instinct that awakened in him every once in a while, made him breathless, eyes darkened, fully engaged. He hunted the old santos painted on hand-hewn boards that we had discovered soon after we came to Taos. No one had ever noticed them except to laugh, but here was an authentic primitive art, quite unexploited. We were, I do believe, the first people who ever bought them from the Mexicans, and they were so used to them and valued them so little, they sold them to us for small sums, varying from a quarter to a dollar; on a rare occasion, a finer specimen brought a dollar and a half, but this was infrequent. The naivete of the santos was of the most genuine kind, their wistfulness utterly touching. They were pressed out of nowhere by inarticulate and untutored men in their extreme need for something to answer their religious needs, something to hang their love upon, something tangible that would picture the inner image.

Andrew was soon absorbed in saint hunting. He managed to hire an old horse and buggy, and he went all round the valley, looking for them. He became ruthless and determined, and he bullied the simple Mexicans into selling their saints, sometimes when they didn't want to. He grew more and more excited by the chase, so that the hunt thrilled him more than what he found, and he always needed more money to buy new santos. I usually bought from him each night some of the ones he did not care for, so those and the ones I found for myself made a real collection before long. I had them in our house for years, until I gave them to the Harwood Foundation, for I finally came to feel they should be kept together and never leave this country where they were born.

It was Andrew who started a market for them, and people began to want them and buy them, and I was always giving one or two away to friends who took them east where they looked forlorn and insignificant in sophisticated houses. People always *thought* they wanted them, though, and soon the stores had a demand for them. Stephen Bourgeois finally had a fine exhibition of them in his gallery. All this makes them cost seventy-five, a hundred, or two hundred dollars today.

On one of the first false spring days that come sometimes in March, William encountered Manby on the lawn. I was unfortunately in the rear of the house, where we lived, and the lawn was near the front fence, so I missed the preliminaries. But afterwards, William said he said: "Good morning, Mr. Manby."

And Mr. Manby said: "Don't speak to me, you goddamned Hun!"

That afternoon Maurice was summoned to the house of the ex-mounted-policeman Bates to meet an inspector from Albuquerque, who, we were told, had come to investigate us. Maurice looked so helpless that I went with him.

"Well?" I said.

"Well, lady, a report has been sent to our office about your household, and I was delegated to come up here and look into the matter. You are suspected of pro-German activities. It is said you are receiving arms and ammunition almost weekly in large boxes and storing them in your house, that one member of your family is going among the Mexican population and enrolling them, that you, lady, are inciting the Indians to rise. . . ."

I was amused and I was mad and I was also scared, for I knew what a village like this one could do to us if it were allowed to get going. "Well, what is the idea?" I asked, smiling in a friendly way. "What are we supposed to be doing all this for?"

"Why, this is the gate to Colorado and the rest of the states, up this Rio Grande canyon," he answered.

"The gate for whom?" I cried, not understanding.

"For Mexico!" exclaimed both the Bateses and the inspector simultaneously, in a great burst.

I broke out laughing loudly. "Well, really! So we are arranging an invasion, are we? Well, listen. The boxes we receive are filled with groceries, the member of our household who is visiting the Mexicans daily is collecting old paintings, and I, I am sorry to say, instead of inciting the Indians to rise am teaching them to knit! Furthermore, I should like you to know that my stepfather is Rear Admiral Reeder, several of my relatives are majors and colonels in the army, and I demand an immediate apology from your office for this ridiculous accusation! I shall report you immediately to Washington for stupidity, for libelous accusations, and for invading our privacy upon insufficient evidence. Who turned in this ridiculous report, that's what I want to know. Who did it?"

"Lady, we don't know. It came in a roundabout way."

"Oh, there's been a lot of talk going around here," Bates broke in, blusteringly. "They say you got that German cook that ain't no cook, and that he's putting up provisions for the future. You got one of them war maps in the house, and it's the German armies you watch. Don't you *know* we been watch-

ing you? Besides, people heard you all talking. . . . Don't you know, when those
lady visitors you had went away, Judge Moore went along with 'em in Oscar's
car and opened that there box at the station they took along before they got
on the train?"

"Oh, I see," I said frigidly to Bates. "You've been watching us, have you?
And this 'investigation' is the climax! Do you know who that friend of mind
was, whose bags you had examined? It was the sister of B——." Already his name
was one to conjure with in America. "Well," I went on, "we'll have another investigation soon. We'll have this inspector inspected, and these smart investi-
gators investigated. We'll go home now, and if you care to come and search our
house, you're at liberty to do so!"

"Lady, I guess we just made a big mistake!" The inspector seemed quite
crumpled now.

We walked across the muddy road and into the house, and Maurice was
looking rather queer. I marched up to that map and pulled out the little flags
and threw them on the floor. Then I sat down and wrote a letter to the War
Department in Washington; just tossed it into the air to fall to earth, I knew
not where. But it had George Creel's name on it!

"As for the inspector . . . I heard he lost his job," said Mr. Manby. "Another
incompetent." I never let him know that I knew that he had started the whole
thing, and that *he* had done a lot of "inciting" among our neighbors. He never
realized how much I knew of all his underground treacheries.

CHAPTER FIFTEEN 🍃

One night Mr. Phillips brought some people to call on us. They were English,
and the woman was nice looking, though she had restless brown eyes and her
smile was held up at the corners determinedly. The man was tall and attractive, with a very youthful air. They had been in Taos only a day and had fallen
in love with it: one of those instantaneous affinities that happen occasionally.
We saw each other sometimes after that; Jack Young-Hunter had a longing to
know the Indians, which had been awakened in him when he was a little boy
in London and Buffalo Bill had taken his circus over there.

It wasn't long before Jack began to talk about buying a little piece of land
here, for he thought this valley was the most beautiful place he had ever been
in. One day Tony said to him: "I show you a place quite near to here—east.
Nicest place, I think."

So we three went together and Tony led us back beyond the house and along
the curving, tree-lined avenue. We walked across a low-dipping field of alfalfa
and up over a wide, dry ditch to the big cottonwood tree. Tony said: "This is

the nicest place I know 'cept the Pueblo. Little bit high up, good air, and you see all over."

"Oh, yes! This is a lovely place," Jack murmured. "I like that little house with those apple trees in front." He pointed to the two-roomed adobe a little distance away to the south, along the level space above the curving ditch line. "There is another big tree over there, too."

"That the place I thought for you," said Tony, leading us towards it over the bare ground. "Jack going to buy over there, and you going to buy here."

I laughed aloud. The idea attracted me, and at the same time frightened me a little, too.

"What do I want a house for?" I queried, wondering at him.

"Don't you want a studio?" Tony asked seriously. "I thought all Americans have to have studios. The field and the apples go with this last house. That why I like it," said Tony.

Heavens! Did he think *I* wanted an alfalfa field and some apple trees? Well, perhaps I did.

"That Mexican want fifteen hundred dollars for all this," he said, waving his hand. "Pretty good house. Good piece of land."

"Well . . ." I hesitated.

"Never mind. Don't have to decide today. That Mexican, he named Tru-jillo; they call him old Chimayo; he my friend. He live there with his sons and grandchildren. We come and talk some other time. First Jack buy this place, then you."

When we were at supper that night, I said suddenly, "I believe I'll buy a little piece of land here and have a studio of my own."

Maurice looked up quickly. "We aren't going to stay here forever," he said. "I have to get back east by August, anyway."

"Well, maybe I'll stay on," I said noncommittally.

I kept thinking about the big tree and how nice it would be to rest under it in the summer and drink the nice water from the stream. Tony didn't say anything more to me about buying it, but while he helped Jack secure the other little house, the idea of it worked in me.

CHAPTER SIXTEEN 🖎

Now when the spreading apple tree in the center of the lawn was white with blossoms, I asked Tony to make a dance in the garden and I invited all the Taos people I knew to come to it. I asked them for tea, not for an Indian dance, and the Indians were asked for a dance, not for a tea! I did not conceal the charac-ter of the occasion from these people. I didn't realize at all that they were not accustomed to meet "socially" as it is called, and that never before this time had the Indians danced at anyone's place in town.

Later, I found out what a strong line of demarcation was drawn between the Americans and the Indians who lived so short a distance from each other but in different worlds, and that this separation was as acceptable to one group as the other. The Indians, I knew, had friends among the artists for whom they posed for twenty-five cents an hour, and they had friends among the merchants where they spent their small earnings or traded their grains for groceries, but any deep confident intimacy or understanding was quite absent between them. There was a varying scale of vague distrust that arose from the great difference in their values and that made them mutually unable to get at each other. Perhaps Mr. Manby's conception expressed the most antisocial viewpoint to Indians in this valley, "You have to watch 'em every minute, thieving rascals," and likewise Candelaria's [Tony's wife] dictum when the flu broke out among the Americans and Mexicans the following January. "That is *theirs*," she said to Tony, who repeated it to me.

Those two opinions marked the lowest common denominator of human separation. But how could there be anything but misunderstanding between these groups, when one set of them had lived here always and raised all they needed off their land and had only the most sketchy monetary system, which was still in the process of being imposed upon them by the other group, who had arrived a short three hundred years ago and who were here to make money?

Upon the third of May in the early morning, an Indian race took place. By this time all the wheat was planted. Now the children raced along the track in relays, to give power to the earth before the corn planting would take place. They were bare and brown, with little loincloths and feathers tied on their black heads, and yellow, red, and white earth paints decorated their bodies.

In the afternoon the first corn dancers of the spring and summer corn drama appeared in the open space before the church. There was a strange medley of spring invocation and the Holy Cross. The saints' days and church celebrations seemed to come with convenient simultaneity as the agricultural crises. In the little church at the entrance to the Pueblo, Tony's father had painted the Queen of Heaven standing upon a crescent moon with the sun rolling large in the sky and ruddy at her right hand, and before the race the Indians were given a mass at the altar before her.

In May, the whole valley was filled with calves and lambs and little chicks. Everywhere they tumbled and scampered and peeped in field and barnyard. The foals stood in pastures and gazed with huge, liquid surprise at their surroundings. The young grass was succulent and tender for them all. Sweet, sweet, the fragrance of growing things, the natural juices of trees and fields as well as garden flowers, hyacinths and daffodils and irises and all the narcissi and tulips. Behind us the desert sage was powerfully strong on the breeze, before us the sacred mountain wafted down its pine and balsam, so we were forever in the delight of good smells, always sniffing, hardly believing it could be real. For in other places odors are not so poignant as here, as flavors are not so keen on the tongue. The seasons were more powerful here than those that I had loved before, in the pleasant moderate days of Croton or Florence, or Buffalo. I had never known anything like this intense, piercing-sweet, flashing assault called spring up in Taos Valley. It seems that here the cup runneth over.

And little by little the hard-pressed store of discontent that had caused me so much irritability and uneasiness melted and evaporated away and was dissipated upon this fresh desert air, swallowed up so that it was as though it had never been, and lighter and lighter beat that heart in me that had seemed old and worn out with more than years, with a kind of distemper of youth never outgrown but perpetuated in its forlorn and persistent infantilism. How much of this melting and cleaning must have been due to Tony? It is not easy to estimate the influence of a person like him. We have no scale to determine the benefit or detriment of presences. Just as some people are allergic to certain constituents, so may others react in some positive and virtuous way when they are brought in contact with the one who can change them.

What a miracle and how little we understand it that a human being will be brought across a continent to the right one, that she may be changed truly almost in the twinkling of an eye by being with him. I would not have understood that such a power is the result of what we call love or being in love, though it is perhaps natural that true love would come out of such an experience. It is *true* love, however, that if it arose, would follow this mysterious change, this revivification and metamorphosis; true love not necessarily entangled with the senses, but true in gratitude, appreciation, even awe, and by a stirring new sense of security, happy and confiding. Only twice in a lifetime have I encountered this mystery of influence and change, and I have been told that many, most, do not ever encounter it. But perhaps they do not need to as I needed to, dying of starvation as I was, the dwindling forces in the organism atrophying from enforced inanition.

CHAPTER EIGHTEEN

More and more, I felt that my real home was in the Pueblo. All through the spring, I hurried out there every morning, and it was like entering into another and a new dimension. I spent part of the time in Tony's house, and part in other houses nearby his. Next door, an old man named John Archuleta lived, married to Tony's sister. There were a lot of children in that house, but none in Tony's. These nephews and nieces used to gather round us when I sat next to Candelaria and, hands on hers, directed the ivory needles into the tangled wool.

Tony's wife didn't like his sister and his old mother. They never came into her house, though the young relatives did, but they watched everything that went on next door, to the best of their ability. Candelaria often stood in her doorway, looking haughty and smiling—a beautiful woman, always spick-and-span in her clean calico and shawl—and ignoring her in-laws, standing in the doorway next to hers. Only a wall separated their houses, but a world of different feeling kept them apart. Candelaria's house was always orderly and shining and she had a slightly malicious, sharp humor, but not real warmth, while in John Archuleta's house there was a confused and crowded atmosphere, many children, much love and warm tenderness.

One Sunday morning I was sitting there, knitting, when Tony came into the house wrapped to the eyes in a white sheet. He came and stood before me, looking down for a while, and I didn't know why. His eyes showed deep and dark under the visor of the white folds. Finally he said in a faraway, dreamlike voice:

"N-i-i-ce color!" He was looking at my purple ribbon, and I knew he saw more in it than I did.

Soon he sat down beside the fire on a little wooden stool and, staring into the flames, he began to sing in a low voice while he beat upon a small metal water drum. A queer magic that opened windows in my imagination soon filled the room and, drifted upon it, leaving my regular life, my known, circumscribed, real life—the understandable, rational kind of living, which was all I had known, except for occasional strange hours of instability when things turned queer and frightened me by their alteration.

But Tony did not turn things queer. Instead of that, he was deepening the reality of life by his present magic and his singing. The limitations of the senses were spreading out and lifting higher, so that I suddenly saw, too, what purple could be, though there are no words to tell it here. And I heard his voice joined to other sounds that had been unheard or unnoticed before now, the actuality in the crackling fire, the voice of the wind outside; and the life inherent in these common sounds was shown to me so I heard them like new voices speaking. There is a live hearing and a deaf one. We are mostly deaf all our lives long, and blind to real seeing.

I didn't know that Tony was absent from us that day in the world peyote opens up to those who have eaten it. But somehow he was able to take me with him where he went. Was it any wonder he drew me to the Pueblo day after day? He shared with me more than magnified and enhanced sense impressions that he experienced. It was the Indian life I was entering, very slowly, a step at a time. I was becoming acquainted with a kind of living I didn't know existed anywhere. I had heard, of course, of the Golden Age, and of the Elysian fields, but they had been only words to me. Now I found out what they meant.

There was a broken wall around the Pueblo, and it enclosed a most lovely and potent way of living. I rarely heard any angry or harsh-toned voices there, never anything but courteous and dignified exchange between neighbors whose houses joined wall to wall. They must have evolved politeness, I thought, as a necessary protection from contacts so close and intimate, for were there not some guarantee of privacy, they would end by killing each other from sheer exasperation. But maybe I was mistaken. Perhaps there is a relatedness I could not conceive of that needs no protection, that is held together in a happy combination of stimulating strains, that is positive, life-giving and taking, like that of bees in a hive. Certainly there was a honey sweetness in their daily bread that I never knew in mine.

When I trudged back home, down the road past the close-cropped, community meadows, where the horses grazed on the fresh green just appearing, down the road and over the two little bridges that crossed the gay, small, sparkling Pueblo creek that came tumbling from the sacred mountain, my heart was not so full of anticipation as on my journey out, and I was reluctant to arrive. I ran in, always just in time for lunch, but with none to spare. I assumed a bright, noncommittal expression, which I supposed was the way Indians looked. I wanted to be like them and felt, in an obscure say, that if I looked and acted the way they did, I would be. The family were usual' ner gathered in the living room or washing up: Maurice with a clo . on his face, Andrew with a frown on his face, John with a frown on his e. Why did all these men frown so much?

"Mother, why do you have to go out to the Pueblo every ty? Do you think the Indians like that? I bet they wonder about it."

"Really, da-a-r-rling, are you teaching those girls anything? I am afraid you are wasting your time!"

Lying on the couch, I tried to exclude my companions from my consciousness, and to remain in the other world I had left behind me, in that Pueblo, where the women sat quietly in full, starched calico dresses, or silently walked down to the river with shawls over them, to fetch water, which they carried home in round, clay pots balanced upon their heads, one arm stretched up with the long shawl line falling straight down in lovely folds. The Indian women were sheltered in their shawls, seeming so comfortable and encompassed within them, so that their whole being was contained, not escaping to be wasted in the air, but held close and protected from encroachments. How exposed we live, I thought, so revealed and open! I longed for the insulation of the shawl and wore mine whenever I could.

CHAPTER NINETEEN 🖎

John Archuleta's oldest daughter, Marina, was a beautiful girl with soft, black eyes and thick hair as soft and black as a raven's breast. Her short nose jutted out like a young eagle's, and her hands were beautiful. She had the same look in her eyes her father had, a steady, faithful, glowing gaze, and I came to know she was Tony's favorite niece. She was always helping Christina, her mother, to take care of the numerous smaller children who tumbled over each other in the family room, and who gave it the aspect of warm disorder that Candelaria's neat, childless room never had.

One morning Tony took me in to see Marina, who was lying down beside the fireplace on her mattress, which was usually rolled up when I got out there. Her face looked swollen and her eyes were too bright.

"He catch cold," her father said, laughing. I saw what short hard breaths she took, and I thought she looked very uneasy.

"Why don't you have the doctor?" I asked him.

"The doctor don't come to the house," he replied in an informing tone, as though I ought to know better. "He go to the schoolhouse twice a week and if the Indians want medicine, they can go get it. We got our own Indian doctor. She coming to see Marina pretty soon."

I thought something had better be done and I told Tony so when he went outside. When I came back the next day, she lay in the same place, and she was breathing like someone who has been running a race. Her head turned from side to side, and her eyes searched the corners of the room with a frenzied look in them.

"The doctor *must* come and see her!" I exclaimed to Tony in a whisper. "I'm going over to the schoolhouse and telephone him."

[Dr. Bergman] finally knocked at the door and came in with a self-conscious look, as though he were unaccustomed to visiting in the Pueblo, as of course he was, and he acted very professional. He felt Marina's pulse and counted it and murmured, "Hum-m-m . . ." in a surprised tone; then he opened a black bag and took out a stethoscope and listened to her heart. Dr. Bergman took out a bottle marked Aspirin and rolled some tablets into a piece of paper. He gave instructions when she should have those. He said they had to give her a complete bath every four hours. I went outside with the doctor when he left and asked him what the matter was, and he told me she had double pneumonia. He drove away with the woman who waited in his car and never came back. Marina died that night towards morning.

I went home and wrote a letter that noon to the Indian Bureau in Washington and told them the doctor had neglected a girl whose case he had diagnosed to me as double pneumonia; that anyone with any knowledge and humanity would have worked over her a little, would have stayed with her that night. Presently they sent out an inspector who called upon me and to whom I told more details. He looked sympathetic, but he said: "This man can be removed to somewhere else, but the chances are the same kind of man would replace him. They can't get any better for the salaries they pay."

In the late afternoon, I took a walk along the road to Placita and I met Tony coming towards me with his blanket over his bowed head. The sun shone behind him and made him look tall and broad and like a biblical figure. He stopped and I saw how haggard he was.

"I been walking a long time," he told me. "I feel so bad."

I didn't know what to say to him. What can one say? So I walked along beside him in silence.

CHAPTER TWENTY

While we waited for spring to deepen, Tony told me of places he would show me, and I could hardly wait until the roads dried up so we could go. Finally, one morning, he came for us in his two-seated buggy to drive over to the hot spring. It took the whole morning to drive northwest across the desert, passing through some scattered hamlets. Tony told us their names: Placita, Prado. We had turned left off the main road and wound up and down over some hilly places until we came to the road down into the Rio Grande Canyon, and there it plunged right downwards, looking terribly steep. We reached the bottom after a mile of curving descent, and there was a stone house built along the brink of the stream.

I stepped into the water and gave a great breath of delight. "Oh, it's wonderful!" And it was, so hot and enveloping and having, besides, some mysterious properties that I had never known before and could not define, but that my flesh and bones accepted, not bothering to name them. The water gave one a new feeling of content. It solaced and satisfied the restless, questing nerves and blood, and when I came out into the world again, I felt made over, and newly put together. I laughed and shook my wet hair in the sunshine.

I found a place in the sand and lay down. Tony came up to me where I was, and all of a sudden a small flash of red passed from him to my hand, where it lay open. Alas! I was not quick enough. It rolled away and fell down over the rock ledge several feet below. Maurice turning at that instant spied it, picked it up. When it was in his hand, I had a chance to see what it was: a little round bag of something in red silk.

I couldn't stay with the others that evening. I went to bed early and tried to read, but Tony's face kept coming before me as it had in my dream in New York. When Maurice came to bed, I pretended to be asleep until I knew he slept, and then I got up and went through his clothes that lay on a chair in the dark room. I found the little bundle by its perfume. It was a rose-sweet bag of scent of some kind I had never known except when a breeze blew it off Tony. I slept with it under my pillow.

Maurice missed it from his pocket when he was dressing the next morning, and I saw an expression of annoyance on his face as I sat up in bed, drinking my coffee.

"Is that a *love token* that Indian was giving you?" he demanded menacingly. Upon this, I burst out laughing.

"Oh, Maurice! What a word! Love token!" He flushed darkly at my ridicule.

"You'd better be careful," he threatened, though he did not say of what.

I didn't answer him and he went out to his breakfast. I wore it inside my dress for a long time—until Tony gave me another one, late in the summer.

CHAPTER TWENTY-ONE 🌿

In our house, from that time on, a new strain was apparent. I walked up to the Pueblo as usual every morning, for the sake of sitting in that happy neighborhood, and to share its warmth and gaiety, but my heart sank a little when I reached home, for Maurice just glowered at me now when I came in. He did not actually take up the issue with me, nor did he hide his feelings until we were alone. No, he brought them to the table, and with his strong personality he spoiled our meals, sitting there frowning and not speaking to anyone.

I did not care, really. I was truly content inside myself, not thinking of present or future, or of those around me. It was as though my old self had ceased to be, or had run away and hidden and left the place open to another. I did not feel myself or feel like myself, yet I seemed to feel more alive than I ever had, and in a different way, and I seemed to understand things I never had before.

It was at this time that I began to open my hands and let things slip away. Things! One sunny day I was looking at the whitewashed wall in Tony's house: it was perfectly bare, one whole side of the room, except for the sunlight that moved upon it.

"How nice an empty wall is!" I exclaimed.

"Indian houses are empty," he answered, "because God said Indians cannot have *things.* White people have *things,* but God give the Indians just what grows on the mountain."

Candelaria laughed a silver, ringing laugh, and said something that made Tony smile, so I asked him what she said.

"He say God give white people things and Indians watch them go under them. You know. Wheel turning." He made a large, round gesture. "So many things carry the wheel down, with the white people underneath. Pretty soon Indians come up again. Indians' turn next."

Right from the beginning I had had the power to see into his mind and catch the pictures he saw, and so now I saw the huge wheel turning slowly, weighted down with all the accretions of our civilization: the buildings and machinery, the multitudinous objects we had invented and collected about us, and ourselves fairly buried under that heavy load, muffled, stifled, going under. On the other side of the wheel, rising bare limbed and free, heads up bound with green leaves, sheaves of corn and wheat across their shoulders, this dark race mounting.

I grew careless with my few possessions, and gave Anita many of my clothes and things. The little sack of perfume had a greater value for me than jewels. My own belongings seemed meaningless now, and without association, but when Tony brought me a branch of evergreen, I treasured it. We did not have much talk together, and when we did there were always others there. But I slowly learned something about the Indian point of view in the occasional moments when we were sitting in his house or driving somewhere in the two-seated buggy. I remember once he gave us a dissertation when he was driving up to Glorieta, an old sacred grove of cottonwoods up the canyon beyond the Pueblo.

"You know, God put all the little and big animals on the earth each in his own place and with his own way. The birds, and the fishes, and the ones on the land. And they all stayed where he told them to stay. Everything wants to stay in itself. God told them not to change.

"Then after the animals, God put the Indians on the earth, and after that the white people. But they were separated by something. By time. Indians have no time. They have never had no time. Now the white people, God He told them to change. And so changing began when the white people came in the world. But He told the Indians to stay themselves, not to change. He never put change in the Indians. The white people have to change, that is their way. So they have to try and change everything. They take God's animals and change them from one thing to another. Now, only a bad witch Indian work this change, and go into a coyote sometimes and out again or be something different. Good people among Indians never work changes. But good white people do because God put it in them to do it. So even they want to change people and nations and will not let them be. Their religion is in machinery to change things and now they come to want to change the Indians though God told them to stay Indian."

"Well, what is the religion of the Indians?" I asked.

"Life," he answered.

My awareness of the people around me in our house had grown so dim by late spring that I cannot remember who was there and who was not, but I think Andrew and Bobby had gone away, and that Julia had returned from Chicago, where she had been spending the winter with her brother. Julia said she wanted to ride horseback and Tony must take her. Tony brought two horses saddled, so I went riding with them. When he and I rode, side by side, forgetting Julia for a moment, behind us, it was the first time we had ever spoken alone.

He said, "I saw you before you came. I dreamed you, but you had long hair."

"Yes. John cut it off the first night I was here."

"Too bad. You look nice with your hair, here on each side." He touched his ears in the place where I had coiled the two strands of long hair for years.

"I saw you in a dream, too," I told him, "before I left New York. It made me come here."

"Yes," he agreed, simply.

CHAPTER TWENTY-TWO

The day came when Julia had to return to New York, and she had the idea of taking Tony with her. She said she knew her brother would like him, and it would be so interesting to show him New York, and maybe she could take him to Washington to meet the president.

The evening before he went away, he walked down the road and stopped beside the house. It was the loveliest hour. The sun was just setting and the air was full of golden light and birds were singing quietly and calling to each other. The mountain had deep purple shadows upon it, and there was a bell tolling down in the village. I was out in the garden when Tony came up to me.

"I bring you these," he said in a low voice. He brought out two pale pink wild roses from somewhere within the folds of his blanket.

"How *sweet* they smell!" I sniffed with amazement at the strong fragrance. I was learning step by step through this new year all the deep flavors and scents that came out of the earth here in this place.

"They the first ones," Tony said in a low voice. He had walked those miles to bring them.

"Oh, I wish you were not going away tomorrow!" I exclaimed.

John and [his tutor] McKenzie drove up in the Ford and I suddenly felt nervous and walked out to meet them, dropping the roses heedlessly as I went.

The next morning several members of his family drove down with him to see him off on the stage with Julia. Candelaria sat beside him; the shawl over her small, neat head was her best black one. In the back, nephews and nieces were crowded together.

From the moment the car drove away, the light faded right out of everything. Until he left, was gone where I could not reach him, I hadn't known how completely I lived through him now, and through him alone. When your whole life is planted in another, and he leaves, you go with him. There wasn't any of me left behind in Taos in my empty body.

"He who loves with passion lives on the edge of the desert!" I thought I was going crazy, because I found out how little the real life around me meant. I sat in the garden and scarcely knew when the others spoke; yet I do not think they noticed anything strange in me.

The days are blank when I look back: nothing at all written on them. One day I got a letter from him. It was a scrawl of unaccustomed, barely formed hieroglyphics, put together in broken fragments; meaningless phrases that he had tried to recover from the meager schooling he had received and never used before. There was not a word in it of actual meaning from himself to me; yet there was carried in those imprints some of his essential self, as though the flow of his loving heart had struck through the pencil that faltered across the cold page and been registered there. This was so evident, he spoke in so direct a way to me behind the masking symbols of words written in lead, that I recognized for the first time in my life there is a mystery in the transmission of feeling across wide space; the fact that individual essence may be poured out of one and carried on a sheet of paper faithfully to its goal, may run through the living fingers, a stream of vital energy, and that one receives messages with some receptive organ besides the elementary ones of eye and ear. Every signature contains the whole creature in miniature, and is a complete picture of him at that instant of his outpouring life.

We are all so differently conditioned that we do not see the same aspect of any human creature that our neighbor sees. When Julia arrived in Chicago with Tony, her brother was horrified, seeing only his bright striped blanket and his brown skin!

And Julia, as I gathered from her account afterwards, had a sudden awakening, and made one of those painful transitions from one point of view to another. For a little while, in Taos, she had seen Tony as himself, a creature in space, endowed with certain attributes and qualities, having a dignity and an authority that were incontestable. But she seemed to awaken from a dream in Chicago. Tony changed in the twinkling of an eye into an Indian in a garish blanket at whom the curious crowd was staring. So, quickly, she allied herself with her own blood, deserted in spirit the embarrassing object and walked rapidly alongside her brother, leaving Tony to follow the best he could.

By the time Julia had deserted Tony, her companion had managed to accept him. "I think it would be better if you get him a suit of clothes and a hat," he said kindly. So Julia, wishing she'd never gotten into this, led Tony to the men's department and let him select what he wanted.

"It was terrible, Mabel!" she told me. He picked out a kind of light green suit, and a blue shirt—and the hat! Well! The clerk took him off to put them on, and when he came back, I wouldn't have known him."

So she had no more pleasure out of him. But he enjoyed the new clothes until the thick, smoky air of Chicago got to the better of him and made him feel weak and sick. Added to that, he had a constant longing to return to Taos, and a feeling he had never known before, about a woman. He told me: "I never miss anyone in my life. I like a woman when I see him, but I don't think about it, 'cept as I would about a nice saddle. But when I leave you there, seems like my heart cryin' all the time."

Julia didn't stay but a day or two in Chicago, then they went to New York, stopping off for a day in Buffalo. She thought the Carys would like Tony, because they were supposed to have Indian blood; they looked like Indians, and their mother had been taken into the Iroquois tribe in Batavia. But when she arrived at the ivy-covered house on Delaware Avenue, she with bobbed hair, and Tony in a green suit with long, black braids, the Carys had nearly died laughing at the strange pair. So she got no comfort there.

So Julia didn't know what to do with him. It was summer in New York and already the pavements were smoking hot. She lived down near Washington Square, where there was less air than uptown, so she thought a ride on top of a bus might make him feel better, for he seemed very sad. Tony looked more and more stoical and heroic and sad as they slowly made the long journey—fifty, sixty, seventy blocks of suffocation and burning lungs! When they reached the Metropolitan Museum, Julia thought she ought to take him in there and show it to him. That was Tony's limit. Statuary might be the saving of Maurice, but it was deadly for Tony. He looked about him at the great, motionless figures, and Julia said he turned a pale gray color and he began to sway. He said: "All dead. No life anywhere," and she thought he was going to faint, so she quickly led him to a marble bench where they sat for a little while, and then drove home in a taxi.

Of course she gave up the idea of taking him or even of sending him to Washington. She saw he couldn't exist away from home, that he grew more tragic looking every hour, so she decided to send him home right away.

When he came home, he got out of the stage in the plaza and walked up to our house. I was there when he came in. "I back," he said, and held out his hand and made a little bow. He had on the green trousers and white shirt and his blanket hung over one shoulder like a toga. With him, life flooded back into the room, into every corner of it, into the chairs and tables, into the bowl of wild roses and into me, too. I didn't say anything, but I looked at him and he returned the look and gave a nod and sat down.

"Home," he said, "be better. What for I leave here?"

"I'm afraid I can never leave here now," I said—but jokingly, of course.

"That good. That right. Here is more power, here is more powerful. You know that nice piece of land I show you? You fix the little house on it . . . you goin' to be happy there."

Then he looked at the flowers on the table and said: "You threw away the roses I bring you."

CHAPTER TWENTY-THREE

When I saw Tony was hurt, something happened. I felt for the first time in my life another person's pain and perhaps this was the instant of birth, certainly the awakening of a heart asleep since childhood. Before that day I had only *seen* things going on in other people and been able to feel only my own sorrow or discontent. Was it heredity or was it environment that had conditioned me so that I had gone all through the years like one cut off from life and other human beings? I had been something like an octopus with many arms, a psychic belly, and a highly developed pair of eyes, for I could see everything with my mind, though I felt nothing of what I saw. I could reach out and grab practically anything I thought I wanted, stuff it into what Edwin used to call, ruefully, my "insatiable maw," and assimilate it, if assimilation is a blotting out of extrinsic values by "understanding" them.

I had been grabbing things for years, to try and satisfy an unnameable hunger. I had been trying to understand others for years so that I could find out what was the matter with myself, and I had always thought that understanding came from seeing. I comforted myself by believing that my capacity to be unhappy, and to feel my own misery acutely, was a sign of superiority. I had been proud of an adolescent *grande passion* lived through and, as I believed, survived in Buffalo years ago and I often quoted to myself: *"Rien ne nous rends si grand qu'une grande douleur"* ["Nothing makes us so great as a great sorrow"], and though I had been rather dissatisfied at times with a sense of sterility in my sorrows, I had blamed the poverty of human nature for that.

Now, over this little matter of a couple of wild roses there occurred in the tight, hard heart a stirring I can only liken to the first surprising involuntary orgasm that Karl caused to break in me on the hardwood floor of my mother's house, how many years ago. Since that, actually nothing real had happened to me or in me. I had been merely repeating that experience or repressing it, and I was as immature as I had been at eighteen.

As I stood there facing Tony when he spoke to me, perhaps it was only an instant in time, yet I was by grace born in that flash as I should have been years, years ago; inducted into the new world. For there is a new world here, though few seem to have the luck to penetrate it. I must assert that what I am telling of myself is not a single strange case of one egotist isolated in the crowd. It is the story of many, it is the familiar, the usual, the accepted. Who reads this knows it to be true. The world is an alien place to nine-tenths of those who live in it or who appear to live in it but who merely go through the motions. Adaptation! It is called adaptation to act *as though*. As though one were alive throughout. As though one liked what is going on around one. As though one felt the ways one pretends to. As though one were good, beautiful, and true when the reverse is the case and one can't help it.

Was it not strange that I, who was nobody in myself, and in whom instinct had never been awakened, should have been brought so far to one who was all good instinct and who, besides that, possessed a magical power of Being? This was the true *participation mystique* I had read about and understood in a way, yet never realized before. Now I found it was one of education's most powerful and mysterious instruments.

"Oh, Tony," I cried, throwing my hands out to him, "excuse me."

He bowed his head gravely. "That's all right," he answered. There was dignity and generosity in him, and always from that moment to this the faint air of a teacher's authority, to which I have submitted with recognition and gratitude. No one has taught me as he has, no one else but Tony has modified or helped me to modify the crooked, strangled, stupid results of environment, though to be sure it will take more than a lifetime to eradicate them completely, just as perhaps it will take ages to change such environments as produced me and the others whose story I tell here as well as my own.

In the same hour of which I am telling, the hour of Tony's return, there quickly followed two other realizations that were also momentous and radical, and were obviously the consequence of the birth of feeling. One was that I was his forever and he was mine, and the other was that I could leave the world I had been so false in, where I had always been trying to play a part and always feeling unrelated, a world that was on a decline so rapid one could see people one knew dropping to pieces day by day, a dying world with no one appearing who would save it, a decadent unhappy world, where the bright, hot, rainbow flashes of corruption were the only light high spots. Oh, I thought, to leave it, leave it all, the whole world of it and not to be alone. To be with someone real at last, alive at last, unendingly true and untarnished. These quick thoughts went through me as feelings, so they were changes in the blood, and I turned to see if he were going through it, too.

"I comin' with you," he said, nodding his head gravely. We were in that dark house but all around us there were flying clear light waves of good feeling so that it seemed as fresh as dawn in the room. A moment, no, a flicker of pain:

"Can you leave your people and can I really leave mine?" I asked.

"Perhaps we help more when we go back, leavin' for a little while," he said.

I had not meant that. I had not felt any moral or ethical responsibility towards *my* people. I had meant was it possible for me to get away from them, throw them off, lose them, lose their influence, get out from under, and wash away from myself the taint of them, the odor of their sickness and their death? Could I who was of these ever be other than they? I hated them in myself and myself in them, and I longed to blot them out in this other. But as a matter of fact, his answer answered my question, as I found out later.

Those who have followed this story up to this time must come upon a change of values now, and in consequence a change of attitude because I cannot continue to write about Tony and the Indians as I have written of others. In other volumes of these memories I have written more like an anthropologist than like a human being. I wrote observantly and coldly like one recording his findings, having returned from an unknown island, telling about an undocumented race of beings. In that manner, revising them in memory, I have told of the habits and customs of myself and my own people. With the passionate curiosity of the hunting anthropologist and with his single-minded willingness to throw away honor, loyalty, and integrity, if only he can get to know and tell about them, I have studied and sacrificed my people and myself in order to tell about us. And as the true anthropologist is driven by pure scientific fervor of knowing and understanding and adding something to the knowledge of the human family by his sacrifices, so have I been.

But I am not an anthropologist where Tony and his people are concerned! Where my scientific brother takes it up I leave off! That I could "write a book about Indians" is the least that might be said: that I may not write one is the most.

Yet for my purpose in this work, it is not necessary to be unreticent about ourselves. If I can get any part of the truth out to others it will not depend upon the intimate details of Tony's life and mine together. But if only I can translate into words something of all I have learned from him! For I have a deep conviction that we were brought together for this purpose, and that my reason for living is to show how life may be, must be, lived.

CHAPTER TWENTY-FOUR

The Indians were working now all over the wide country that was theirs and sometimes they bound their heads with thick wreaths of cottonwood leaves to keep off the hot sun, or wound the white sheet round and round in coils like a huge turban, so their dark faces became Asiatic. But I never believed they were Mongolian as the scientists insisted they were. It seemed to me more likely the Far Eastern peoples and themselves had descended from a common stock; that from one of the great continents sinking in the oceans, parts of those earlier races had migrated east and others west. Why should not the Indians have dwelt on this continent as long as the Orientals upon theirs? I can never think otherwise.

I could close my eyes and see them on this side of the earth, stretching all the way across North America, and down over Mexico, Central and South America. Hunting tribes living in the open, agricultural peoples living in villages of earth shaped like pyramids, worshiping the sun and growing things; then the stonecutting people, artists worshiping imagery, building great temples, and more pyramids, and carving serpentine creations, all the way to the heated zones; and these miles of continent were permeated with the Indian psyche as the Far East is saturated with the Indian psyche, which too has its mountain tribes, its high magnetic centers, its stone-carved temples, engraved with symbols of creation. Only scattered and isolated groups of Indian influence are left up north here in these states that we Nordics have swarmed over and fought to own and call united, but below us millions upon millions of undamaged Indian souls wait the moment of awakening; they wait until the European element has worn off. Their five hundred years of quiescence has been like a twilight sleep in which their forces accumulate in the great racial reservoir. They are sleeping while their brothers here in these mountains keep the true fire burning and alive till the morning of emergence.

It was one day after lunch when the round, low apple tree outside my black-barred window was still all white with blossoms and full of bees, and a heavenly scent was filling the house that I said to Maurice: "Well, I'm going to buy a piece of land over next to Jack Young-Hunter's and fix up a place to work."

What did I know about work? I didn't think this; I just said it because I was moved to do so, without calculation or realization or any conscious process. Maurice looked rather airy and nervous at the same time. We were sitting under the apple tree.

He said, "But—here it is nearly June—darling! I want to do a head of that Indian girl, and go back to New York in August."

"Well, you go," I said, and I was as surprised as he was to find it all settled.

"You really wouldn't let me go without you?" he asked, looking incredulous.

"Yes, I would," I answered gently, and that was all there was to it. No explanations or discussion. I just got up and went in the house and found my hat, and then I started to walk to the Pueblo to find Tony, to tell him. I almost ran, I was so happy and excited and glad to be able to tell him, but when I got there he wasn't home.

On the way back to town, at the corner of the Mexican graveyard, I met Tony driving home in his wagon, and I stopped him. "I was looking for you," I said. "I'm going to buy that piece of land and fix up the house."

He nodded. A light came into his face, and brightened his eyes.

"Get up," he said, moving to one side of the high seat.

On that high spring seat beside Tony I felt full of my own life, which was different from his, and it was as though I could let go and just be, and feel ample and protected and free to be myself, because he would cope and act and determine things. This gave me a most comfortable freedom of feeling, unworried by thinking, scheming, planning, trying, or being efficient and practical.

So it was as though my life was unimpeded and could rise richly in me and flow roundly about us both, while I just sat there and let it, and he, holding the reins, would drive us along taking all the responsibility. Nothing could happen to us so long as he was in charge, I felt, and this was a wonderful and luxurious feeling. I glanced sideways at him and I saw how he was at home in the universe and with me, balanced and strong, and able to do anything. Step by step we had come to each other until the moment I climbed up into his wagon seat and drove along beside him, and then we reached an equilibrium together that sustained itself, and that we did not have to bother about.

Now I bought the place Tony wanted me to have and no purchase ever gave me such a feeling of satisfaction. Edwin had secured the villa and the *podere* in Florence while all I did there was to hunt for chairs and tables, velvets and brocades and all kinds of little boxes, and objets d'art, so I never really felt the house and land were mine, and the other years of my life since I left my mother's house I had lived in rented houses. Here was a big field and a lovely old orchard, an adobe box on the upper edge of the place, and it was my own, bought with the money that had accumulated in the bank since we had been in Taos, for living was so simple we had practically no expenses except the rent of Manby's place, and our food. When I moved to my first very own house, all I had to take to it were my santos!

I could not help a feeling of unfairness at buying those acres and orchards and the home of a family for so little money but Tony told me old "Chimayo" was satisfied. Besides, he said, they were going to build another house outside on the lane, and they would like to work for me when I needed extra men. There were three brothers and several daughters in the family—one of the nicest families in the valley. Very soon José was helping us, and he has worked here ever since.

Palmists had always looked somewhat puzzled at the life line in my left hand because it broke in half right in the middle, and now I can see from this distance of the years that the second half of my life began when Tony made me buy that piece of land. For the first time I ceased hovering over the earth, where I had only landed from time to time to taste and try a flavor of neighborhood or of race, of person, place, or thing. I had lived like a dilettante, like a visitor to this planet, and nothing had been more real to me than food in new places is to travelers. But when I bought the Taos place my feeling for Tony made me take root in it and I began to live in a way that was new to me. This does not mean that I stopped putting out feelers, or that I was through with curiosities, for one does not really change; one only develops. I will always be trying to penetrate into the mysterious varieties of human nature, though with perhaps a different motive.

Of course acquiring a piece of this land here was a symbolic move, a picture of what was happening inside me. I had to have a place of my own to live on where I could take root and make a life in a home. This earth and Tony were identical in my imagination and his, and I wanted to become a part of them, and the day the place became mine, it was as though I had been accepted by the universe. In that day I became centered and ceased the lonesome pilgrimage forever.

CHAPTER TWENTY-FIVE ❧

When Elizabeth Duncan's School was over, she came out to visit us [just as] the work on my new place had begun. At the end, where there was only a plain adobe house of three little rooms, Tony wanted to add a large room. That was all at first. Just one large room. At the east end it would reach to the edge of the desert Indian land. We could not cross or touch the reservation boundary line; in fact, the Trujillos, from whom I had bought the property, had gone nearly to the border but had not quite reached the iron peg in the ground that showed the Indian line, but we meant to go all the way, a few feet more; in the front we could go almost to the ditch but we could leave enough space for a wagon and horses to drive around. This would make a wing and we decided to build a long porch to join it and shelter the other rooms, and we began to build it with old seasoned wood that was of a pale dry powdery gray color. Tony found old long-cut trees for the columns, and Luis [Suazo] cut the corbels to support the roof beams out of the pieces we had left. The curves and points of these corbels looked raw on the inside when they were hacked out, so I invented a mess of wood ashes mixed with kerosene oil to rub on them and it made a perfect match, and blended with the dry weathered outside surface.

CHAPTER TWENTY-SIX ❧

It is impossible to tell adequately what surprises came to me in this new life. For instance, there was not the high, exciting exaltation I had often enough known before, when after a dismal interval, during which I had been submerged in a twilight depression, I emerged like a rocket into another stimulation. No, this time it was as though a gentle organic growth was taking place, and actually in my heart I felt small, imperceptible movements, like tiny leaves unfurling; a wonderful evenness marked my days and nights, so that waking or sleeping I felt a sweet balance that was delicate and strong.

To know this equilibrium was such a positive experience that every hour I renewed my consciousness of it, turning to it, feeling it in wonder and humility. When I was with Tony, I was in tune with all outdoors and with myself as well, for the first time in my life. I felt real at last, not a pretended reality such as one may feel when one blots our pain against another and loses the sadness of one's own cravings. No, a true reality of my own was coming into being within me. Not since I had been pregnant with John had I known this blessed fullness of being.

CHAPTER TWENTY-EIGHT 🦋

In the years gone by, yearning and unsatisfied in Italy, I had had preoccupations that had absorbed all my thoughts and I called them love. Then in New York I had learned to use the name of sex for the strong autonomous serpent in the blood that once unleashed took full possession of all my other activities, and rode me unmercifully.

Here in Taos I was awake to a new experience of sex and love, more mature and more civilized than any I had known before. It is difficult to define the difference but here Tony was providing me with an enveloping kindness that was of the very nature of security and protectiveness, a warmth that relaxed one, delivering one from the anxiety and the tension of life even while it stimulated and made one more aware of living. The feeling that came to me from Tony and that in return grew stronger daily in me made me more wide awake than I had ever been before in my most conscious moments, but with this difference: that there was growing in my awareness of all about me a tenderness, a sensitiveness to things outside myself, that had been peculiarly reserved before now for my own quandaries. I had been keenly aware of myself and I had been sorry for myself often enough, and perhaps there had been plenty to feel sorry for in my repressed and injured existence; I had also been very alert and intuitive about other people and what went on in them. But I had been a cold observer.

Then the men I had known had been of the same material as I, of the same environment and social system. They, like I, had been in various ways competitive, restless go-getters. Of course, they thought of themselves as dynamic, for they went so far and so fast in their efforts to escape themselves.

Everything they did took them away from the contemplation of the inner man. They would create new art forms, they would remake the world, but they would never come to grips with their own solid crystallized deformities. This world of escapists I had lived among, this crowd of reformers, artists, writers, labor leaders, philosophers, and scientists, they had been terribly busy all the time "doing the job" as they were wont to call it, the job, in fact, of avoiding the responsibility of themselves, and of getting onto themselves, and their activities had not left them time or leisure to be: for merely being. They reasoned and they rationalized, they fed themselves and they made love, they wrote, painted, telephoned, and talked at a furious rate—but they never radiated. They had not the time *to be:* to be anything much, and never the time to be kind, kind, as, I was learning now, a man could be.

Evidently it took time and leisure for one to well up perpetually from the source as the water from a spring, and to color and enrich the space around one, and to warm and console those near one as Tony did, in his static fashion, unconcerned and whole. It was like sunshine falling. The essence of his mode of being was kindness, disinterested, involuntary, and unceasing. But it takes time to be kind and my other friends and I had never had that, just as we had never had any culture in the real sense of the word and for the same reason, for kindness and culture are closely related and require the same soil. Yes, we had all been too busy for the kind of love I was learning to know in Taos.

Not a day passed that Tony did not make me realize how rough and insensitive I was, and that all my past sensitiveness had been employed in self-feeling and never in fellow-feeling. When he saw I suffered from this dawning awareness of myself as an isolated egotist, he consoled me. There did not seem to be anything he did not understand. He was unresponsive, becoming faintly aloof and disapproving at any appearance of self-assertion, of snappy authoritativeness, and he disliked cocksureness. But at the smallest sign of embarrassment or mortification at a blundering break that I made, he was right there with a helping hand to lift me up and comfort me. It was as though he gauged all the handicaps of my past years and what they had done to condition me, and wanted to help me disentangle myself from their effects.

CHAPTER TWENTY-NINE 🖎

I learned first from Tony to respect the inviolate unspoken mysteries but I did not learn all at once. I had to knock my head against the stone wall of his silence for a long time before I could accept it, and all during that hard time he did not try to make submission easy for me. His attitude was "take it or leave it" and I could not go away, so I finally gave up and resigned myself. When Lorenzo [D. H. Lawrence] came, years after, I was already schooled and ready for his passionate doctrine of the "dark gods." I knew what he meant, for Tony had taught me to respect the unseen and undisclosed gods, dark in their dark inviolate mystery. Lorenzo's doctrine had always been: let the unknown remain unknown.

It may be imagined that for one as avid of life and experience and mystery as I was, the Indian cosmos never ceased to fascinate and attract me. Whenever I was with Tony or when I was in the Pueblo, I felt I was up against an

indefinable organization of physical and spiritual faculties that couldn't be explained even if one succeeded in defining them. They couldn't be proved as
any sum in arithmetic can be; cause and effect did not work out according to
the usual simple logical formulas. Nothing made sense as I recognized sense,
for there were different laws at work all the time. So at first I pestered him a
good deal with my questions and he was very patient with me but absolutely
unshakable. He didn't seem to be able to answer a direct question for one thing;
he couldn't answer my questions about how things were done, for another;
and he wouldn't tell anything about anything even if he could, so from the
start I was stumped.

That peculiarity about Indians never seeming able or willing to answer any
direct question got on my nerves at first until I realized that it was uninten-
tional. They were not putting one off, dodging an issue, being contrary, or trying to hide anything. They were that way about the simplest interrogation,
and I finally understood that that mode of question and answer does not even
exist in their system. They do not use such means as that for *finding out* anything. When I came to that realization, I began to surmise faintly what our
type of education must have done to the makeup of Indian children sent to
the schools as they have been these many last years at a very early age, for our
method of teaching is based altogether on question and answer. Theirs, I knew
later, is founded upon suggestion, example, divining, drawing out, showing.

Tony, luckily for himself, had for the most part escaped the school training. He was Indian, whole, uninjured, and unsplit by the torture of combin-
ing in himself two opposing modes. What made him so patient with me? I
have never known, unless it was that he accepted the bitter with the good in
a situation that from the beginning he recognized as arranged by God for a
purpose hidden from us both. There was always that deep conviction in it for
us both and possibly we did, after all, have our sense of inevitability.

CHAPTER THIRTY 🌿

There was a pleasant ease in the way the Indians worked and it took me a long
time to get accustomed to it, for I was used to another kind of labor. I had
seen other houses in construction. I had watched Italians working on the Villa
Curonia with a foreman dogging them. And all my life I had been half aware
of an unpleasant atmosphere in the areas where workmen were engaged.

But here in Taos it was delightful to be with these workmen, for there was
no indignity in raising a house, and nothing sordid in either the materials or
in their use of them. Mud was mud, yes, but mud was earth, something living and precious to be handled with understanding and care. Mud was earth

and somehow it was not dirt. It was clean and kind and possessing an importance. Working with earth was a noble occupation. To loosen it and make the adobe bricks, mixing the wheat straw from last year's harvest with it thoughtfully, laying them in rows to dry while the rock foundation is being built, and then fitting them carefully upon each other with the rich dark mud between that will turn as hard as stone, all of it is a sacred matter, for the wonder of creation is in it, the wonder of transformation, which always seems to be of greatest significance to Indians.

To take the living earth from under their feet, undifferentiated and unformed, and shape it into a house, with length and breadth and height, each person's house different, yet always basically the same as others, to bring the trees from the mountain and spread the long, round beams across the walls, to cut the young saplings and lay them close and even, either straight or in the ancient herringbone design, and with more earth and mud to form the roof and so have a shelter that will last forever if it be taken care of, this, it must be admitted, is wonderful.

Here we were in July and Maurice was leaving on the first of August without a word about it passing between us. Tony and I waited for that departure. He knew that we would belong to each other then and I knew it too. It seemed necessary for me to have the change absolute and clear-cut, and for Maurice to be gone completely out of my life before I could take this next inevitable step, and that no faintest overlapping of these two people should occur. So, though day by day the intimacy between Tony and myself had grown deeper and we had become ever more sensitive to each other's thoughts and feelings, our closeness was psychic; physically we remained strictly apart. It was like a period of probation and preparation.

This narrative about Tony and me grows more and more difficult to tell, for I feel increasingly obliged to leave most of it unwritten, not only the secret aspects of his religious life and experience, but the secret intimacies of our own personal life together. Was it I who had believed so short a time ago there are no secrets, no privacies? Were all my beliefs to be made over in this new world? Not only my beliefs but the actual soil in which they had grown must be turned over and over, fertilized and cultivated. Let no one believe that a rebirth takes place in one bright convulsive flash. It is a slow, dark passage in time accomplished with blood and sweat, and not only by one's own but these vital juices of another, who loves one enough to work upon this creation, are wrung from him too, in patient agony.

I can only write now about the superficialities of our life, and still hope that

the most valuable lesson of all will reveal itself here somehow of its own accord. The lesson is said to be an old and hackneyed one but it was new to me:
that love can finally overcome all the conditioning of the years gone by, and all
the crystallizations of heredity and environment.

The pages I must write, as well as the ones I must not write, are all about
this miracle. It seems to me I have to let others know there is a true and possible change of being that can take place, and that I have passed the latter part
of my life in this work of change. If I who was nobody for so long, a zombie
wandering empty upon the earth, could come to life, who cannot? My empty
memories must have shown what life had done to me, my recorded thoughts,
reactions, and motivations and how they were, and what they were (underneath the mask of the persona) are not so different, I fancy, from many other
typical products of our time.

It is for those desperate and frightened people I am trying to write now as
it was for them I wrote before. Revelations of the hidden distortions, the crip-
ple under the veils of civilization, the mind breaking under its strain, and the
heart atrophying in its insulation—those were the intimate memories of my
life until I came to Taos, where I was offered and accepted a spiritual therapy
that was cleansing, one that provided a difficult and painful method of curing
me of my epoch and that finally rewarded me with a sense of reality.

CHAPTER THIRTY-ONE

The morning we started on our journey up to Blue Lake was one of those days
that seem dark with sunshine. There is a sunniness so deep and so mellow it
is like a cloak. The big trees on either side of the Pueblo road hung their branches
heavily dark and still and their shadows were profound, with the thick gold
splashing through. Deep July, deep summer day in July, with the green grass
black in the shade and sparkling with dew in the open places!

This landscape made me think of a painting by Constable with its thick,
soft, faraway clumps of trees, and then I was impatient because I did not want
to connect this new world with the old familiar things. Was one to be forever
reminded of something else and never to experience anything in itself at firsthand? My mind seemed to me a wastebasket of the world, full of scraps that I
wanted to throw away and couldn't. I longed for an immersion in some strong
solution that would wipe out forever the world I had known so I could savor,
as though it were all there was to savor, this life of natural beauty and clarity
that had never been strained into Art or Literature.

It had begun to appear to me that there had always been a barrier between oneself and direct experience; the barrier other people's awarenesses and perceptions translated into words or paint or music, and forever confronting one, never leaving one free to know anything for oneself, or to discover the true essence in anything.

We meant to reach Twining that night but about three o'clock the habitual afternoon shower descended upon us in such torrents that we were soaked through before we could untie our yellow slickers and slip them on. The rain was heavier near the mountains than down in the valley, and we were skirting the base of the Arroyo Seco range on our way to the Hondo Canyon. After a discussion with his friends, Tony told us we would not try and climb up to Twining that night, that we would stop and camp below the waterfall.

We crossed the Seco creek and it was brown and full from the rain, and then we started up towards the hidden waterfall. The horses slid and left long gashes in the sticky clay of the little trail we were on, so we had to go slowly, watching every step, but finally, after we wound our way up through a magical grove of symmetrical bright green, dripping Christmas trees, we came to an open place of emerald lawn where a brook was running deep through round, green grassy banks, the overflow of the waterfall that we could hear now wildly, continuously, thundering above us at this spot.

Tony turned in his saddle and announced: "We camp here." All unexpectedly, his face was a little stern and serious and he looked like a person compelled to some ordeal, though able to go through with it and even to smile while doing so, for as I looked at him somewhat anxiously, I suppose, he got off his horse and walked up to stand beside me, saying gently, "Come on. We got to stay here," in a tone of voice that assured me he would see me through it.

He put it in my mind that I was the cause of something that had changed his mood and that gave him some concern, but that he was going to stand by just the same. Perhaps in that moment I was given at last a complete feeling of security in someone outside myself, and that has never once failed me since that day, so, if I have succeeded in a measure in gaining confidence in myself, and a partial deliverance from evil, it dates from that hour below the waterfall.

[After making camp] the Indians began to sing in low voices and soon we grew drowsy and wanted to sleep. I asked Tony to put a heap of pine twigs under a tree away from the others, and he took the old wagon sheet that the blankets had been rolled in and he hung it on the lower branches and let it fall to the ground so I had a small shelter inside it. As I bent to go in, he said in a low voice: "Sleep well. I be right here to help you."

It seemed I was going to need help, for soon I was racked with pain that shot through me with knives, and presently I had to get up and go outside. Tony was lying on the ground nearby, wrapped in a blanket, and as I staggered out he sat bolt upright.

"I've got an awful pain," I whispered to him as I picked my way past. I had to go some distance to get far from the camp but the moon was shining brightly so every step was plain to be seen. I felt I was battling in the night, for my bowels writhed in me and I was on the rack of a new pain that I had never had before. After a while I weakly made my way back to my bed and found Tony standing beside the flat red embers of our fire.

"Come warm yourself," he said in a voice like a doctor. He did not make any move to help me. He just offered the fire as though that were all he could offer.

[The next day] we slowly wound our way up the Hondo road, back and forth, over nine bridges, crossing the cold, rough stream again and again. I felt weak, and I could hardly hold myself upright on my horse, but Tony was solicitous and tried to make me forget myself by calling my attention to the red-winged birds that flitted into the shadows, or the brightly singing invisible birds in the higher branches. Once he dismounted and gathered a few huge mauve columbines and brought them to me and they were like large butterflies. When we finally reached Twining at four o'clock, it was raining again and all I wanted on earth was to lie down.

The old white abandoned hotel was there, empty, and Tony and Juan Concha helped me into it while the others unpacked. I don't know how long I lay there. Finally Tony and Juan Concha appeared, carrying a lighted lantern. Juan Concha knelt down beside me and offered me a tin cup, saying, "Here. Drink this. Help you."

"What is it?" I asked them, raising up on my elbow.

"Medicine Juan fix for you. Better drink," Tony told me.

"What *is* it?" I sputtered

"The medicine," Tony said gravely.

Peyote! Well!

The medicine ran through me, penetratingly. It acted like an organizing medium coordinating one part with another, so all the elements that were combined in me shifted like the particles in a kaleidoscope and fell into an orderly pattern. Beginning with the inmost central point in my own organism, the whole universe fell into place; I in the room and the room I was in, the old building containing the room, the cool wet night space where the building stood, and all the mountains standing out like sentries in their everlasting attitudes. So on and on into wider spaces farther than I could divine, where all the heavenly bodies were contented with the order of the plan, and system within system interlocked in grace. I was not separate or isolated anymore. The magical drink had revealed the irresistible delight of spiritual composition, the regulated relationship of one to all and all to one.

Was it this, I wondered, something like this, that *artists* are perpetually trying to find and project upon their canvases? Was this what musicians imagine and try to formulate? Significant Form!

I laughed there alone in the dark, remembering the favorite phrase that had seemed so hackneyed for a long time and that I had never really understood. Significant form, I whispered; why, that means that all things are *really* related to each other. These words had an enormous vitality and importance when I said them, more than they ever had afterwards when from time to time I approximately understood and realized their secret meaning after I relapsed into the usual dreamlike state of everyday life.

The singing filled the night and I perceived its design, which was written upon the darkness in color that made an intricate pictured pattern, not static like one that is painted but organic and moving like blood currents, and composed of a myriad of bright living cells. These cells were like minute flowers or crystals and they vibrated constantly in their rank and circumstance, no one of them falling out of place, for the order of the whole was held together by the interdependence of each infinitesimal spark. And I learned that there is no single equilibrium anywhere in existence, and that the meaning and essence of balance is that it depends upon neighboring organisms, one leaning upon the other, one touching another, holding together, reinforcing the whole, creating form and defeating chaos, which is the hellish realm of unattached and unassimilated atoms.

Though I had just had a lesson in the invisible coherence of all human beings, it did not seem illogical that I felt entirely separated from the others out here. There was a new faculty of detachment from them dawning upon me, a different kind from the solitary, unbalanced attitude that was the only one I had ever known. It is difficult to define. There was the beginning of objectivity in it, a realization of our oneness and dependence upon all others, with, at the same time, the realization of the need for withdrawal, for independence, for nonidentification with the mass. In a new dimension one might, nay must, realize that one is related to and identified with this universe and all its aspects, and yet that one must become more than that, more than a bright neighborly cell in the great organism.

That long, wakeful night was the most clarifying I had ever had, and the momentary glimpse of life I was given by an expansion of consciousness always remained with me, though it was often forgotten.

Just before dawn, when I was lying down again in the bare room, Juan

Concha returned and knelt beside me, and he said in the kind, gentle Indian way, "Come now! Drink again and you be well and strong." He put the cup to my lips and I drank the hot infusion obediently. Then he left me, and soon I heard the camp awakening outside, someone chopping wood, and low voices speaking together in the high, clear morning stillness. I had never had an awakening like that one. Though I had not actually slept, it was as though I had, as though I had always been asleep and was awake now for the first time.

The release from the troubled, senseless, nightmarish night my life had been, the relief at coming back to the reality of the bright, confident day, was overwhelming. I could feel my quivering nerves and my loud, frightened heart gradually compose themselves after a lifetime of concealed apprehension and alarm.

The setting was so full of splendor and majesty I wondered how we could bear it. How could we endure the sight of these great pine trees *growing,* living in growth, pulsating in their deep, green-springing upward urge, vibrating through and through with life and making their low strong music? How support the shining sky and the torrential stream, knowing their relation to each other, perceiving their mysterious connection? No, not knowing it, being it, experiencing all that in oneself because one was not cut off from life anymore.

So that from now on one would not look at life again and read it as one reads in a book, and learn its constituents as one learns lists; all this learning in the brain and never in the blood was ended. One could really learn only by being, by awakening gradually to more and more consciousness, and consciousness is born and bred and developed in the whole body and not only in the mind, where ideas about life isolate themselves and leave the heart and soul to lapse inert and fade away. Yet never to cease watching was imperative also; to be aware, to notice and observe, and to realize the form and color of all, the action and the result of action, letting the substance create the picture out of abstract consciousness, being always oneself the actor and at the same time the observer, without whom no picture can exist.

This new way of perception was speeding through me, informing every part with its message, while outside the business of life went on apparently as accidental and unimportant as ever.

[After breakfast and the long climb to Blue Lake] we stood side by side upon a high peak and Tony was pointing downwards. I looked and my heart stopped, for the face of the Lake gazed up at us. It was directly below, a pool of lambent burning blue. It smiled. It had life, it had conscious life. I knew it.

We dismounted and sat beside the deep blue water for a long while. The pine trees sloped steeply down all around its edge except at one end, where it flowed out forever, down the long decline of the canyon, down the mountain, down the canyon, turning, twisting, persisting upon its course until it came to Taos Valley, crossed it, fell into the Rio Grande, and ran down to the Gulf of Mexico, where Indians like these drink it, and it binds them further into one flesh and blood.

"I can see life whole," I said to Tony, beginning to talk again after the silent day.

"Yes," he answered.

CHAPTER THIRTY-TWO

We had bought a little tepee to take to Blue Lake with us, and now I had Tony put it up in the garden for me. I liked to go out and lie upon the cool grass inside it and be alone. Maurice was delayed in completing the head of Albidia [Marcus]. Soon it would be the first of August and he was not by any means ready to go, and we all seemed to be living in a period of suspension. Finally he was almost ready to leave Taos, though it would be sometime after the first of August.

I had heard from Tony of a big corn dance that would be going on all day on the fourth of August in Santo Domingo Pueblo and I decided to drive down to it. I thought while Maurice was going away I would absent myself, for I had a tender, soft, sorry feeling for him now. Poor Maurice. I was sorry he had to plunge back into all that old turmoil with his two black wax Indian heads, while I would be here in this happy place learning how to be human! I let the sadness bubble up and up in my heart but I could not show it to him and he never knew I felt it.

CHAPTER THIRTY-THREE

[After returning from Santo Domingo] I knew that I must really face life. My heart was beating anxiously when I woke up the next morning and I had an apprehensive feeling when I turned into the heavy shade of the curving lane to go over to my own place. Tony was sitting under a tree, waiting for me halfway over, and as I came along, I saw him pondering, as though in a deep meditation. He sat on the ground, leaning against the trunk of the tree, his knees drawn up and his hands clasped upon them. I reached him and dropped beside him.

"Maurice is gone," I said.

He nodded, but answered nothing.

"Tony, I'm worried," I began uneasily.

"Worried about what?" He looked full at me to search my face. There was a kind, helpful look in his eyes, as though he would do all he could for me.

"About that peyote. It frightens me. What do we know about it? I know now that it seems to magnify something in one's mind, and to make everything stronger, colors, sounds, tastes . . . but I sort of feel we should be able to do that by some power in ourselves and not through any outside thing. How do you feel about it, really?"

"Sure. The Peyote is a big power. Why that frighten you?"

"Well—it's about consciousness. Anything that tampers with consciousness always frightens me—consciousness is all we have—just as it is. We have some faculties in us that, maybe, can increase our consciousness if we would learn how to use them. Then there are the things outside us to increase it or to change it or diminish it, like drink, and drugs, and kinds of love affairs. But somehow I feel we make a big unnatural mistake to influence our consciousness from anything outside like those things. Don't you see? Peyote seems to be one of those things. That frightens me. I mean it frightens me to think that you would go away from me in your consciousness and I could not follow you or know where you are. Do you understand what I mean?"

"Sure, I understand. Then what?" he persisted, trying to help me get it all out.

"Tony! You know if we come together now there's no turning back. Do you feel that?"

"Yes." He nodded. "I know this not play. This forever."

"I mean, I know it is like going across a deep gulf on a bridge that goes with me, is gone when I reach you. I will not be able to return because you will make all of my own kind of life unreal for me. It has always been more or less unreal—you will make it impossible."

"I give you a new life, a new world—a true one, I think."

"Oh, *yes!* I know that—but don't you see? Because it will be true and what I want, I am afraid of the peyote. I am afraid the peyote will make it unreal, make you seem unreal if you are using it. If I come together with you, won't you give up the peyote?"

"I guess you not makin' a bargain with me," he replied as though announcing a fact. "No. We not makin' a trade together. I always goin' to do things because that help you, make you happy, make you feel life good. You goin' to do the way I want because you want to make life good. No need to bargain, us!"

Well, this was making me feel a little ashamed now. Why could I not take a big, broad view of things as he always did—trust him? I knew I could trust him. Why did I not act on my trust?

He went on after a silent moment. "It's not important, that Peyote. I mean it's not important to use it. One must know it is a big thing God put here in the world, but one doesn't have to use it. Better not to use it than not to use it right. Ever'thing must be used right. I have seen that. Trouble. Danger. But you not be worried. Ever'thing goin' to be all right. You see."

He rose and pulled me to my feet. "We go see the new room now," he said. "That be nice?"

I spent the day at the house, going home at noon to fetch some lunch and to see John for a few moments. He seemed occupied with his own concerns and I went quickly back to the place that was coming to feel like a home.

When Tony walked home with me at five o'clock, he stopped in the garden beside the tent, which was already set up under the trees. The day had been smooth and full of certainty, and the reassurance I had learned to draw for myself from the poise of the Indians was deep in me. They could always drive away the peculiar nervousness and anxiety that waited beneath the surface ready to lay assault upon my composure. It is true they had great direct problems to face, problems connected with the welfare of their crops, their children, their land, and their religion. They had always had an uncertain tenure of peace since the Spaniards had first broken their ancient adaptation to life. But they did not go about ridden by fears and worries; they were free in their souls. When a difficulty came they took issue with it but they never anticipated it. They lived in the here and now, giving little energy to past or future.

They were not neurotic. The word is out at last. The Indians were not neurotic, for they had not lost their vision of creation. They had not any phrase about life in their language, like ours when we speak of "the creation *myth*"! They were too healthy for words like that. Now I had come to the place where one life ends and another may begin. The old mythical life could end at last. I looked up at Tony, where he stood so serious, sure, and strong. For the first time in my life I had discovered I could trust someone always and that I could be trustworthy to someone always and that this would be true in spite of anything we could do!

He bent a firm, gentle look down upon me and held out his hand, and I took it.

"I comin' here to this tepee tonight," he said, "when darkness here. That be right?"

"Yes, Tony," I said, "that will be right." And it was right.

Afterword

Luhan tells us in her last volume of memoirs that her life "broke in two" after her arrival in New Mexico; yet she provides us with only a brief glimpse of what was to become the most productive and sustained part of her life as a writer, patron of the arts, and advocate of Pueblo land rights and culture. Nor does she bring to closure her relationships with her mother, her son, or her "adopted" daughter, Elizabeth. Luhan and her mother visited each other during her Taos years, although I don't know how frequently, and her mother helped to support Mabel financially, often doubling with cash grants the $24,000 in annual interest that Luhan received (in the 1920s) from her inheritance. With her marriages to Sterne and Luhan, Mabel feared being "cut off" by her mother, but this did not happen. Sara Ganson died shortly after the publication of *Background,* a death that some of Luhan's Buffalo friends and relatives believed was hastened, or even precipitated, by its publication.

Luhan makes mention of Elizabeth's being at school and coming to visit during her early years in Taos, but I have not been able to find out what happened to her. Mabel's relationship with her son, John, was a very complicated and difficult one. Although Luhan took good care of the education John received (he attended Yale University), she was no more able a mother than her own. It is chilling to read that her inability to mother began at the moment of John's birth, but it is not surprising in the light of her own maternal deprivation and the continuing trauma of her relationships with men. As an adult John had a variety of occupations, including being a banker in Buffalo and working for the Bureau of Indian Affairs in Albuquerque; he also published two novels. He was twice married—first to Alice Corbin Henderson's daughter, "little Alice," whom he married in 1923 (the same year that Mabel wed Tony) and whom he divorced in 1932; his second wife was the writer Claire Spencer, whom he married in 1933. The two marriages produced five children. Evans died in Maine, in 1977.

Luhan's relationship with Tony did and did not fulfill its initial promise, mostly due to her inability to accept him for who and what he was. He was as emotionally solid as she was frenetic, but his silence and illiteracy sometimes frustrated and irritated her, as did the remoteness of her life with him in Taos, which is one of the reasons she traveled (often with Tony) to Mexico and to the East and West Coasts, typically for several weeks each year. Luhan continued throughout her life to need the stimulus of intellectual men and women, of artists, philosophers, and spiritual gurus, such as the poet Jean Toomer, a follower of the Russian mystic Gurdjieff, with whom she at one point fell in love, causing a painful rift in her marriage.

Tony's relationship with Mabel was clearly a mixed blessing for him. Not only were there serious stresses between them because of their dramatically different personalities, education, and interests, but their marriage also created friction at the Pueblo. Tony divorced Candelaria in order to marry Mabel, who provided her with $35.00 per month (presumably for life). Because intermarriage was proscribed by tribal law, Tony was marginalized for a time from certain tribal practices. But Tony remained active in tribal politics, and his access to the powerful friends that Mabel brought to Taos who fought for Pueblo cultural and land rights gave him the opportunity to serve as a liaison to other Pueblo tribes. During the 1920s he became a valued and trusted adviser to John Collier, who was later appointed Commissioner of Indian Affairs under Franklin Roosevelt. It is clear that he attained a degree of wealth and influence that would have been impossible without his marriage to Mabel. In 1935 the spiritual leader of Taos Pueblo publicly announced his benediction on the Luhans' marriage. Their marriage lasted until Mabel's death in 1962. Tony died a year later, in 1963.

At their best, Mabel and Tony Luhan did serve as "the bridge between cultures" that she imagined they could become during the year after they first began to live together. Their initially modest adobe home grew into a multi-storied, seventeen-room hacienda, with a 1200-foot gatehouse for their staff; in addition, they built several guest houses on their twelve acres of property. Luhan devoted much of the rest of her life to what Maurice Sterne had prophetically suggested was her mission: to bring her fellow Anglo-Americans to an understanding and appreciation of the Pueblo way of life and of the Southwest as a region of cultural significance. She envisioned her home in Taos as the center of "a new world plan" that would redeem Anglo civilization from its urban-industrialist bias, its individualist and materialist credo, and its Eurocentric vision of culture.

Luhan called many artists and visionaries to Taos to help celebrate and preserve the paradise she believed she had found in New Mexico, among them painters and photographers Marsden Hartley, John Marin, Georgia O'Keeffe, Ansel Adams, and Paul Strand; writers Mary Austin, Willa Cather, D. H. Lawrence, Jean Toomer, Robinson Jeffers, and Frank Waters; theater designers, musicians, and dance choreographers Robert Edmond Jones, Leopold

Stokowski, and Martha Graham; and anthropologists and social reformers Elsie Clews Parsons, Jaime de Angulo, and John Collier. She published numerous articles on Taos and the Pueblo Indians from 1918 through the early 1950s, as well as three other books besides her four-volume memoir: *Lorenzo in Taos* (1932), a biography of D. H. Lawrence; *Winter in Taos* (1935), a utopian domestic novel about the daily rhythms of life at her home, *Los Gallos* (named for the roosters she brought from Florence who were perched on the roof); and *Taos and Its Artists* (1947), one of the first histories of the Taos art colony. Luhan, of course, never fulfilled her messianic dream, but over the course of the second half of her life, she captured northern New Mexico's spirit of place in her writing, and she drew to her home many men and women of achievement and vision who did the same.

Glossary of Names

Bernard Berenson (1865–1959)

Raised in Boston and educated at Harvard, Berenson moved to Florence in 1900. He was a leading art connoisseur and critic, especially of the Italian Renaissance. He left his villa, I Tatti, to Harvard University, along with a distinguished art collection and library, where it serves as a center for the study of Italian Renaissance culture.

Alexander Berkman (see Emma Goldman)

Jacques-Émile Blanche (1861–1942)

A traditional French portrait painter, writer, and art critic, Blanche immortalized Mabel as a Renaissance lady in two oil portraits he did of her in 1911. In his novel *Aymeris* (1923), Mabel served as a model for his heroine, Gisell Links, a Jamesian American who represents the clash between the brash naivete of a new world and the rich traditions of the old.

A. A. Brill (1874–1948)

An Austro-Hungarian immigrant who settled in the Lower East Side in 1889, Brill was, by 1917, the American leader of the psychoanalytic movement in the United States. He was the first practicing psychoanalyst in the United States, the first to translate Freud's major works into English (see his *Basic Principles of Psychoanalysis,* 1921), and the most influential early popularizer of Freudian psychology. A highly successful clinician, Brill was pragmatic, tolerant, and cosmopolitan, a man who enjoyed the company of reformers and artists. His relationship with Luhan, as both friend and therapist, lasted through much of her life.

Arthur Brisbane (1864–1936)

Like Luhan, Brisbane grew up in Buffalo, the son of Albert Brisbane, a reformer interested in the utopian socialist ideas of Charles Fourier. Brisbane became a newspaper editor and writer who boosted circulation through his use of sensationalistic headlines and popular editorial columns. In 1897 he became managing editor for William Randolph Hearst's *The New York Journal* and helped to promote the Spanish-American War. He was the highest-paid newspaper editor of his time.

Pen (Robert) Browning (1849–1912)

The son of Elizabeth Barrett and Robert Browning, he grew up mostly in Italy and Paris, where he trained as a painter and sculptor. More of a dilettante and spendthrift than a serious artist, Browning was interested in housing decoration and renovation (he owned five houses in Asolo, Italy). In his later years he had a successful lace-manufacturing company in Asolo.

Louise Bryant (see John Reed)

Paul Burlin (1886–1969)

Raised and educated in England and New York, Burlin studied painting in Europe and moved to Santa Fe in 1913 because of his interest in finding "the primitive" in his own country. Influenced by Matisse's use of decorative color and Cézanne's structure, he painted the cultural and physical landscapes of the Southwest in an expressionist idiom. He met and married Natalie Curtis in 1917 in Santa Fe, where they built a small home, which they occupied until her accidental death in Paris in 1921.

Witter Bynner (1881–1968)

Bynner was a poet, one of the first translators of Chinese poetry in the United States (noted especially for his translations of the T'ang poets) and a devotee of the philosophy of Taoism. Bynner visited Mabel and moved to Santa Fe in 1922, where he continued to write poetry and became a supporter of Native American arts and culture. Bynner's play *Cake* (1926) is a bitingly satirical, protoabsurdist drama, loosely based on Luhan's life and character, about a woman who is the solipsistic queen of her own universe.

Edward Carpenter (1844–1929)

English reformer and writer, Carpenter was a socialist associated with William Morris's late-nineteenth-century Arts and Crafts movement, who was also influenced by Havelock Ellis's new theories of sexuality. Author of the influential treatise *Love's Coming of Age* (1896), Carpenter claimed superiority for woman by virtue of her closeness to the "unconscious processes of Nature" and called for her liberation from bondage as man's private property. But he also argued that woman's primary role, once liberated, was to serve as an energy source and muse to men of creative genius.

Willa Cather (1873–1947)

One of the great fictionalizers of the pioneer experience on the Great Plains (see *O Pioneers!*, 1913, and *My Antonia*, 1918), Cather was a critically acclaimed and highly popular American novelist during the first half of the twentieth century who also published numerous short stories, poetry, and book and music reviews. Cather stayed with the Luhans in Taos during the summers of 1925 and 1926 while working on her novel *Death Comes for the Archbishop* (1927). Her character Eusabio is thought to be modeled on Tony Luhan, who served as her guide during her visits.

John Collier (1884–1968)

Born in Georgia, Collier moved to New York in 1907, where he became general secretary of the People's Institute at Cooper Union, a multicultural community development organization devoted to educating immigrants in the utopian theories of the Russian anarchist Kropotkin and the socialist theories of William Morris and in promoting ethnic pride through organized festivals and pageants. Collier visited the Luhans in Taos in 1920 and shortly thereafter began his work as a leader in the battle for Pueblo land and religious rights. Appointed U.S. Commissioner of Indian Affairs under Roosevelt in 1933, he drafted the Wheeler-Howard Indian Reorganization Act of 1934 (the Indian "New Deal").

George Cram ("Jig") Cook (1873–1924)

A midwesterner who began his career as a professor of English literature at the University of Iowa, Cook cofounded the Provincetown Players in 1915 with his wife, the novelist and playwright Susan Glaspell, as a radical experiment in the communal writing and staging of American plays that would have contemporary social import. In two summers in Provincetown and six seasons in Greenwich Village, the Players produced ninety-seven original plays written by forty-seven American playwrights, Neith Boyce, Hutchins Hapgood, Mary Heaton Vorse, Ida Rauh, John Reed, and Louise Bryant among them.

Edward Gordon Craig (1872–1966)

English actor, visionary theater director–designer, dramatic theorist, and graphic artist, Craig's influential aesthetic focused on simplicity, movement, light, and the unity of design in theatrical presentations. Craig founded the first theater journal (*The Mask*, 1908), experimented with moving screens (one of his designs was used by William Butler Yeats in the Abbey Theatre in Dublin), and coproduced *Hamlet* with Stanislavsky at the Moscow Art Theatre in 1912.

George Creel (1876–1953)

A midwestern journalist in the 1890s, Creel started his own newspaper, the *Kansas City Independent,* in 1899. His writing for the *Denver Post* and *Rocky Mountain News* (1909–1911) established his reputation as a "muckraking" investigative reporter and progressive reformer. In 1917 Woodrow Wilson appointed him head of the Committee on Public Information, the propaganda arm of the federal government that helped to foment public support of the U.S. involvement in World War I.

Natalie Curtis (1875–1921)

Curtis was a musician and musicologist who first traveled to the Southwest in 1900, where she became interested in Indian music. She collected and published Indian songs, her best-known work being *The Indians Book: Authentic Native American Legends, Lore & Music* (1907; rev. by Paul Burlin, 1923). The book introduced Native American myths, music, and songs from many different tribes to popular audiences.

Andrew Dasburg (1887–1979)

One of the most avant-garde of the postimpressionists in prewar New York, Dasburg painted a series of abstract (synchromist) portraits of Mabel (*The Presence and Absence of Mabel Dodge*), with whom he maintained a lifelong friendship. During the 1920s Dasburg lived and taught part-time in Woodstock, New York, and in Taos and Santa Fe, settling permanently in the Taos area in 1935. In New Mexico he rooted his cubist-derived abstractions in the landscape, emphasizing through strong rhythmic lines the organic connection between the human and natural environments. Dasburg is considered the "father of modern art" in New Mexico because of his influence on many of the artists who visited and settled there in the post–World War I era.

Jo Davidson (1883–1952)

Born in New York, Davidson moved to Paris in 1907, where he became a portrait sculptor known for his bold naturalistic style. His subjects included Mabel Dodge, Gertrude Stein, Woodrow Wilson, Mohandas Gandhi, and Franklin Roosevelt.

Arthur Davies (1862–1928)

Davies was a painter, printer, and tapestry designer whose early work was in a romantic, decorative tradition. Intensely interested in the avant-garde, he was appointed president of the Association of American Sculptors and Painters in

1912 and was a leading organizer of the Armory Show, the first major exhibition of European and American postimpressionist artists in the United States. One of the most controversial art exhibitions in American history, the show displayed some thirteen hundred works in the Sixty-ninth Regiment Armory on Lexington Avenue in New York City before moving on to Chicago and Boston, with an estimated attendance of some three hundred thousand in all three cities. Frederick James Gregg was in charge of publicity for the show.

Muriel Draper (see Paul Draper)

Paul Draper (?–1925)

Paul Draper, a tenor singer, went to Europe in 1909 to study piano but because of a hand injury ended up studying singing in Florence. He had recitals in London and New York City and soloed with the Boston and Philadelphia symphonies. Muriel was a leading London salon hostess at their home, Edith Grove, where she organized musical soirees and entertained friends, such as Henry James and Artur Rubinstein.

Elizabeth Duncan (see Isadora Duncan)

Isadora Duncan (1878–1927)

A pioneer of modern dance who was born and raised near San Francisco, Duncan lived most of her life in Europe. She broke with traditions of classical ballet to form her own original style of dance. Duncan was an outspoken champion of women's emancipation, supported the Russian revolution, and established a school of dance in Moscow in 1921. As Luhan explains in *Movers and Shakers,* Elizabeth worked with young dancers for many years in Germany before founding her school in Croton-on-Hudson, which Mabel helped to fund.

Eleanora Duse (1858–1924)

A world-renowned Italian actress, "The Duse" formed her own acting company and toured the world. She was best known for her great interpretive roles, especially in the plays of Henrik Ibsen and Gabriele D'Annunzio, a poet, novelist, and dramatist noted for his verbal virtuosity and celebration of eroticism. In 1909, suffering from ill health, Duse left the stage and stayed at Mabel's villa for a time while she was recuperating. Mabel wrote a moving story of her affair with D'Annunzio, "The Eye of the Beholder" (published in *The Masses,* October 1917), which focused on Duse's self-destruction as a result of devoting her life to an artist who devoured it in his work.

Max Eastman (1883–1969)

A radical journalist and socialist philosopher, Eastman founded the first men's league for woman suffrage (1910) and served as editor of *The Masses* (1912–1918), one of the best left journals of the pre–World War I era, which attempted to link a radical libertarian consciousness with a commitment to labor journalism and women's rights. He published books and essays on a wide range of subjects, including humor, art, and Marx and Lenin. Mabel served as a model for his heroine "Mary Kittredge," a mother-muse figure to young male radicals, in his novel *Venture* (1927).

André Gide (1869–1951)

One of the towering figures of French literature in the twentieth century, Gide advocated the claims of individual conscience and liberty in defiance of conventional morality. His novels and journals probed deeply into psychological and moral conflicts (see *L'Immoraliste* [*The Immoralist*], 1902) and boldly confronted contemporary political and social issues, including homosexuality (see *Les Nourritures Terrestres* [*Fruits of the Earth*, 1897]). He received the Nobel Prize for Literature in 1947.

Emma Goldman (1869–1940)

Anarchist, women's rights activist, writer, and symbol of working-class militancy who lectured on birth control, free love, free speech, and economic revolution, Goldman was born in Lithuania. She came to the United States in the 1880s, joined the German anarchist movement, and took Alexander Berkman as her lover. Berkman's attempted assassination of steel magnate Henry Clay Frick during the Homestead Steel Strike of 1892 led to fourteen years of imprisonment for him. During this time Goldman lectured nationwide, edited the anarchist monthly magazine *Mother Earth* (1906–1917), published books on anarchism and modern drama, and was repeatedly arrested, imprisoned, and finally deported (with Berkman) from the United States during the Red Scare of 1919.

James Gregg (see Arthur Davies)

Emilie Hapgood (see Hutchins Hapgood)

Hutchins Hapgood (1869–1944)

A Chicagoan who became a columnist for the *New York Globe,* Hapgood wrote about the sufferings of society's outcasts in such books as *Autobiography of a*

Thief (1903) and *Anarchist Woman* (1909). Though not an activist himself, Hapgood supported revolutionary causes of every variety and strongly identified with the ethnic working classes, as can be seen in such books as *The Spirit of the Ghetto* (1902), about Jewish immigrant life on the Lower East Side. He also wrote *Story of a Lover* (1919) about the difficulties in his open marriage with Neith Boyce. Emilie Hapgood was Hutchins's sister-in-law. She was an advocate of African-American culture, best known for her financial support of the production of three plays on African-American themes by Ridgely Torrence, which were performed by the Coloured Players at the Garden Theatre in Madison Square Garden in April 1917 (settings and costumes by Robert Edmond Jones).

Neith Boyce Hapgood (1872–1951)

Born and raised in Indiana and Los Angeles (her father cofounded the *Los Angeles Times*), Boyce became a journalist and short-story writer, playwright, and feminist novelist, one of whose major themes was the struggle of the "New Woman" over the terms of heterosexual intimacy (see her novel *The Bond*, 1908). Boyce was one of founding members of the Provincetown Players and author of the first play they performed, *Constancy* (1915), which was closely based on Mabel Dodge's love affair with John Reed.

Marsden Hartley (1877–1943)

Born in Maine, but spending much of his adult years in Europe, Hartley was one of the foremost American Modernist painters. He met Mabel at the Stein salon in Paris and she became one of his supporters in New York, where he was a member of the Stieglitz circle. Hartley visited Mabel in 1918, spending some eighteen months in Santa Fe and Taos, during which time he painted between fifty and a hundred pastels and oils. Well known for his powerful expressionist paintings, as well as for his poetry, criticism, and essays on American art, Hartley was an advocate of the importance of Native American art and Hispanic folk culture as shaping influences on the formation of a national culture.

William (Bill) Haywood (1869–1928)

Haywood was a labor organizer who headed the Western Federation of Miners and became the leader of the International Workers of the World in 1905, which he called "the Continental Congress of the working class." He played a leading role in the successful "Bread and Roses" textile strike in Lawrence, Massachusetts, in 1912 and the unsuccessful but important silk strike in Paterson, New Jersey. The Wobblies, as they were known, were anarcho-syndicalists, who advocated revolution through workers taking control of industrial unions, but their work mostly involved nonviolent labor organizing and, during the anti-radical hysteria of World War I, free speech crusades. Because of their outspoken opposition to the war, Haywood and most of the union's leaders were arrested under the 1918 Sedition Act, and he was sentenced to twenty years in prison. In 1921 he jumped bail and fled to the Soviet Union.

Alice Corbin Henderson (1881–1949)

Henderson began writing poetry in Chicago, where she spent most of her formative years and where she became associate editor of *Poetry: A Magazine of Modern Verse* (1912–1916), one of the finest avant-garde journals of the prewar era, among the first to publish Robert Frost, Carl Sandburg, Amy Lowell, Ezra Pound, and T. S. Eliot. She moved to Santa Fe in 1916 with her husband, the artist and architect William Penhallow Henderson. Here she continued to write and publish poetry (see *Red Earth*, 1920, and *The Sun Turns West,* 1933). Henderson supported the work of many modernist poets, including Carl Sandburg, Vachel Lindsay, and Witter Bynner and worked on behalf of Pueblo land rights and Native American arts. Her daughter, "little Alice," married Mabel's son, John Evans, in 1923.

George D. Herron (1862–1925)

[Luhan refers to him mistakenly as "John" in European Experiences]

Clergyman, lecturer, and writer, Herron began his professional life as a Congregationalist minister, interested in Christian Socialism. He resigned a professorship at Iowa College (later Grinnell) in 1899 because of his increasingly radical politics. Partly through his influence, the Rand School of Social Sciences was founded in New York City by Mrs. E. D. Rand, whose daughter Carrie he married in 1901. Deposed from the ministry because of the scandal of his divorce and remarriage, Herron fled the United States and took up residence with his wife and mother-in-law near Florence. Herron was active in Socialist Party politics, helping to write the 1904 platform. It may have been from him that Mabel received her first lessons in radical social philosophy.

Marie Jenny Howe (1871–1934)

Howe was a Unitarian minister, suffragist, and founder of Heterodoxy, a feminist social club (1912–40), where women came to discuss everything from political and social reform to their daily lives and interests. She was the wife of Frederick Howe, who was appointed reform Commissioner of Immigration in 1914.

Smith Ely Jelliffe (1866–1945)

Neurologist, psychoanalyst, and medical editor, Jelliffe authored over four hundred articles and books (he coined the phrase "psychosomatic"). Trained by A. A. Brill, in 1912 he helped bring Jung to New York for a lecture series that precipitated Jung's break with Freud. For forty-three years he owned and edited *The Journal of Nervous and Mental Diseases* and coedited the *Psychoanalytic Review,* the first English-language psychoanalytic journal. While approaching his patients as individuals and from a broadly eclectic theoretical viewpoint, he held a conservative social morality and was very much opposed to what he viewed as the mannish "New Woman."

Robert Edmond [Bobby] Jones (1887–1954)

Born in New Hampshire and educated at Harvard, Jones became one of the most innovative and influential stage designers in modern American theater, noted for his articulation of the importance of symbolic designs and of the scenic designer as a collaborator in script interpretation. He began set designing in New York City in 1911 and was one of founding members of the Provincetown Players in 1915. Mabel supported him for many years, giving him rooms at 23 Fifth Avenue and Finney Farm. His visit to Taos in 1919 influenced his stage designs. In 1926 Luhan raised funds to send him to Switzerland for analysis with Carl Jung.

D. H. Lawrence (1885–1930)

One of the foremost English Modernist writers, Lawrence established himself as a prophet of sexual liberation with his books *The Rainbow* (1915) and *Women in Love* (1916). In 1921 Mabel invited him to Taos, hoping he would write her life's story, which he started but never finished. However, she became a model for many of the female heroines of the short stories and novels he wrote during his New Mexico years (1922–25), including "The Woman Who Rode Away," (1925), *St. Mawr* (1925), and *The Plumed Serpent* (1926). Mabel gave the Lawrences a small ranch up on Lobo Mountain, north of Taos, for which Lawrence's wife, Frieda, gave her the manuscript of his first novel, *Sons and Lovers* (1913).

Arthur Manby (1859–1929)

An Englishman who settled in Taos in 1883 with the idea of creating a fortune for himself through mining and land speculation, Manby was notorious in the Hispanic community for his unscrupulous land deals, through which he enriched himself at their expense. A man of violent and paranoid fantasies, he is rumored to have formed a secret society during the 1920s to collect "intelligence" on locals; members who failed to perform were presumably to be sentenced to death in a ritual that included beheading. In 1929 Manby was found dead (and decapitated) in his home; his murder was never solved.

John Marin (1870–1953)

A painter and printmaker, known especially for his semiabstract cubist expressionist landscapes, Marin was born in New Jersey and studied at the Pennsylvania Academy in Philadelphia and the Art Students League of New York, traveling in Europe from 1905–1910. Upon his return to New York City he joined the Stieglitz circle and became regarded as one of the finest American Modernist watercolorists. He visited for two summers in Taos at the Luhan house (1929–30) and created more than a hundred watercolors during his time there.

Henri Matisse (1869–1954)

French painter, sculptor, printmaker, illustrator, and designer, Matisse was one of the most important innovators in twentieth-century painting: a Fauvist (from *"Les Fauves,"* French for "wild beasts"—so named by an art critic who first reviewed his and his colleagues' works at the 1905 Salon D'Automne) in his dramatic and sensuous use of color, dynamically flowing line, and distorted forms assembled in flat patterns. His work demonstrated a joyful view of man and nature, with sunlit landscapes and richly colored and decorative interiors his most common subjects.

Joseph O'Brien (see Mary Heaton Vorse)

Agnes Pelton (1881–1961)

Born in Germany, Pelton grew up in New York, studied at the Pratt Institute, and was one of the few women artists exhibited in the Armory Show (see Arthur Davies). She visited Mabel in Taos in 1919, where she concentrated on realistic portraiture and landscape paintings. In the 1920s she settled in southern California; in 1938 she became one of the founding members of Santa Fe's Transcendentalist Painters Group, known for her highly original lyric and symbolic abstractions.

Bert Phillips (1868–1956)

One of the Anglo founders of the Taos Society of Artists, Phillips came to Taos with Ernest Blumenschein in 1898. He primarily painted naturalistic and romantic images of Indians, Hispanics, and the landscape, some of which were used by the Santa Fe Railroad in their national advertising campaigns. The

Taos Society of Artists, which had an exhibition in New York in 1917, was very likely Mabel's first introduction to the region and its Native peoples.

Pablo Picasso (1881–1973)

Born in Spain, Picasso was a painter, sculptor, printmaker, ceramicist, and stage designer who is considered by many art historians to be the greatest and most influential artist of the twentieth century. With Georges Braque, he was the creator of cubism (1907), a new pictorial language that relied on an intellectual conception of form and color and emphasized a two-dimensional pictorial surface and the geometric interrelation of forms. Picasso's synthetic cubist style influenced Gertrude Stein's "Portrait of Mabel Dodge at the Villa Curonia" (1912).

Ida Rauh (?–1970)

Rauh was a feminist, socialist, actress, sculptor, poet, member of Heterodoxy, and one of the founding members of the Provincetown Players. Married to Max Eastman and to Andrew Dasburg, she visited Taos in 1924 with Dasburg and did a portrait bust of D. H. Lawrence while he visited there.

John Reed (1887–1920)

An Oregonian who was educated at Harvard, Reed settled in Greenwich Village in 1910. A contributor to *The Masses* and *The Metropolitan,* he helped to organize the Paterson Strike Pageant and covered the Mexican war (*Insurgent Mexico,* 1914) and the Bolshevik revolution (*Ten Days that Shook the World,* 1919). He founded the Communist Labor Party in 1919, which merged with the Communist Party in 1920 to become the United Communist Party. He died in Russia of typhus and was buried in the wall of the Kremlin. Louise Bryant met Reed in Oregon, where she was a journalist who also contributed poetry and sketches to left-wing magazines. She left her husband to join Reed in New York in 1916 and went to Russia with him in 1917. Bryant's work covering the Russian revolution launched her fame as a writer (see *Six Red Months in Russia—An Observer's Account of Russia Before and During the Proletarian Dictatorship,* 1918). Although Luhan dismisses Bryant as a rider on Reed's famous coattails, she was at this time a serious journalist and committed radical.

Arthur Rubinstein (1886–1982)

Born in Poland, Rubinstein studied piano in Berlin, having debuts in Berlin and Paris in the early 1900s. One of the foremost concert pianists of the twentieth century, he was an ardent champion of composers such as Stravinsky,

Debussy, Ravel, and Prokofiev. He was especially regarded for his interpretation of the nineteenth-century Romantics, in particular Brahms and Chopin. Muriel Draper brought him to the Villa Curonia during the summer of 1914.

Margaret Sanger (1879–1966)

Trained as a nurse, Sanger became the leading early-twentieth-century advocate of birth control in the United States. She married William Sanger in 1902 and moved to New York City in 1910 with him and their three children, where she worked as a nurse on the Lower East Side, joined the IWW, and supported the Lawrence and Paterson strikes. She published the *Woman Rebel,* a feminist newspaper, and a pamphlet on birth control, *Family Limitation.* In 1914–15 Sanger fled to Europe to avoid arrest for publishing information on birth control, but she returned to lead the birth control movement in 1916. In 1921 she established the American Birth Control League, which became the Planned Parenthood Federation of America in 1942.

Janet Scudder (1873–1940)

Scudder was an American sculptor, a traditionalist who lived in Paris for most of her life and was best known for her fountain groups containing children.

Upton Sinclair (1878–1968)

Sinclair was one of the most prolific and popular socialist writers of the early-twentieth-century United States, the author of numerous novels, plays, and essays that sought to expose the oppressive nature of capitalism and advocate for workers' rights. His best-known work is *The Jungle* (1906), a fictionalized exposé of the meat-packing industry, which contributed to the campaign for the first U.S. Pure Food and Drug Law.

Lincoln Steffens (1866–1936)

A Californian who became a nationally known lecturer, political philosopher, "muckraking" journalist, and "clean government" reformer, Steffens was given the editorship of *McLure's* magazine in 1901, where he worked to expose urban corruption by pointing up the collusion between American businessmen and party machines (see *The Shame of the Cities,* 1904). After the Russian revolution, he became a supporter of revolutionary causes, though he never joined either the Socialist or Communist Party.

Gertrude Stein (1874–1946)

Born in Pennsylvania and educated at Radcliffe College, where she studied psychology with William James, Stein moved to Paris in 1903, where she lived with her brother, Leo, until 1912, when Alice B. Toklas, her lifelong companion, moved in. She and her brother were among the foremost collectors of post-impressionist art, and her Paris home became a salon for the leading artists and writers of the interwar period, including Ernest Hemingway, on whom she had a major influence. One of the most radical experimenters with language among her generation of writers, Stein published essays, poems, plays, and novels; among her most notable works of fiction are *Three Lives* (1909) and *The Making of Americans* (1925).

Leo Stein (1872–1947)

Stein was one of the first prophets of Modernist art and one of the earliest to collect Picasso and Matisse. Although he suffered from a lifelong inability to find a métier for himself, he developed a psychoaesthetic theory, which he termed "radical solipsism" (the act of creating the self through language), that was very influential on Gertrude and Mabel (see his *Journey Into the Self,* 1950). He remained an important friend and confidant of Luhan's during her years in Taos.

Maurice Sterne (1878–1957)

A Russian emigré who spent much of his life in travel, Sterne studied in Paris in the early 1900s but left in 1907 when he became discouraged by the direction in art Matisse and Picasso were leading. He was a conservative postimpressionist whose paintings are marked by a strongly rhythmic and dynamic line. Sterne traveled in the Far East, to India and Java, in search of a "Garden of Eden" where life would be simple and beauty a part of daily living, seeming to find what he wanted in Bali, where he lived from 1912–14. At the time he met Mabel in 1915, he was just beginning to make a name for himself and recognized that Mabel could help his career.

Alfred Stieglitz (1864–1946)

Stieglitz was one of the most outstanding photographers of the early twentieth century and one of the foremost advocates of photography as an art form, who was among the first to show the work of the European modernists in the United States. His "291" gallery and his magazine, *Camera Work,* were major forums for the newest aesthetic theories and practices of his day. Stieglitz was also a patron and supporter of numerous American painters and photographers, many of whom are now recognized as among the most important and innovative of the early twentieth century, including Marsden Hartley, Georgia O'Keeffe, John Marin, Paul Strand, and Arnold Rönnebeck, all of whom spent time at the Luhan house in Taos.

Carl Van Vechten (1880–1964)

Born and raised in the Midwest, Van Vechten arrived in New York City in 1906, where he became a music and drama critic and later a novelist, photographer, collector, and promoter of twentieth-century writers and musicians. He was one of the major white benefactors of the writers of the Harlem Renaissance and the executor of half a dozen of the most important library collections of modern American literature, including Gertrude Stein's. Van Vechten used Mabel as a model for his heroine Edith Dale, who appeared in his Jazz Age novels of the 1920s, most notably *Peter Whiffle* (1922), where she is a wise sophisticate who helps to initiate the young hero into the world of the avant-garde.

Mary Heaton Vorse (1874–1966)

Born to a wealthy New England family, Vorse became a writer of women's popular fiction, an editor for *The Masses,* a charter member of Heterodoxy, and a founding member of the Provincetown Players. Vorse spent most of her life as a committed libertarian socialist, radical labor journalist, and publicist. Joseph O'Brien, a freelance reporter, socialist, and suffragist, met Vorse in 1911; they covered the Lawrence "Bread and Roses" strike together in 1912 and married that year.

H. G. Wells (1866–1946)

Wells was a highly popular English novelist, historian, social critic and reformer, science writer, and author of science-fiction stories, the most famous of which are *The Time Machine* (1895) and *The War of the Worlds* (1898). The book of Wells's that Luhan mentions reading at the end of *European Experiences* might have been *The New Machiavelli,* a novel about social reform that he published in 1911.

Oscar Wilde (1854–1900)

Irish author, playwright, and wit who lived most of his life in England, Wilde preached an anti-Victorian ethic in life and art. He is best known for his satirical plays, especially *The Importance of Being Earnest* (1895), and his novel, *The Picture of Dorian Gray* (1890). In 1882 he made a tour of the United States, which is mentioned by Luhan in *Background* when she tells the story of his revulsion toward a wealthy Buffalonian's domestic interior.

Jack Young-Hunter (1874–1955)

Young-Hunter was a traditional English portrait painter who saw Buffalo Bill's Wild West Show in London when he was a child, an experience that later inspired him to travel to the Southwest. He arrived in Taos in 1918 with a letter of introduction to Bert Phillips. On the land that Tony Luhan helped him purchase, he built a Renaissance banquet hall for a studio, where he brought his wealthy clients whose portraits he painted in the tradition of John Singer Sargeant.